Clean Politics,
Clean Streams

Clean Politics, Clean Streams

A Legislative Autobiography and Reflections

Franklin L. Kury

LEHIGH UNIVERSITY PRESS
Bethlehem

Published by Lehigh University Press
Co-published with The Rowman & Littlefield Publishing Group, Inc.
4501 Forbes Boulevard, Suite 200, Lanham, Maryland 20706
www.rowmanlittlefield.com

Estover Road, Plymouth PL6 7PY, United Kingdom

Copyright © 2011 by Franklin L. Kury

All rights reserved. No part of this book may be reproduced in any form or by any electronic or mechanical means, including information storage and retrieval systems, without written permission from the publisher, except by a reviewer who may quote passages in a review.

British Library Cataloguing in Publication Information Available

Library of Congress Cataloging-in-Publication Data

Kury, Franklin L., 1936–
  Clean politics, clean streams : a legislative autobiography and reflections / Franklin L. Kury.
    p. cm.
Includes bibliographical references.
ISBN 978-1-61146-073-5 (cloth)— ISBN 978-1-61146-104-6 (pbk.)—
ISBN 978-1-61146-074-2 (electronic)
  1. Kury, Franklin L., 1936- 2. Legislators—Pennsylvania—Biography.
  3. Pennsylvania. General Assembly. House of Representatives—Biography.
  4. Pennsylvania. General Assembly. Senate—Biography. 5. Pennsylvania—
Politics and government—1951– I. Title.
F155.3.K87A3 2011
328.73'092—dc23
[B]
                                                                    2011025547

For Barney and Helen Kury,
my parents and the proprietors of Barney's
Shoe Service, an unlikely political incubator.

The power to move heavy objects is increased dramatically by use of a lever on a fulcrum. With this principle of mechanics in mind Archimedes declared, "Give me the place to stand and I will move the Earth."

Contents

Introduction	ix
Prologue: 1701–1952	xiii

Part I: Getting There, 1952–1966

1	Getting Ready	3
2	Cracking Gibraltar, the Lark "Machine"	23
3	Running for the House	27

Part II: The House of Representatives, 1966–1972

4	The Education of a Freshman	41
5	Absentee Ballot Reform	49
6	Ballot Box Reform in Northumberland County	53
7	Clean Streams and the Environmental Revolution	59
8	The Environmental Amendment to the State Constitution	69
9	The Bridge at Sunbury	73

Part III: The State Senate, 1972–1980

10	Defying Gravity: Going to the Senate	79
11	The Senate Is Not the House	89

12	Senate Confirmation of the Governor's Appointments	95
13	The "Bloodless Coup" Bill and the Governor's Disability	103
14	Righting a Listing Ship by Rewriting the Utility Law	107
15	Our Rendezvous with Flood Disasters	121
16	The Thornburgh Administration and Farewell	143

Part IV: Political Life after the Legislature and Reflections, 1981–2010

| 17 | Political Life after the Legislature | 151 |
| 18 | Reflections | 157 |

APPENDICES

A	A Sampling of Basse Beck's "Up and Down the River" Columns	167
B	Robert Broughton's Analysis of the Environmental Amendment	175
C	Questions and Answers Document Distributed Prior to the Public Referendum on the Environmental Amendment	181
D	A Report of the Special Senate Committee to Study Confirmation Procedure, November 1973	187
E	Article IV, Sec. 8 of the State Constitution as Revised to Implement the Committee Report	197
F	The Witnesses and Persons Consulted in the Investigation of the PUC	199
G	Senator Franklin L. Kury, "Rendezvous with Disaster," *Pennsylvania Township News* Magazine, May 1977	203
H	The Study of Historical "Flood Disaster Prevention in the Commonwealth of Pennsylvania," Prepared by Senator Kury and Inserted in the *Senate Legislative Journal*, 1974	207

Acknowledgments	251
Notes	253
Bibliography	267
Index	269

Introduction

Thomas Paine, pamphleteer of the American Revolutionary War, wrote that what Archimedes said of mechanical power might be applied to reason and liberty. Paine observed that the American Revolution made possible in politics what was only theory in mechanics. Thomas Jefferson, Paine's contemporary, went further. In his letter to M. Correa de Serra in 1814, Jefferson declared "the good opinion of mankind, like the lever of Archimedes, with the given fulcrum, moves the world."

It is not easy to get to a place—like a legislature—where public opinion can be used as a lever resting on a fulcrum to effect great change. I found it requires leading in the right cause, persisting to gain the support of others, and—frankly—good luck. I also found that, once at the juncture of the lever and the fulcrum in the legislature, the results can be stunning.

I saw this first-hand time and again in the enactment of the Pennsylvania clean streams law, the environmental amendment to the constitution, reform of the gubernatorial nominations and appointments process, the gubernatorial disability act, the flood plain and storm water management laws, and the rewriting of the public utility law. But the most dramatic example of the power of Archimedes' principle of leverage at work in politics was Governor Milton Shapp's commitment of $20 million to construct a bridge between Sunbury and Shamokin dam in exchange for my vote on a bill that included twenty-five new judges for Philadelphia. In the pages that follow I describe how these things came to pass and my involvement in making them happen.

My story began in the unlikely setting of a shoe repair shop along the railroad tracks in Sunbury, the county seat of Northumberland County,

Pennsylvania. It progressed through Trinity College in Connecticut and the University of Pennsylvania Law School, and then five successful campaigns for a seat, first in the Pennsylvania House of Representatives, and finally, in the Pennsylvania Senate. To get there I had to overcome Northumberland County's dominant political organization, a classic patronage-based "machine" effectively led by an aggressive party chairman.

When I first ran for the House of Representatives in 1966 I had little idea that laws like those cited above could be enacted or that I would play a significant role in their success. But I do not write this story under any illusion that these successes were accomplishments of mine and mine alone. I soon became aware that success in politics requires the help of lots of other people. To win the House and Senate seats I needed and had strong support from volunteers of both parties who had no relationship to patronage. To pass the bills listed above into law I received great help from my party leadership and legislators, both Democrat and Republican, as well as strong public support. My personal contribution rested in the ability to focus public and legislative attention on an issue that called for change and then to work with unrelenting tenacity within the structure of the legislature to get the votes. Old-fashioned luck played a significant part as well. I had the good fortune to serve at a time when my party controlled both the House and the Senate and the governorship. But as I will describe in chapter 15 (on the flood plain and storm water management laws) even the weather can play a cruel but critical role in the legislative process.

In the story that follows I will describe my experience in running for office and then working as a legislator, reporting how the laws listed above originated and how they were passed. But I also will tell what I learned about politics after I left the legislature, when I ran unsuccessfully twice for state-wide office, served as finance chair of the Allen Ertel for Governor Campaign, and was a fund-raiser and delegate organizer in the Walter Mondale for President campaign. Finally, I give my reflections on this experience, comparing the legislature and politics during my tenure to what I see happening now, and the future of the Pennsylvania General Assembly.

I have written this book to record how my experience illustrates, in its own way, that Archimedes' principle of leverage works in the world of politics. But I also want the reader to better understand the relationship between politics and governmental policy, as well as what it takes to bring about reform and how it is accomplished. This story is also for students of state government and politics, those professionally involved with the General Assembly, and those interested in our state's history. Now that thirty years have passed since I left the Senate, I can tell this story in better perspective than if I had done it sooner.

It gives me satisfaction to tell this story, which I do to the best of my recollection and belief. Looking back at it, I agree with President Kennedy's declaration that in politics the only sure reward is a good conscience. I feel that way. I have a good conscience.

> Franklin L. Kury
> Harrisburg, Pennsylvania
> May 10, 2010

Prologue: 1701–1952

On October 29, 1701, William Penn planted a legislative seedling in the political soil of Pennsylvania. In Part II of the Charter of Privileges Penn promulgated that day as governor and proprietor of the colony he provided:

> For the well governing of this Province and Territories, there shall be an Assembly yearly chosen, by the Freeman thereof, to consist of *Four* Persons out of each County, of most Note for Virtue, Wisdom and Ability . . . Which Assembly shall have the power to chose a Speaker and their officers; and shall be Judges of the Qualifications and Elections of their own Members; sit upon their own adjournments; appoint committees; prepare Bill in order to pass into Laws; impeach criminals, and redress grievances; and shall have all other Powers and Privileges of an Assembly, according to the rights of free-born Subjects of England, and as Is usual in any of the King's Plantations in *America*.

Before the 1701 charter Pennsylvania was one of nine "proprietary" colonies in which political power and ownership of the land rested in the hands of the individuals to whom the king had granted the colony. After King Charles II had granted him the colony in 1681 Penn utilized frameworks of government that did not contemplate self-government by Pennsylvania's residents. There were two General Assemblies before 1701, but they were not popularly elected and were viewed by Penn and his deputy as advisors, not as an independent branch of the proprietary government. The Charter of Privileges changed this forever. From then forward the General Assembly would be elected from each county and operate independently of the governor.

The seedling planted in 1701 took root and grew with sufficient strength to thrive through the balance of the colonial era. In the midst of the

Revolution, the then independent colony of Pennsylvania adopted a state constitution in 1776 that replaced the proprietary governorship with a supreme executive council but retained a legislative assembly of one house. In effect, Penn's legislative seedling was grafted onto the tree of Pennsylvania's new and independent government.

After the United States had adopted the national Constitution in 1789, Pennsylvania adopted its second state constitution in 1790. The legislative branch was revised to provide for a second house, the State Senate, and a strong governor with extensive powers of appointment. Following the Civil War a third state constitution, under which Pennsylvania operates today, was adopted in 1873. This constitution increased the membership of the General Assembly and placed limitations on the power of the assembly to enact special legislation and incur debt. Legislative sessions were made biennial, that is, they met once every two years.

The 1873 constitution has been amended a number of times, including a major amendment from the Constitutional Convention of 1968. In its present form Articles II and III provide for the General Assembly, the former providing for its structure and governance, and the latter for the scope and process of legislation.

Three centuries after William Penn initiated a popularly elected legislature as an independent branch of state government, the General Assembly is fully viable, but functions in a way that would surely confound him. Great changes in the political climate that neither Penn nor anyone at the time could foresee brought this about. Through the first century of Pennsylvania's colonial existence there were no political parties as we know them today. Besides executive budgets, the issues dealt with by the legislature were relatively mundane subjects like local government, land rights, and crime. With the election of presidents under the new United States Constitution, political parties became more formal and organized. Jefferson's Democrats and Adams' Federalists commenced a national two-party system. Both parties used patronage through giving governmental positions to their supporters, but patronage was so minimal that it was hardly the basis for party control. Politics was still largely issue driven, both at the national and state levels.

In the first six decades of the nineteenth century the Pennsylvania General Assembly expanded its efforts on new issues such as canals. Its brightest initiatives, however, were in education. In 1834 the General Assembly enacted a free school act that created a democratic system of public education. Twenty-three years later it enacted the Normal School Act of 1857 to provide professional education for teachers in the public schools.

The Civil War brought cataclysmic changes to Pennsylvania government and politics, including the legislature. The Republican Party, which began only a few years before the war, gained a firm grip on Pennsylvania that endured for almost a century. A century and a half after William Penn's government of an agricultural and commercial trade community in the southeastern portion of the state, Pennsylvania's population in the mid-nineteenth century stretched north to Scranton and west beyond Pittsburgh. The state was on the cusp of great industrialization based on coal, steel, and railroads. The war hastened Pennsylvania's industrial development as it rushed to support President Lincoln and the Union cause. Pennsylvania became one of the industrial giants of the world in the decades following the war. Because of the great wealth acquired by the coal, steel, and railroad companies in this period, Pennsylvania's government and its legislature became subservient to their interests.

The financial strength of coal, steel, and railroads assured Republican control so strongly that from 1860 to 1954 only two Democrats were elected governor: Robert Pattison in the 1880s, when the Republican Party split, and George Earle in 1936, part of the Roosevelt landslide. The legislature likewise rested in Republican hands. With the exception of three elections during the Franklin Roosevelt era, Republicans controlled both the House and Senate in the twentieth century until 1954 with majorities of four or five to one from 1906 until the New Deal. Thereafter, the Republicans restored comfortable majorities in both houses from 1943 through 1955. From the end of the Civil War through the Great Depression of 1929 the legislature appeared to equate the public interest with the corporate interests of the coal, steel, and railroads that provided the bulwarks of the state's economy.

Consider the following:

- In 1865 and 1866 the legislature authorized railroad, steel, and coal companies to have private police forces to protect company property.
- The Coal and Iron Police, as they were known, became infamous for their intimidation of union activities by coal miners and other industrial workers.[1]
- The first clean streams law was passed in 1905 and amended four times in the next half century. The coal industry received an exemption from each one, as will be discussed in chapter 7.
- The state legislature created ten state hospitals in the Department of Welfare to treat injured coal miners: at Ashland, Blossburg, Coaldale, Connellsville, Hazleton, Shenandoah, Nanticoke, Philipsburg, Scranton, and Shamokin. Thus the medical care of injured miners was paid for by the taxpayers, not the coal companies.
- Black lung disease, or miners' asthma, was not added to the list of occupational diseases covered by Workers Compensation until 1965.

Coincidental to the domination of its government by the great industrial powers, Pennsylvania saw the emergence of Republican party "bosses" who controlled the nominations on party tickets at the county and state levels. The power of these leaders was based on a new form of patronage. State contracts and jobs were given in exchange for contributions to the party treasuries. The governor, usually nominated by the Republican bosses, became the focus of the patronage system.

> the Governor of Pennsylvania has general authority over more patronage positions than any other governor in the Union, and perhaps even more positions than are available to the President of the United States. By (the mid-1950s) the governor had appointive power over 50,000 jobs . . . outside the civil service or merit system.[2]

While the governor made the actual appointments, county leaders, whose approval was needed before the governor acted, in fact made the selections. Until 1970 governors were limited to one four-year term and the real patronage power went to those "bosses" who dispensed state patronage in their own counties and met periodically to select the Republican nominees for governor and other state offices. The state patronage jobs were spread through every county, as for example, the county highway sheds, where the Department of Transportation employed workers to repair and maintain the state highway system. (This will be discussed in more detail in chapters 2 and 16.) Besides the state patronage, the county leaders also had the patronage for the county courthouse and its row offices.

Until the end of World War I, individual "bosses" like Boies Penrose and Matthew Quay led the state Republican Party. When Penrose died in 1921 without a clear successor the power devolved upon the "bosses" of the strongest Republican counties. By the middle of the twentieth century the power of the Republican Party in Pennsylvania was in the hands of county leaders such as John McClure in Delaware County, Graybill Diehm in Lancaster County, Harold Watkins in Schuylkill County, Harvey Taylor in Dauphin County, and Henry W. Lark in Northumberland County. The Democrats had their patronage organizations as well—in Philadelphia, Lackawanna, and Allegheny Counties—but it was usually limited to the courthouses and was not sufficient to win statewide elections. There was no taint of illegality or immorality attached to the patronage system. Both parties and the public at large generally accepted it as the way politics works.

In November 1950 George M. Leader, a York County poultry farmer who had studied state government at the Fels Institute of the University of Pennsylvania, was elected to the state senate as a Democrat. When he took office in January 1951 he came face to face with patronage politics and its use in controlling state government. The Republican Party controlled the Senate 32 to 18, and the Senate was under the firm hand of its president,

Senator Harvey Taylor. In addition to serving as President of the Senate, Taylor was Republican State Chairman and the de facto "boss" of Dauphin County. Nothing moved in the Senate without Taylor's approval; he ran the calendar and the committees. Governors needed to clear with Taylor their proposed appointments and legislative agendas.

The lobbyists for the Pennsylvania Railroad and Sun Oil Company each had reserved seats on the Senate floor, behind the rail, close the Majority Leader's desk. Other lobbyists were free to walk off and on the Senate floor. The senators themselves (except for the floor leaders) had no offices, no telephones, and no secretaries. The Democrats had no caucus room but, being so few in number, were able to caucus in the office of their floor leader, Senator John Dent.

The source of Taylor's power was the state's insurance contracts. Taylor had become the broker of record for all state insurance purchases. He received a commission on every insurance contract. Leader estimated that Taylor received about $450,000 a year in commissions from the state insurance purchases. For example, Leader pointed out, 1,600 state automobiles were individually insured with a 35 percent commission. Taylor distributed the insurance commissions to Republican senators, House Republican leaders, and the party candidates for state office.

"I found the Senate a very frustrating place," Leader told me. "I introduced 37 bills and not one of them was ever considered by the committee. One bill I introduced was to require fluoridation of public water supplies. Republican Senator Al Pechan, a dentist, joined me as a sponsor. It made no difference. The bill never moved. I was on several committees, including Agriculture and Education, but with the exception of Education, they never did anything. Paul Wagner, Chairman of the Education Committee, occasionally called a meeting in which there was substantive discussion, but other than that the committees were inert." "There was almost nothing for the Democratic senators to do but make speeches and smoke cigars," Leader remembered. "I was bored! When the opportunity to run for Governor came to me in 1954 I eagerly took it."

Leader's election victory by 270,000 voters over the Republican Lt. Governor, Lloyd Wood, was the upset of that year's national elections. The November 12, 1954, issue of *Time* magazine carried a smiling photograph of Governor-elect Leader on its cover and a feature story on his election inside.[3]

About this time the political sparks that had been glowing within me for some time ignited into a flame that led me into Northumberland County politics, direct conflict with the Lark patronage organization, and election to the Pennsylvania House and Senate.

I
GETTING THERE, 1952–1966

1
Getting Ready

BEGINNINGS

In the autumn of 1952 President Truman campaigned for Adlai Stevenson with whistle-stop speeches in the Susquehanna Valley. Starting in Scranton, the president was to speak from the end of his special rail car at stops along the north branch of the Susquehanna River and then in Williamsport. My father, the Democratic candidate for the state House of Representatives, had been invited to board the presidential train at Danville, meet the president, and ride to Northumberland. A sophomore in Sunbury High School, I was excited to go to Northumberland and hear the president. Several buddies and I went to the principal's office and asked for permission to be absent from classes so we could do so. The principal denied our request.[1] Momentarily stunned, my classmates and I talked about it and quickly decided we were going to Northumberland, in spite of the school's decision.

On the appointed day four of us skipped classes and drove to the railroad station in Northumberland. A crowd of hundreds stood around the tracks waiting. Soon the train arrived, the crowd parted to make way, and—when the train stopped—quickly reassembled around the last car. I jostled to a position only a few feet from the car platform from which Mr. Truman would speak. When the president appeared most of the crowd applauded but there were catcalls and some boos from the rear, even some placards telling the president to go home. I suspected the hecklers were sent by the Lark organization. As the president began to speak the catcalls from the rear grew louder. Truman closed his speech book and looked at the audience

President Truman in Northumberland, Pennsylvania, October 22, 1952, campaigning for Adlai Stevenson. Source: Personal file photo.

immediately in front of him and urged his listeners to study American history. A few minutes later he thanked the crowd for attending, and the train departed for Williamsport.

The Incubator

The political fire ignited that day in the rail yard at Northumberland had been smoldering for sometime from sparks struck in Barney's Shoe Service, my father's business. I worked there as a shoeshine boy and peanut clerk for several years before going away to college. I worked a full day every Saturday and hoped to shine fifty pairs of shoes, charging each customer $.15 for the shine (that went into the cash register) and looking for a $.10 tip. On a good day I could make $5.00 for myself.

An unlikely political incubator, Barney's Shoe Service was located immediately adjacent to the Pennsylvania Railroad's tracks at 16 North Third Street, just off Market Street. In the late 1940s and early 1950s people from all over central Pennsylvania came to Market Street in Sunbury on Saturdays to shop. The malls were still some years away, and Sunbury retail outlets offered a wide variety of merchandise. My father, besides repairing shoes, also sold freshly roasted peanuts prepared in a rotating gas fire roaster that

Part of the crowd waiting for President Truman in the Northumberland rail yard. Source: Personal file photo.

stood on the sidewalk. The odor drifted down to Market Street and attracted customers to buy the peanuts, leave shoes to be repaired, get a shoeshine from me or one of the other boys, and—often—talk politics with Barney.

Barney's Shoe Service was a Democratic island in a sea of overwhelming Republicanism. But my father had a good nature and enjoyed political banter with everyone, regardless of how strong their Republicanism. As a result Northumberland County candidates and public officials of both parties frequently stopped by for a shine or a bag of peanuts and a chat with Barney. I overheard a lot of the conversations. I recall, for example, shining the

Barney's Shoe Service on North Third Street in Sunbury, about 1950. Barney Kury is in the window. Source: *Personal file photo.*

shoes of John U. Shroyer of Shamokin, who had been Republican governor Edward Martin's secretary of highways, while he talked with my father.[2]

Not all of the conversations were amicable. The day Truman fired General MacArthur, Lyman Suiter of Sunbury stopped in for a shoeshine and finished by angrily denouncing Truman. He talked to my father as if he were part of the firing decision. When MacArthur returned to the United States and addressed the joint session of Congress, the Sunbury Junior High School interrupted its classes while MacArthur's speech was broadcast live over the school public address system.

My father ran for the state House of Representatives in 1950 and 1952, as well other offices. As a Democrat, he lost every time, but the losses did not diminish his enthusiasm—and idealism—for politics.

My Family

My parents were born in Shenandoah, Schuylkill County, in the first decade of the twentieth century, the children of recently arrived immigrants from Poland who came to work in the anthracite mines in Schuylkill County and start a new life. Father, born April 23, 1911, was baptized Bronislaus Kurylowicz and went by that name until 1936, when he changed it to Barney

Barney and Helen Kury with the first three of their six children, 1942. The author (with the wooden rifle), Wendell, and Bernard. Source: *Personal file photo.*

Kury. My paternal grandfather, Jerzey Kurylowicz, was the treasurer of the United Mine Workers in Shenandoah. He died of miner's asthma in 1924, and my father quit school following his graduation from the eighth grade to help support his mother, two brothers, and two sisters. After working as a slate picker in the local colliery, he went to Baltimore for work, but came back to Pennsylvania in the early 1930s. He married Helen Catherine Witkowski at St. Casimir's Church in Shenandoah on January 5, 1936. Barney's Shoe Service in Sunbury was opened about that time, and I was born ten months later on October 15. Naming me created a stir with my paternal grandmother. She wanted a traditional Polish name like Stanislas, Franjecyk, or Vladislas. But my father took a much different tack. President Roosevelt made a "whistle stop" speech in Sunbury shortly after I arrived, spurring my father to decide that Franklin was the right name for me. About that time he also "Americanized" his name to Barney Kury.

Both of my parents are now deceased, and I have many memories of them. But the one that stands out above the others is their passion to see their six children get the education they each lacked. (Mother had quit school after sixth grade.) They succeeded. My brothers Bernard and Channing, and I, became lawyers; Wendell became a medical doctor; Gloria became an associate professor of art at Yale and is now a fine arts book publisher; and Wilson, after Army service in Vietnam, became a purchasing official for the U.S. Navy Supply Center until his death in 2000.

None of us would have achieved these professional positions without the emotional and financial support of our father and mother. They carefully followed our grades and encouraged us to ascend the academic ladders of places like Trinity College (Wilson and me), Princeton University (Bernard and Wendell), Vassar College (Gloria), Yale (Gloria), Cornell University (Channing) and the University of Pennsylvania (Bernard and me for the law school, Wendell for the medical school.) When my father died in 1958 only Bernard and I were in college. Mother took charge of seeing that we completed our educations. "We will continue," she told us and worked te-

Adlai Stevenson, the Democratic candidate for president, on the steps of the Northumberland County Courthouse in Sunbury in the fall of 1956. Immediately to Stevenson's right is Governor George Leader and the third person to Stevenson's right is Barney Kury. To Stevenson's left are George Lindsay, candidate for Congress; U.S. Senator Joseph Clark; Grant Mertz, candidate for the State House; and Lt. Governor Roy Furman. Eugene Mirarchi, the Democratic County Chairman, is just under Barney Kury's left shoulder. On the extreme left of the photo, under the "Vote Republican" sign is Karl Purnell, later a Republican state representative from Union County. Source: Courtesy of the Sunbury Daily Item.

naciously to help us. Looking back at the effort of my parents to give their children such educations I see my siblings and me as the luckiest kids on the planet to have had such parents.

Although educating us was our father and mother's major passion in life, for Barney Kury politics was a close second. He ran for office five or six times—city council, state representative—without success. The only election he won was to become a delegate to the Democratic National Convention in Chicago in 1952. At that convention he became the hotel roommate of the state senator from York County, George M. Leader. They hit it off and became good friends.

The last time I talked with my father face to face was during the midwinter break from classes in January 1958. We sat and talked in the lobby of the K. & L. Hotel, a property at Third and Market Streets in Sunbury that he and his partner, Lloyd Long, had purchased and which he managed. Dad asked me to consider running for the 108th House District seat that fall, six months after graduation from Trinity. I knew agreeing to do it would mean a great deal to him. We had spent a lot of time together at political events in the past few years, including going together to the Democratic National Convention in Chicago in 1956. I mulled over it for a few moments but declined. I wanted to go to law school. A run for the legislature right after college would derail law school plans.

Education

In my junior year at Sunbury High School I took Mrs. Arlene Hatton's touch typing class to prepare for college. The newly-acquired ability to touch type drew me closer to my father and his political endeavors. Though chairman of the Sunbury Democratic Committee, my father had no office and no secretary. I became his secretary and was soon typing letters and press releases for him. I also began accompanying him to Democratic meetings throughout the county. After I learned to drive my father put that skill to political use by offering my driving services to James Kerwin of Northumberland, the Democratic candidate for County Controller. Kerwin was visually impaired and I was glad to help.

That year I also took Richard Abbott's class in public speaking for two reasons. I wanted to be a lawyer, and I had a stuttering problem. My father thought the stuttering occurred because my mind raced ahead of my vocal chords and mouth. Mr. Abbott worked patiently with me and succeeded in eliminating my stutter. By the end of his class I could recite speeches like Patrick Henry's "Give me liberty or give me death" without a problem.

I also pursued politics at the high school as a member of the Key Club, a service club sponsored by the Sunbury Kiwanis Club. Key Clubs held an annual state and national convention to elect officers. I became secretary of the Key Club and became the campaign manager of my classmate Charles "Chuck" Ulrich's successful effort to become the Key Club State Governor.[3]

My political enthusiasm was so evident that my classmates gave me the nickname "Senator." At the time the thought of a future campaign for the State Senate did not occur to me.

Trinity College

In September of 1954 I entered Trinity College in Hartford, Connecticut, where my political skills were immensely shaped and honed. I had little interest in football, baseball, or other sports and made no effort to participate in those extracurricular activities. Instead I poured my passion into the Atheneum Society, Trinity's debating team. We were coached by Professor John Dando for a full schedule of debates and debate tournaments throughout the school year on such subjects as the diplomatic recognition of Communist China, the guaranteed annual wage, and the ending of nuclear testing. The team had to be prepared to argue either side of the argument. We did not know until just before the debate began which side we would have.

To prepare for intercollegiate competition, Coach Dando put us through rigorous practice debate. At the conclusion of each practice Professor Dando or one of the other faculty crisply criticized the performance of each debater—style, delivery, vocabulary, and logic.[4] In my case the usual criticism was to slow down the delivery, use fewer hand gestures, and focus on the listening audience.

After weeks of practice debates the Trinity teams faced off against other college teams throughout New England. By the time I graduated in 1958, I had participated in over 100 debates against colleges like Wesleyan, Harvard, Brown, the U.S. Military Academy at West Point, and the University of Vermont. Beyond the regular schedule we also took part in debate tournaments in Burlington, Vermont; Brooklyn, New York; and Pittsburgh. My partner, Robert Back, and I did not win all of our debates, but we won most of them. In our senior year we won eighteen in a row. We enjoyed strategizing on how to make our cases and surprise the opposition. By my senior year I took satisfaction in debating without notes or relying on the "card cans" that we usually used to hold our notes. Just as important, I felt comfortable talking and arguing "on my feet" on complicated subjects.

In the autumn of 1956 I participated in the student/faculty debate on the presidential election held in front of the student body. Professor George B. Cooper and I spoke for Stevenson, and Professor Brinton Thompson and Dyke Spear spoke for Eisenhower.

Besides the debate team I also spent my four years in college as an enthusiastic representative from Trinity in the Connecticut Intercollegiate

Student Legislature. Composed of fourteen colleges in the state, the CISL convened annually in the state capitol at Hartford as a mock legislature to elect officers, learn legislative procedure, and act on bills. In my sophomore year I ran for House Majority Leader but lost by one vote. As a senior I successfully ran for state chairman, presided over the session ceremonies and introduced special speakers such as Governor Abraham Ribicoff and John Bailey, the Democratic national chairman.

Two other events during my years at Trinity had an impact on my political development. In the summer of 1956 I served as Governor George Leader's page at the Democratic National Convention in Chicago. Being with the governor for the week, I was inside all of the Pennsylvania delegation caucuses and heard speeches by Senator Albert Gore Sr., Senator Estes Kefauver, and others. I met Democratic politicians from all over Pennsylvania. It was a heady experience, as a nineteen-year-old, to have a seat behind Governor Leader on the convention floor, to see so many nationally famous people, and to take in the full panoply of the convention.

The most traumatic event of my life occurred the first week in March of my senior year at Trinity. On Friday, March 7, the debating team was ready to leave for Brooklyn, New York, to take part in a regional tournament. Just before our departure I dashed into the college post office for my mail and

The student legislators of Connecticut colleges gather to hear an address by the Lt. Governor, John Dempsey, at the podium with his hands together. The author is seated on the left side of the aisle, second row, to Dempsey's right, wearing dark framed glasses. Source: *Personal file photo.*

was delighted to find an acceptance to Yale Law School. Earlier in the week I received an acceptance from the University of Pennsylvania Law School. With the cars to Brooklyn waiting outside I stuffed the Yale letter into my pocket and left with the team. We arrived at the St. George Hotel late that afternoon. I promptly called my father at the shoe shop to give him the good news.

"I've already been accepted at Penn, Dad. Which do you think I should choose?"

"Let me think about it. I'll call you back Sunday," my father replied after he had congratulated me.

We hung up, and I immersed myself in the tournament. Trinity did really well, winning enough to be listed in the prize honors. Our faculty escort, Dr. Robert Meade, took the team to Luchow's German restaurant to celebrate. On the way back to Trinity I fell asleep in a reverie over our debate triumph and the acceptance by Yale.

Sound asleep in my room at Trinity several hours later I was aroused by a loud knock on the door. "Wake up, Franklin, it's Chaplain Thomas." I pulled myself out of bed and noticed it was about 4 a.m. I opened the door and Rev. Thomas entered and told me to sit down.

"Franklin, your father has been killed. We're sending you home."

Stunned and speechless, I dressed and followed the chaplain to his house, where he provided some breakfast and then drove me to the railroad station. All the way home, through Connecticut, New York, New Jersey, and the fields of Pennsylvania, I stared out the window in disbelief. When I arrived in Harrisburg and found my brothers Bernard and Wendell waiting for me, I knew it was true. I cried for a long time.

My father, home from a long Saturday at the shoe shop, had gone down the cellar stairs to check the anthracite furnace. One of the wood steps broke and he pitched forward, hit his head on the concrete wall, and snapped his neck. Dr. Daniel Solomon, our family doctor, pronounced him dead on the spot.

My life, and that of my mother, brothers and sister, was changed forever. I did not realize it then, but my father's premature death at age forty-six intensified the fire inside me that fueled my drive in the political arena.

Moving On

When Governor Leader learned of my father's death, he called my mother and offered to provide summer jobs for my two older brothers and me. My brothers got work on Department of Highways' survey crews, but I was assigned to the governor's office, where I worked on the budget and with the governor's scheduling office

Graduation from Trinity College three months after father's death. Left to right are Gloria, Bernard, Helen, Channing, Franklin, Wilson, and Wendell. Source: Personal file photo.

That September I left the governor's office and entered the University of Pennsylvania Law School in Philadelphia. I chose Penn over Yale because of a scholarship and its being closer to home.

Politics continued to attract my efforts. Although I took no part in the 1958 campaigns after starting law school, in 1960 I re-entered politics to become the Pennsylvania Co-Chair, along with William Wister, a Penn Law School classmate, of Students for Kennedy and Johnson. After meeting with Mayor Richardson Dilworth, Chair of Citizens for Kennedy and Johnson, and his executive assistant, Natalie Saxe, we organized Students for Kennedy-Johnson chapters on about sixty Pennsylvania campuses. Avid support for Kennedy did not prevent me from hearing Nixon. When Nixon and Henry Cabot Lodge, his running mate, spoke on the corner by the law school, I went to hear them. I also went to their rally in Center City that evening. Shortly after Nixon's appearance in Philadelphia my law school classmate, David Norcross, an avid Republican, and I debated Kennedy vs. Nixon before students at Bryn Mawr College.[5]

During the 1959 and 1960 summer breaks in the law school years I worked as a reporter for the Sunbury *Daily Item*. Although the editor, Harry H. Haddon, was a staunch, conservative Republican, he respected my father and, learning of my typing ability, offered me a job that included covering the Northumberland County Courthouse (located just across the street from the paper) and writing a weekly "wrap-up" of what happened in the state legislature. To do the wrap-up every week the legislature was in session I queried by telephone the House members from our area, including Louis Pursley of Union County and Arthur May of Snyder County.

The Attorney General's Office

Following graduation from law school in 1961 I took the Pennsylvania bar examination in July and then reported to work as a clerk in the attorney general's office in Harrisburg. I did not know any lawyer in Northumberland County well enough to get a clerkship and thus went to Harrisburg. My political contacts from working in Governor Leader's office were enough to get the job. Attorney General David Stahl of Pittsburgh assigned me to work with two deputy attorneys general, Frank P. Lawley, who handled criminal cases, and John D. Killian, counsel to the Department of Education. Both assignments threw me into a significant experience related to the legislature.

The author at work as a courthouse and legislative reporter for the Sunbury Daily Item *in the summer of 1959*. Source: *Courtesy of the Sunbury* Daily Item.

The legislature determines penalties for violation of the state criminal code and none is more controversial than the death penalty. In early 1962 the state had scheduled an execution by the electric chair for Arthur Grover Schuck, who had been convicted of murdering two people. Schuck, in a fit of jealousy and influenced by alcohol, lay in wait with a rifle for his girlfriend and her new lover to drive by. Seeing a car with two persons he took to be his girlfriend and her lover, Schuck fired several shots into the car and killed the driver and passenger. The deceased were not the ones Schuck wanted to kill, but they were dead.[6]

On the Monday of the execution, the attorney general received calls from lawyers and others seeking to stop the electrocution, set for nine o'clock in the evening. Lawley was unexpectedly absent and Mr. Stahl assigned me to find the cases cited by those who called as a reason to stop the proceedings. He reviewed each one and found no reason to stop. Governor Lawrence had given his instructions that, barring a court order, the execution was to be carried out.

At eight o'clock that evening Attorney General Stahl and I went to the governor's office and opened a telephone line to the prison warden in the execution room. This was done so that, if the governor changed his mind or a court order received, the warden could be told immediately. Mr. Stahl was on one phone and I was on an extension, so I heard the entire execution proceeding. A few minutes before nine the warden asked Stahl if there was any reason not to proceed. Stahl replied in the negative. Moments later we heard a clergyman reciting the Twenty-Third Psalm as Schuck was led into the chamber. Soon the warden informed us that the prisoner had been strapped into the chair and he was ready to carry out the warrant for execution signed by Governor Lawrence. Stahl told him to continue. Seconds later we heard a loud "BZZZ," followed by a pause, and then another "BZZZ" that seemed longer in duration than the first. When the "BZZZ" stopped the warden told us that the prison physician was examining Schuck. A minute or two later the warden returned to the phone and said the condemned was dead, the warrant had been implemented. We said goodnight and left the governor's office. I walked to a bar on Third Street, ordered a double scotch, drank it, and went to my apartment still shivering from what I had just experienced on the telephone. That experience shook my views of capital punishment such that, as a state representative, it was relatively easy for me to be against it.

Another assignment from the attorney general's office proved much less traumatic. Deputy Attorney General John Killian was preparing to defend in the U.S. Supreme Court an act of the legislature requiring Bible reading in the public schools.[7] Killian asked me to prepare a memorandum showing the status of Bible reading in public schools in the other forty-nine states. With today's computer technology that assignment could be done in a matter of minutes. In 1962 no such help was available, so I went to the state law library, which had the statutes of every state in sets of volumes. Starting with Alabama, I checked the index, found the citations, read the statute or court decision, and copied the relevant portions by hand onto my legal pad. After manually locating, reading, and recording the information on all of the other states, I wrote a memo showing the legal status of Bible reading in the public schools in every state. A summary based on my memorandum was attached to Killian's brief that went to the Supreme Court. I had no other involvement in the case. But running for the House of Representatives in a conservative religious area in 1966 I was able say that I had helped to defend Bible reading in Pennsylvania schools.

Working in the attorney general's office also brought about the most important meeting of my life—with my future wife. Elizabeth Heazlett of Wilkinsburg had been a student of Attorney General Stahl when he taught at the University of Pittsburgh Law School. In the spring of 1962 Beth, as she is known, entered the James A. Finnegan contest at the suggestion of Mr. Stahl in hopes of winning a summer internship in state government. On the day the winners of the contest were to be announced I accompanied Mr. Stahl to the governor's reception room to hear the results. Standing in the back of the room, I watched as the winners of the contest were introduced. The third place award went to Beth, who stood up in a dark red skirt and jacket with a fox-fur stole draped around her shoulders. As Beth walked forward to accept her award Robert Sabbato, an assistant to Internal Affairs Secretary Genevieve Blatt, tapped me on the shoulder and said, "See that girl in red? You ought to meet her. She's your kind of girl."

As soon as the ceremony was completed I walked up to Beth and her mother to introduce myself. My stuttering revived. "Heh . . . Heh . . . Hello, I'm Franklin Kury." My verbal awkwardness did not stop Beth and her mother from accepting my offer of a tour of the attorney general's office. When the tour was over Mrs. Heazlett asked if I could show them where her father's name was engraved on the Education Building. In a few moments we were walking through the Soldier's Grove east of the main capitol between the Education Building and the Finance Building. On the frieze around the top of the Education Building are engraved Pennsylvania's first school code and the names of prominent Pennsylvania educators, one of whom was Mrs. Heazlett's father, Samuel Hamilton, superintendent of schools in Allegheny County during World War I and the author of numerous books on mathematics and logic.

We found Samuel Hamilton's name on the northeast corner of the building. Neither Beth nor her mother had seen it before. I was ignorant of it until that day. Mrs. Heazlett and Beth thanked me and left to return home. But a spark had been struck. Fifteen months later—after six months in the army and being admitted to law practice—Beth and I were married in Heinz Chapel on the University of Pittsburgh campus.

Congressman George Rhodes

Another turn of events while working for the attorney general had a significant impact in preparing me to run for the legislature. In the summer of 1962 Congressman George Rhodes of Berks County called and asked me if I would work in his Washington office. Rhodes' opponent that fall was another congressman, Ivor D. Fenton of Schuylkill County, who had represented his home county and Northumberland County for over twenty-five years. Fenton was popular in Sunbury because, following the 1936 flood, he secured federal funding for a flood wall to protect the city from a future flood rampage by the Susquehanna River.[8] Rhodes too had been in Congress for a number of terms but his district was confined to Berks County. Rhodes and Fenton were forced to face off in 1962 when congressional reapportionment combined their districts.

Attorney General Stahl agreed to let me leave to work for Rhodes. I went to Washington and worked in his office until I reported to the army in November. I had not met Congressman Rhodes before. I found him to be mild-mannered, conscientious, hard working, and dedicated to his constituency. Most of my work involved assisting in responding to queries from residents of Northumberland County, researching related issues, and providing suggestions as to whom the congressman should contact there to help in his campaign.

The congressman's office provided a fascinating workshop on representing a legislative district. Constituent requests received the highest priority. Every one received a personal response. Equally impressive was the attention he paid to bulk rate mailing. Congressman Rhodes personally checked many of the envelopes and how they were packaged and bagged to insure delivery by the post office. The importance of attending to the details in bulk rate mailing stuck firmly in my mind. The lessons learned from Congressman Rhodes were put to good use in the bulk mailings I did in my legislative campaigns. I used bulk rate mailings effectively in every campaign.

Rhodes defeated Fenton in that election, and I reported to the U.S. Army Basic Combat Training School at Fort Knox, Kentucky, to begin my stint in the Army Reserve.

Starting Law Practice

Shortly after I went to Fort Knox, Samuel B. Wolfe, the state senator from the 27th District, died. I had met him once and interviewed him by

The author with Congressman George Rhodes, a conscientious congressman and legislative mentor. Source: Personal file photo.

telephone as part of my legislative reporting for the Sunbury *Daily Item*. He also had provided me a one-year scholarship to attend law school at the University of Pennsylvania.[9]

Shortly after Senator Wolfe's funeral the Senate announced a special election to fill the vacancy to be held in January 1963. Through the aggressive leadership of the Northumberland County Chairman, Henry Lark, the Republican committee people of the district selected Preston B. Davis of Milton as their nominee.[10] The Democratic committees designated Dr. John Linnet of Shamokin. I didn't know Linnet, but I was aware that Davis was close to the Lark organization. He served as Northumberland County solicitor when the Lark organization commissioners controlled the courthouse. Davis defeated Linnet easily to become the new senator.

When I completed the six month active duty portion of my Army Reserve service, I returned to Sunbury, was admitted to law practice in Northumberland County, married Beth, and opened a law office in the old Bittner Building at Fourth and Market Streets. Soon I was back in politics, starting by being elected as the Democratic precinct committeeman for the First Ward, a position I held for four years. In 1965 Samuel Haupt, a friend of my father's, decided to run for mayor of Sunbury, a position the Democrats had not held for many years. The last Democrat before Haupt was Morris Michaels, who served during World War II. A popular salesman for the Sears store in Sunbury, Haupt had good political talents that served him well in meeting people. I became active in his campaign, focusing on strategy, advertisements, and brochures. Haupt won in an upset and took over city hall. One of his first appointments was to make Beth the city solicitor.[11]

Meeting Henry Lark

In early 1965 I received a telephone call from Henry Lark, the Republican chairman, to tell me he would like to meet with my wife and me. Lark was regarded as the "boss" of the Republican organization that dominated the county. I was surprised by his call. He would come to my law office. He came that afternoon to urge me to run for judge of Northumberland County that year. Lark had a political problem to solve and saw me as the way to do it. Since the incumbent judges, Robert Fortney and William Troutman, were not seeking re-election, both of the county's judgeships were open. Lark wanted to elect Frank Moser of Shamokin and Senator Davis. The sprag in Lark's plans came from Michael Kivko, a popular Sunbury lawyer born and raised in Mt. Carmel, a Harvard Law School graduate, and a relatively independent Republican. Because judicial candidates could cross-file for both parties' nominations, Lark feared Kivko would win a Democratic nomination and be a formidable general election opponent for Moser and

Davis. Lark had no doubts about Moser and Davis winning the Republican nominations. Lark was sure I could defeat Kivko in the Democratic primary.

> "You'll win the primary and we will beat you in November, but it will be close, respectable. When the Democrats next get a governor they will make you a workers' compensation referee, like [Clair] Groover in Union County."
>
> "I'm kind of young to be a judge," I replied.
>
> "No, you're not. John Fine was elected judge in Luzerne County when he was about your age."
>
> "Let me and Beth think about it. I'll let you know."

Beth and I quickly decided to decline. I had less than two years of law practice experience and simply was not ready for a judgeship. There was a second reason. I have never had any desire to be a judge at any point in my career. Being a judge has never interested me in the least. The next day I called Lark and gave him the decision. As Lark feared, Kivko defeated Davis in the Democratic primary and then defeated him again in the general election.

Meeting Basse Beck

I continued with my law practice and soon had an equally unexpected but more interesting visit. Basse A. Beck, a friend of my father and the copublisher of the Sunbury *Daily Item* and the principal owner of radio station WKOK, stopped by my office. He asked me to help him in his work as chairman of the North Central Division of the Pennsylvania Federation of Sportsman's Clubs. For several years Beck had been publicly calling on the legislature and the electric power companies to undo the environmental damage inflicted on the Susquehanna and its tributaries by the discharge of mine drainage and the blocking of shad migrations by the Conowingo and other dams on the lower Susquehanna. He wrote numerous columns titled "Up and Down the River" for the *Daily Item* that highlighted environmental damages to the streams. (See appendix A for examples of his columns.) Intrepid, he went to Pennsylvania Power and Light company shareholder meetings to raise environmental questions. Indefatigable, he persisted in speeches to groups like the sportsman's clubs. I did not realize until later, but Basse Beck was one of the first to challenge the coal and electric power companies on behalf of the environment.

I agreed to become his "secretary," much like I was for my father. We traveled together to sportsmen's meetings throughout central and north central Pennsylvania. He preached the environmental gospel, and I listened. In 1965 Mr. Beck brought me a copy of H.B. 585, a bill to bring the coal companies completely under the state's clean streams law. As stated in the

Prologue, the legislature had passed five clean water laws since 1905, but each one gave an exemption or special provisions for the coal companies. Beck asked me to read the bill and give him any suggestions I had for improving it. I noted that the bill had no declaration of purpose, a provision often used in legislation to make clear the purpose of the bill. I recalled that President Eisenhower had made a speech calling not just for the stopping of Communist expansion, but to roll it back. Why not something comparable to this for the rivers and streams of Pennsylvania? So I drafted a declaration calling not just for the ending of pollution discharges, but also for the reclaiming of every polluted stream in the state. There were about 2,500 miles of mine-polluted streams in Pennsylvania at that time.

Mr. Beck liked my amendment and arranged for us to appear before a House Conservation Committee hearing on the bill to be held in Berwick. Rep. John Laudadio, a state leader in the Sportsmen's Federation, was chairman of the committee and the chief sponsor of the bill, which had 114 co-sponsors from both parties. Rep. Tom Foerster of Pittsburgh, another environmentally active legislator, was also active on the committee. At Beck's suggestion I testified and presented the amendment. Foerster and Laudadio

The author before the House Conservation Committee in 1965 presenting the amendment calling for the rolling back of pollution. Top row, left to right, are Representatives John Laudadio, Stanley Meholchik, Tom Foerster, and Ray Wilt. Bottom row, left to right, are Representatives Francis Kennedy, Thomas Tiberi, Budd Dwyer, and William Renwick. Source: *Personal file photo*.

thought it was a good suggestion, and they later added the amendment to the bill.[12]

It read:

Declaration of Policy:

1. Clean, unpolluted steams are absolutely essential if Pennsylvania is to attract new manufacturing industries and to develop Pennsylvania's full share of the tourist industry;
2. Clean, unpolluted water is absolutely essential if Pensylvanians are to have adequate out of door recreational facilities in the decades ahead;
3. *It is the objective of the Clean Streams Law not only to prevent further pollution of the waters of the Commonwealth, but also to reclaim and restore to clean, unpolluted condition every stream in Pennsylvania that is presently polluted;*
4. The prevention and elimination of water pollution is recognized as being directly related to the economic future of the Commonwealth;
5. The achievement of the objective set forth requires a comprehensive program of watershed management and control.(Italics added.)

Later that year H.B. 585 came to the House floor and passed 190–6. One of the six to vote against it on final passage in the House was Adam T. Bower, the representative from our district and a loyal soldier in the Lark organization.[13] Beck was livid, furious that the legislator from his district could vote no. He came to my office. "Franklin, you run and I will head your campaign."

I did not need persuasion. I was ready.

Just married. Leaving Heinz Chapel on the University of Pittsburgh campus. September 14, 1963. Source: Personal file photo.

2

Cracking Gibraltar, the Lark "Machine"

On January 20, 1967, Beth and I stood on the steps of the capitol with other newly-sworn-in legislators of both parties for the inauguration of Raymond Shafer as governor.

Shafer was one of the few lieutenant governors who succeeded in becoming governor.[1] Before joining Governor Scranton's team he served as senator and district attorney for Crawford County. In World War II he was skipper of one of the boats that returned General MacArthur to the Philippines.

Following the swearing-in ceremonies the traditional inaugural parade moved out and marched up Third Street past the capitol and the reviewing stands. I was surprised to see, in the middle of the parade, Henry Lark, Representative Paul Ruane, and other Northumberland County Republicans carrying a long banner that stretched ten or twelve feet across proclaiming "Northumberland County—Gibraltar of the GOP." For some years the declaration on the banner was true. Northumberland County had been solid for the Republican Party. What the banner did not say was that the Republican Rock of Gibraltar had a large crack.

LARK AND HIS ORGANIZATION

Henry W. Lark, county chairman since the 1950s, was deeply rooted in Northumberland County business and Republican politics.[2] His father, Henry W. Lark Sr., known as Wilson Lark, had prospered as a manufacturer of overalls, coats, and shirts. He was a founder of the Dime Trust and Safe Deposit Company in Shamokin, later the National Dime Bank until its acquisition in 1970.

He married Isabelle Witmer, daughter of Charles Witmer, an active Republican lawyer who served as county solicitor, U.S. Attorney, U.S. District Judge, and Northumberland County judge. His sister, Emeline, married William I. Troutman, who became a U.S. congressman at large from Pennsylvania, state senator, and Northumberland County judge.[3]

Lark was not in politics for personal financial gain. Economically comfortable from significant coal land holdings, ownership of Shamokin radio station WISL,[4] and ownership of the Sunbury Wire Rope Corporation,[5] he never ran for public office or held a position in government. Lark was a Republican zealot motivated by the strong desire to see his party control the government. He thrived on political power, which he exercised aggressively from his position as chair of the Northumberland County Republican Party. And he was successful. No one gained a county Republican nomination without his approval. By winning consistently in the county, Lark became one of the Republican county leaders who met to choose their candidate for governor and other state offices.

Lark's leadership produced a classic political "machine" based on patronage, giving government jobs to the party faithful in exchange for voting loyalty and financial contributions from their government paycheck. The County Courthouse row offices and the state Department of Transportation highway maintenance shed provided the core of the patronage. To work in either place, the employee agreed to a 5 percent contribution from his or her salary to the Republican County Committee and have each voting-age member of his family register Republican. At that time this system was generally accepted in the community as "just politics." There was no taint of illegality attached to it.

With the voting registration base and steady flow of campaign funds from the patronage system assured, Lark took the initiative in putting together slates of candidates, circulating petitions for them, rebuffing primary election challenges, and running the campaigns.[6] He obtained respected community leaders, such as the mayors of Sunbury and Shamokin, to be his candidates. He organized rallies and handled all of the advertising. In the last ten days before the general election Lark sent a bulk-rate letter to every household in the county denouncing the Democratic candidates in harsh language as untrustworthy and urging a straight Republican vote. For Lark's organization a straight Republican vote meant a single X in the party bloc on the paper ballot, not putting an X for the party candidates for each individual office.

Party loyalty was a dominant characteristic of the party's candidates. There was little or no reason to focus on the issues to be dealt with once in office. The party organization elected them and when sworn into office they would implement the party platform. (There is virtue in this. The party is accountable for its candidates and their performance in office. The British

House of Commons has a similar system, absent the patronage. British parties select their candidates, who run on the party manifesto.) There is, however, a major weakness in the system. The party relying on patronage and party loyalty is vulnerable on unexpected issues. I am convinced Chairman Lark and Representative Bower were completely surprised by the way my campaign used Bower's "no" vote against him on bringing coal companies under the clean streams law.

The Lark organization had discipline and a sense of direction. Together with the fact that the county Democrats had little comparable in terms of leadership or patronage, this produced consistent electoral success. When I began my law practice in Sunbury in 1963, the Lark organization candidates filled every position in the courthouse except for the statutorily mandated minority county commissioner, George F. Perles, and the Prothonotary, Larry V. Snyder, a Democrat who lost a foot while serving in the army in the Battle of the Bulge.

For state offices the Lark organization held the State Senate seat through Preston B. Davis, a respected lawyer from Milton who had been county solicitor, and Adam T. Bower, who was first elected to the 108th House of Representative seat in 1938. Democrat John F. Stank represented the eastern portion of the county in the other House seat. Although a hardworking neighborhood campaigner, Stank lost in 1964 to Paul Ruane, a schoolteacher from Coal Township on the Lark slate. Ruane held the seat until defeated by Democrat Joseph Bradley in 1974.

Equally important, the Lark organization produced substantial regular pluralities for statewide and national Republican candidates. Lark himself had become a leader in the state Republican Party and played influential roles in choosing statewide candidates.

Lark had a valid reason to call Northumberland County "the Gibraltar of the GOP."

The first cracks in the seeming invincibility of the Lark organization came in the 1960s. Aggressive Democratic candidates like Oscar Kehler, a businessman from Trevorton, and Dr. William Rumberger, a dentist from Sunbury, ran as Democrats determined to win. In the 1963 election for county commissioners, Kehler ran 297 votes behind Fred Kohler, one of the two Lark candidates, but 483 ahead of Fred Hoffman, the other Lark candidate. The second Democrat, George Perles, came in fourth, 96 votes behind Hoffman. This kept Lark in control of the courthouse, but it showed that Democrats could defeat Lark candidates.

In 1965, Rumberger ran for county coroner against Dr. Henry Ulrich, the Lark candidate, and seemed on election night to be the winner by 15 votes. Rumberger was confident he had won, but Lark himself told him "no Democrat wins in Northumberland County by 15 votes." Lark contested the election and the results began to change with every ballot box that was opened. When Ulrich's lead went over 100 Rumberger conceded, but privately vowed—with Kehler—to run for county commissioner in two years and take control of the courthouse.

Rumberger and Kehler did run successfully as a team for county commissioners in 1967 and became the first Democrats to control the courthouse in fifty-two years. But it took eighteen months after the election—in June of 1969—for them to take their seats. In the year and a half between the election and their taking office, the voters of Northumberland County were subjected to an election contest, including questioning of the absentee ballots, that revealed the irregularities that had marred the county's election system. On absentee voting, it became clear that the sheriff's office personnel hand delivered absentee voting applications to the residents of the county nursing home and brought back a unanimous Republican vote, even when Rumberger's aunt resided there. As for the ballots in the precinct boxes, expert testimony stated that boxes were opened and ballots changed after the polls were closed.

The voting public had the picture of a county election system of questionable integrity that seemed annually subject to protracted election disputes. It was a painful experience for both the political parties and the public. In the first election contests, the ballot boxes were stored in the bowels of the courthouse basement. Guards employed by both political parties sat by the door to the storage room in round-the-clock shifts to protect against tampering with the ballots. In the 1967 contest for county commissioners the ballot boxes were stored in the vault at the First National Bank of Sunbury, eliminating the possibility of ballot tampering and the need to hire guards.

The litigation over the votes count dragged on for days, ballot by ballot and precinct by precinct, as the vote counters on the courtroom floor reviewed each ballot while lawyers for both political parties looked on. When a question arose about a particular ballot, the lawyers took it to the judge, who would make a ruling. The proceedings produced huge expenses for each party in fees for lawyers and handwriting experts. The public was tired of it. Even the Republican-leaning Sunbury *Daily Item* editorialized that a reform of the process was needed.

I paid close attention to these contests, as my discussion in chapters 5 and 6 will show. To win a seat in the legislature I would need to challenge and defeat the Lark "machine" and do it with enough votes to preclude an election contest. I would have to crack Gibraltar.

3

Running for the House

In contemplating the 1966 campaign for the House seat I recognized the magnitude of the challenge. The incumbent, Adam Bower, was the senior Republican in the House, first elected in 1938 when I was two years old. He was chairman of the House Republican caucus, important to the administration of Governor Scranton and an integral part of the Lark organization. My father had opposed him twice and did not come close. Yet I thought Bower had made a serious political mistake in being one of only six Representatives to vote against H.B. 585, to bring the coal companies under the clean streams law.

I planned the campaign on several principles. First, I would put together my own "organization" but do it entirely with volunteers. Even if I wanted it, there was no patronage available to me or any other Democrat in Northumberland County. Second, the campaign would be issue oriented, with heavy emphasis on clean streams and Bower's negative vote. Thirdly, the campaign would make an aggressive effort to get Republican votes. There was no other way to win. The Republicans had a registration lead of 60 percent to 40 percent in the new 108th House District of western Northumberland County and all of Montour County. Finally, I would make personal contact with as many voters as possible. I needed all the Democratic votes and a good number of Republican ones too.

I also appreciated the opportunity created when Montour County was added to the 108th House District for the first time, a result of legislative reapportionment. The Lark organization and Bower had no prior involvement with Montour County. We therefore would give special attention to Montour County, where politics was more a matter of personal initiative and personality and much less party organization than in Northumberland

Basse Beck, center, with the author and James Frederick of Watsontown. Source: Personal file photo.

County. Although the Montour County state representative was Republican Harry Kessler, the Democrats held several courthouse offices. Clara Van Kirk was register of wills and my friend, Richard C. Brittain, was the district attorney. Both Van Kirk and Brittain agreed to help me. Esther and Frank Cotner of Washingtonville became active supporters.

Basse Beck became chairman of the Bipartisan Citizens for Kury Committee, just as he had promised. His stature as a businessman and his well-known advocacy for environmental reclamation put significant heft into the campaign. For committerer treasurer I was fortunate to get William T. Deeter, president of the Danville National Bank, who diligently handled paying the campaign bills from the $7,500 my wife and I put into the campaign. It was awkward for me and Beth to ask for campaign contributions, so we just paid the bills, all of them.

But first I had to win the primary election. Paul Becker, the chair of the Montour County Democratic Committee, became a candidate. We had a spirited and nonhostile campaign which I won handily. The primary raised my visibility in Montour County, and Becker became a strong ally.

Between the primary election in May and the end of July I developed the entire general election campaign that would be launched the first week in

August. In that period I drafted every newspaper and radio advertisement, completed campaign brochures, and designed a public opinion questionnaire for the district based on one used by Representative John Pittenger, a Democrat elected from Lancaster. Beth and I also prepared a schedule for a door-to-door campaign that would put me in every precinct for the time proportionate to the number of voters in the precinct. The voter total in the entire House district was divided by the number of precincts, and the result was laid out against the number of days available for campaigning.

We calculated that a precinct of 500 voters was worth a day of door knocking, a precinct of 1,000 voters two days. On that basis a door-to-door campaign was scheduled and begun the day after Labor Day. I also worked with Harriet Klingman, an enthusiastic Democrat from Sunbury, who agreed to lead the volunteers' efforts. She called together the Democratic women of Sunbury, including my mother, and others to operate the campaign headquarters, keep my schedule, and—most important later—address envelopes for a mailing to every voter.

Harriet Klingman, standing right, and the volunteers who formed the base of the volunteers in the 1966 House campaign. Left to right, Gloria Neidig, Beverly Fiedler, Pauline Huey, Pearl Haupt, Pauline Bickel, and Mrs. Klingman. Source: *Courtesy of the Sunbury* Daily Item.

I spent August walking up and down the main streets of Sunbury, Northumberland, Danville, Milton, and Watsontown handing out the public opinion questionnaire suggested by Pittenger, asking that it be completed and returned to me. Between the handouts and a random mailing we distributed 3,500 questionnaires. I promised to read every returned questionnaire. I kept the promise and acknowledged receipt of every one.

The results were encouraging. Five hundred forty-five, about 15 percent, were returned, a sufficient basis for a press release of the results that received good coverage. The *Danville News* ran the results, together with a photograph of me reading the responses behind a large stack of them. The paper said it believed my questionnaire to be the first ever distributed by a local candidate for the legislature. Just after Labor Day the campaign ran a newspaper advertisement with the same photo of me reading one of the questionnaires.

The returned questionnaires proved quite informative. By reading every one I developed a better "feel" for the voters of the district. The large number of responses that had handwritten notes or comments impressed me. These voters appreciated communicating directly with me. They wanted to be heard, and I was happy to listen.

While passing out questionnaires in a bank in Milton, Northumberland County, I got the first tangible evidence that I could win the election. One

Reading the answers to the public opinion questionnaire distributed in August of 1966. The response was surprisingly strong. Source: *Personal file photo.*

of the tellers asked me who my opponent was. "Adam Bower," I replied. "Hmm . . . we haven't seen him up here for years," the teller responded. The answer hit me like an injection of adrenaline. I left the bank feeling enormously buoyed.

Another pleasant surprise came in August. I received a telephone call from K. Leroy Irvis, the House Democratic caucus chairman, inviting me to have dinner with him. We met in Harrisburg a week later and talked about my campaign. Irvis showed great interest in our efforts. He gave me a number of bits of information about Bower, as well, as tips on how to conduct the campaign for greatest effect. He wished me well and we parted. Realizing that the House Democratic leadership was paying attention to my efforts, I returned home with increased confidence.

We launched the formal campaign right after Labor Day, starting with the opening of the campaign headquarters in several rooms next to my father's shoe repair shop (closed several years before) on North Third Street in Sunbury. A large banner declared, "For Clean Streams and Clean Politics. Kury for Representative." Harriet Klingman organized the volunteers and managed the day-to-day operations. We also opened a Montour County headquarters on Mill Street in Danville that was run by Clara Van Kirk, Mary Brittain (mother of the district attorney), and Nancy Whitney.

The initial radio and newspaper advertising focused on clean streams. The timing of the ads and my campaign fortuitously coincided with newspaper stories of fish kills from pollution on the north and west branches of the Susquehanna.

"Poison Kills 100,000 Fish in North Branch" declared the Sunbury *Daily Item* in a front-page story on August 1, 1966.

The *Danville News* editorialized on August 8, 1966:

> Well, here we go again.
> Anywhere between 70,000 and 100,000 fish in the north branch of the Susquehanna . . . are destroyed by what was believed to be acid mine drainage.
> Doesn't it all sound familiar?
> And will it ever end?

"Mahoning Fish Kill Probed" appeared in the Sunbury *Daily Item* on August 10, 1966.

"Sludge Dam Kills 95% of Kettle Creek Fish" reported the *Daily Item* on September 6, 1966.

With so many people in the district relying on the river for fishing, boating, and swimming, these fish kill reports proved to be a political godsend for the campaign. The public became increasingly receptive to our environmental message. And 1966 was not the first time such stories had appeared.

In the late summer of 1965 a major fish kill devastated the west branch from Clearfield to Northumberland and Sunbury. In September of 1965 the Milton and Sunbury papers carried front page stories headlined "Susquehanna Due For Slug of Acid" (*Milton Standard*, September 3); "Susquehanna Acid Slug Takes Heavy Fish Toll," together with photos of the dead fish (*Milton Standard*, September 15); and "West Branch Fish Kill Arrives at Northumberland" (Sunbury *Daily Item*, September 16).

These are examples of the stories. There were many more. These newspaper reports graphically documented the arguments that Basse Beck had been making for several years in his "Up and Down the River" column in the Sunbury *Daily Item*. (See appendix A for examples of these columns.) With Bower's vote against bringing the coal companies under the clean streams law, the cumulative impact of these stories, and Basse Beck's columns that preceded them, was to hand me a ripe issue that few candidates receive. We recognized that and we used it to the fullest advantage.

Basse Beck recorded and paid for a radio ad in his own voice declaring that he sat in the hall of the House of Representatives and watched Adam Bower vote "no" on the bill to bring the coal companies under the clean streams law. We also ran newspaper ads with photos of the recent fish kill. One photo showed a boy with sad look, his collie dog next to him, holding a dead fish. This was not a posed photo, but one we took from news stories published earlier.

Another photograph, taken by Beth, showed me holding two large jars of water, one clear and taken from our kitchen tap and the other coal black, taken from Shamokin Creek, that flowed into the Susquehanna just south of Sunbury and was badly polluted with coal drainage. The ad, with the photo in the center, made a simple declaration, "The Choice is Yours!"

While the ads were running, Beth and I began the door-to-door campaign we planned in July. We always worked with the current voter registration lists so that we only called on homes of registered voters. When Beth campaigned, she took one side of the street and I took the other. If someone was home, we made a brief introduction and asked if we could give them a brochure. For those not home, I left a brochure in the mailbox with a card attached, saying, "Sorry you weren't home when I called. I will appreciate your vote on Election Day, November 8. Thank you. Franklin Kury." This message, in blue handwriting, was printed in advance so I didn't have to take the time to write it personally. The other side of the card was a formal calling card showing my name as a candidate for the House, as well as the headquarters address and telephone number.

We also marked the registration sheets to indicate the name of anyone we spoke with and the names from homes where no one came to the door.

The "Choice is Yours" photograph taken by Elizabeth Kury and used as the basic campaign photograph in 1966. Source: Personal file photo.

These lists were given to Harriet Klingman at the headquarters, who arranged to have follow-up letters to those we met, as well as to those who weren't home. The volunteers couldn't do letters for everyone, but they did enough to make a significant impact. I signed every letter and occasionally added personal postscripts.

Chapter 3

Political campaigns are a roller coaster ride of ups and downs. In early October I was flying high. Genevieve Blatt, the secretary of Internal Affairs and a popular statewide figure, agreed to do a coffee klatch at the home of Paul and Nancy Whitney in Riverside. The Whitneys sent three dozen invitations to meet Miss Blatt and me. At the appointed hour only one couple arrived. I felt hugely embarrassed. My self-confidence, which had been growing steadily, crashed. Miss Blatt, however, took it in good stride and told me not be discouraged.

In mid-October we ran a series of radio ads to make a preemptive strike on a fundamental tenet of the Lark organization, the straight Republican vote. Lark always preached that the only safe vote was a single "X" in the Republican Party block on the Northumberland County paper ballot. This meant a vote for every Republican candidate. The first preemptive strike was a radio ad done by Richard Brittain, the district attorney of Montour County, and went like this:

Announcer: With me in the studio is Richard C. Brittain, the district attorney of Montour County. Attorney Brittain, is a split vote as valid as a straight party vote?

Brittain: Certainly. A split vote is just as good as a straight party vote.

Announcer: So, if I want to vote Republican but split my vote to elect Franklin Kury as state representative, will my vote be counted?

Brittain: Absolutely. It would be a criminal offense not to count that ballot.

Announcer: Thank you, Attorney Brittain. The preceding was paid for by the Bipartisan Citizens for Kury Campaign.

The campaign ran that ad on every radio station that served the district several times a day for the rest of the campaign. In retrospect, I believe that ad, together with Basse Beck's ad, had an enormous impact on the results.

Two weeks before the election the campaign made a second preemptive strike on the Lark organization and the county commissioners, who were in charge of conducting the election count. Through my friend Dean Fisher, a lawyer in Williamsport, we obtained the services of Thomas C. Raup, a lawyer in Fisher's office and a part-time assistant district attorney of Lycoming County. We issued a press announcement that Raup had been appointed special counsel to the campaign. Raup personally went to a County Commissioners' meeting on my behalf and reviewed with them the procedure for tabulating the votes and guarding the ballot boxes. Raup's appearance served notice that we were ready to challenge any questionable items in the vote count.[1]

The Lark organization now put its full efforts into the Bower campaign. It began to run newspaper advertisements touting the incumbent's seniority and experience, pointing out that he was an important member of Governor Scranton's legislative team.

Bower then announced that he had, using his seniority, obtained funds to build a fabridam across the Susquehanna River at Sunbury. A fabridam is a collapsible dam made of neoprene that stretches completely across the stream, is raised in warm weather to give deeper water for boating, and lowered in cold weather to allow the passage of ice and debris. Bower had, with the governor's approval, put together the state's commitment to the longest fabridam in the world (at that time). This was Bower's counterattack to my clean streams issue.

My campaign responded with a new advertisement with the photograph of me holding the two jars of water. This time the question asked became, "What kind of water will the fabridam hold?"

The Lark organization went into full attack during the two weeks before the election. Lark sent his annual election year letter to every Republican household on October 28. Printed on Northumberland County Republican Committee stationery and signed by him as the chairman, the first paragraphs heaped praise on outgoing Governor Scranton and Lt. Governor Ray Shafer, the candidate to succeed Scranton. Lark then demonized the Democratic candidate, Milton Shapp, as a wild spender and then sang the praises of Congressman Herman Schneebeli, Senator Davis, and Representative Paul Ruane (in the other Northumberland County house district), all seeking re-election.

The next two paragraphs focused on me—and my wife.

> A greedy young payroll Democrat, not quite 30 years old, is trying to defeat Adam Bower, Chairman of the House Republican caucus, and the original proposer and leading advocate of the Sunbury fabridam.
>
> Adam's opponent is out-Shapping Shapp, brazenly contradicting official state records in his untruthful advertising. On the Democratic payroll at more than $5,000 per year for the last six years (he's only 29), and with his wife getting another $1,700 political handout, he can really taste political money.

October 31 Bower sent his own personal letter to the voters. He reiterated his senior position in the House and his close relationship with Governor Scranton. He asserted his success in obtaining $960,000 for the fabridam and that my clean streams charges were a smokescreen. He denied voting against the clean streams bill and said he voted for every clean streams bill since the administration of Governor Duff.[2] Bower also explained that prior to the letter his duties in Harrisburg prevented him from campaigning throughout the district.

The Shafer for Governor campaign sent a postcard to every voter urging a vote for Bower because of his leadership on clean streams issues. The front of the card carried a color photograph of Shafer and his family. The

Governor Scranton signing into law H.B. 535 as the author looks on. Seated to the right of Scranton are Representatives Tom Foerster (glasses with dark frames) and John Laudadio, the prime sponsors of the bill. The right half of this photograph was used in a brochure sent to every Republican voter in the 1966 House campaign. Source: *Courtesy of Outdoor People of Pennsylvania and the Pennsylvania Federation of Sportsmen's Clubs.*

Northumberland County Republican Committee also distributed a hand card with a photograph of Bower with Governor Scranton when the governor approved the fabridam funding.

My campaign had two carefully planned last-minute surprises. The first was a red, white, and blue brochure sent to every Republican household signed by Basse Beck as Chairman of the Bipartisan Citizens for Kury Committee. The front of the brochure featured a photograph of Governor Scranton signing H.B. 585 while I looked over his shoulder. The photograph was taken and published previously by *Outdoor People of Pennsylvania*, the newspaper of the state Federation of Sportsmen's Clubs. Since I worked on the bill with Basse Beck, I was invited to the signing ceremony by the Sportsmen's Federation and took full advantage of the opportunity. The paper willingly provided me a copy of the photograph. Inside, the brochure urged a vote for me for "Clean Streams and Clean Politics" signed by Basse Beck. The top half of the back panel showed how to split a Republican ticket to vote for me. In bright red in the middle of the page appeared:

TAKE THIS BROCHURE INTO THE VOTING BOOTH WITH YOU ON ELECTION DAY, NOV. 8 AND USE IT AS A GUIDE IN MARKING YOUR BALLOT.

The lower third of the pages had the following quotation.

> ". . . in this election it isn't enough to vote as your grandfather did or as your father did. It isn't enough simply to say, 'Well, this is is my party label and I'm going to vote that way because the other fellow has the same label.' You've got to look beneath the labels. It isn't enough to vote as somebody else tells you, someone who is the head of an organization to which you belong . . . JUDGE THE CANDIDATES ON THE BASIS NOT OF WHAT LABELS THEY WEAR, BUT WHAT'S BEHIND THEM . . . WHAT DO THEY STAND FOR?"
> —RICHARD M. NIXON
> Former Vice-President of the United States
> (Caps and bold are as used on the brochure.)[3]

Considering the nasty attack on Democrats in the annual letter Chairman Lark mailed every election eve, as well as his always urging a straight Republican vote, I took considerable satisfaction in sending this brochure to every Republican household in the district.

The other surprise was a mailing to every voting household containing a general brochure with photographs, my biographical information, and a statement of the issues. Harriet Klingman and her volunteers made both mailings possible by hand-addressing over 18,000 envelopes, stuffing them, and getting them ready for a bulk mailing the week before the election. Harriet's husband, John, a retired postal employee, helped to insure that we complied with all of the rules for a bulk mailing.

The campaign also ran large advertisements in the Sunbury, Milton, and Danville papers showing "Three Ways To Vote for Franklin Kury"—a split Republican vote, a straight Democratic vote, and a candidate-by-candidate vote.

Having received a tip to watch the ballot boxes from Watsontown, I also employed several reliable supporters to follow the ballot boxes from their polling places in Watsontown to the courthouse in Sunbury. I was concerned that these boxes might be opened before they got to Sunbury.

Election day proved to be another roller-coaster ride. Late in the afternoon rain began. By suppertime, when most of the voters went to the polls, the rain became quite heavy. I became despondent, fearing that the rain would keep my voters at home. My fears proved unjustified. I won by a vote of 10,564 to 9,625, a plurality of 939. The size of the plurality removed another fear. Based on the experience of Dr. Rumberger and others, I ran the campaign on the assumption that if my winning margin was less than 500 votes on election night I would never take the seat.

The victory became a statewide story. The *Philadelphia Daily News* carried a photograph of me and Beth holding the election results and reporting that I had "pulled the major upset of the Pennsylvania election." Similar stories were carried in Pittsburgh and other areas. Beth and I were elated. We had truly cracked Gibraltar. I was on my way to the House of Representatives. The exhilaration of the election victory was, however, soon shattered by the news that Basse Beck had suffered a stroke that incapacitated him for the rest of his life. He died in 1974.

That night I also thought of my father. His legislative aspiration for me, the one broached in the hotel lobby eight years earlier, had been fulfilled. All of the time we had spent together in politics, my experience in Harrisburg and Washington, hard work by dedicated volunteers, and good planning—plus the luck of running on the burning issue of fish kills in the Susquehanna—came together in a way that I could not have foreseen on that January in 1958 when my father asked me to run that year. In the years I spent in the House and Senate my father was never far from my mind.

II
THE HOUSE OF REPRESENTATIVES, 1966–1972

4

The Education of a Freshman

As a newly elected representative, I went to the state capital in December 1966 for the organization meeting of the Democratic House caucus for the new legislative session. I felt excited by my election victory but also apprehensive about what lay ahead. The Republicans controlled everything—the Governorship, the Senate (27–23), and the House (104–99). Adam Bower, who I had just defeated, had been named chief clerk of the House. I was certain he would use that position to undermine my work in the House.

I was surprised by the lack of accommodations that awaited the new representatives. There was no office, no secretary, and no telephone for me or the other new legislators. Our only seat was the one assigned to us on the House floor. The salary was $7,200 per year. In addition, legislators received a $4,800 nonaccountable expense account, and a reimbursement of $.10 per mile for travel to and from Harrisburg.[1]

How would I get my legislative work done, especially constituent services? Fortunately for me, I had a law office in Sunbury and used that to full advantage, at my own expense, to answer the mail and make many of my phone calls.[2] I knew from my experience in working for Congressman Rhodes the critical importance of responding to constituent letters, telephone calls, and problems with the government.

Before long Herbert Fineman, the Democratic floor leader, hired Gertrude McNeill and several secretaries for House members. For the first year there was one secretary for about twenty members. We were encouraged to write out responses before we took our turn with the assigned secretary.

The party caucus is critical to the working of a legislative body. Limited to elected party members and leadership staff, caucuses are held before each voting session to explain and discuss the bills that will be acted on. To run

The author takes the oath of office as a freshman representative. Mrs. Kury holds the Bible and Judge Sidney Hoffman administers the oath. Source: Personal file photo.

a legislature without caucuses would be like playing football games without huddles. Always closed to the press and public, the caucuses permit each party to discuss and strategize on the legislation they will be voting on. In the caucuses the leaders count the votes so they know what will succeed and fail in the voting.[3]

At the first House Democratic caucus, the new members were introduced and the caucus proceeded to elect as our leaders for the new session Herbert Fineman of Philadelphia as minority leader and K. Leroy Irvis as minority whip. The Philadelphia and Allegheny County delegations, which had 49 of the 99 Democratic representatives between them, had worked out the slate in advance of the meeting. No one else was nominated, and we had little choice but to go along with their candidates. Fortunately, both Fineman, whom I had not previously met, and Irvis, proved to be intelligent, articulate, and effective leaders for whom I developed considerable respect.

When the House was in session our caucus met at least once a week to go over the legislative calendar, get a briefing on each bill, hear the leaders' views on the bills, discuss amendments,[4] and discuss party strategy when

Swearing-in day at the House 1967. Helen Kury with three of her children. Left to right; Channing, Mrs. Kury, Wilson, and the author. Source: Personal file photo.

that was appropriate. The great bulk of bills did not involve party positions. Those were usually confined to the budget bill and significant policy proposals from the Republican Shafer administration. Attendance at caucuses, however, was essential to understanding what forces were at play on the bills to be considered. To go to the floor without participating in the caucus put a legislator at a considerable disadvantage and political risk. Missing a caucus could mean voting in ignorance of significant political and substantive information.

The caucus provided a great education for me in the diversity of Pennsylvania and the manner in which politics was practiced outside of Northumberland County. Philadelphia, for example, had 29 members in the caucus, all of whom solidly supported Fineman and provided his base to be floor leader. Their view of Pennsylvania struck me as being quite parochial. I got the impression that, for some of them, the western boundary line of Pennsylvania was the Schuylkill River, which flows into the Delaware River just south of Philadelphia. The members from northeastern Pennsylvania and the southwest also came from strong, if smaller, Democratic organizations, but their focus was on undoing the damages to the people and environment of their areas from the ravages of coal mining and steel making.

The area between Philadelphia and Pittsburgh had sent about two dozen members to our caucus. These "rural" legislators were not elected by party organizations like the one in Philadelphia. The upstate legislators rejected the suggestion that they follow the lead of the Philadelphia caucus in their votes.[5] Kent Shelhamer, an apple farmer from Columbia County, became a leader of a group of upstate Democrats that frequently questioned the party leadership on its policies and showed their independence from Philadelphia.

But I learned quickly the importance of not surprising my party leaders on the House floor with a vote or speech contrary to their position on bills of importance to them. The time and place to reveal differences was in the caucus. The leaders did not always like dissent, but they usually respected it as long as they had advance notice. Fineman and Irvis recognized that to regain a voting majority in the House they needed to elect upstate Democrats not produced by strong party organizations and not inclined to support the policy objectives of urban Pittsburgh and Philadelphia.

Since my party was in the minority for the 1966–1968 session, there was little we could do to pass significant bills. We could make speeches, offer amendments, and occasionally work with someone on the Republican majority side to develop and enact proposals that were not on party line

Newly elected Governor Raymond P. Shafer at the Milton Bi-centennial. To the right are Senator Preston Davis and the author. Source: *Courtesy of the Milton* Standard.

bills. (See my discussion of the absentee ballot reform legislation in the next chapter.)

MY POLITICAL EDUCATION DEEPENS

The most startling education, however, came from none other than Adam Bower himself. Early in 1967 I received a phone call asking me to call on Mr. Bower in his office. The call came as a total surprise. I couldn't recall ever speaking to him before. During the entire campaign of 1966 I never met him or saw him. When I met with him, he asked me to sit down.

"Franklin, there is something going on you ought to know about."

"What is that?"

"Your leader, Fineman, has put your county chairman, John Mazur, on the House payroll as a research assistant." He showed me the papers documenting Mazur's appointment.

I was stunned. I barely knew Mazur and was just getting to know Fineman. Why would Fineman do that without talking to me first? Mazur, a resident of Mt. Carmel, was not in my district. But I realized at once that Bower had just done me a significant favor. If I had continued in ignorance of Mazur's position on the House staff, the Lark organization would likely use it against me when I ran for reelection. Why would Bower help me? I should have asked him, but failed to do so.

We chatted for a few moments, I thanked him, and left. I knew what had to be done. I went directly to Fineman's office and demanded that he issue a press release announcing that he had hired Mazur and was taking responsibility for it. Fineman did that, the Northumberland County papers carried the story, and Mazur's employment was not an issue in my reelection.

I came away from that experience with an enhanced respect for Adam Bower that remains to this day. Several years after his death, Representatives Merle Phillips and Russell Fairchild passed a bill to name the fabridam the Adam T. Bower Fabridam. They asked me to be the speaker for the dedication, and I was pleased to do it. At the dedication I acknowledged Bower's years of service to the district but also described the help he gave me after I had defeated him. I thanked him again.

Another part of my education in state government also came from a Republican. I had received a complaint from a constituent about a matter involving the Department of Labor and Industry. To deal with this, I sent a letter to the department. A week or so later I received a telephone call from the secretary of the department, Clifford L. Jones, who told me how the department would resolve the problem. I was impressed that a Republican governor's cabinet member would personally call a freshman Democrat. That may just have been Clifford Jones' way of dealing with legislators, but it showed me that political differences should not obstruct solving governmental problems. In Jones I met a Republican politician who did not hesitate to reach out to Democrats in the public interest. This encounter also started a friendship that endured until Jones died in 2008. In 1976, when I ran for my second term in the Senate, Jones had become president of Pennsylvanians for Effective Government and endorsed my candidacy.

The Mazur appointment aside, Fineman made a number of excellent appointments to his leadership staff that greatly benefited the caucus. For example, he hired John Pittenger, defeated for reelection in Lancaster, as research director for the caucus. One of the brightest and most issue-knowledgeable persons ever to serve in the legislature, Pittenger taught political science at Franklin and Marshall College, later became Governor Shapp's secretary of education and then dean of Rutgers Law School, as well as co-author of a book on Constitutional law.[6] As our policy "guru," Pittenger provided valuable insight and information on the bills before us. Fineman also helped the caucus by finding more secretarial help and, later, office space. Four to six members shared offices on the top floor of the capitol, and it was appreciated as a step forward.

Reviewing legislation with John Pittenger, Policy Director for the House Democrats.
Source: *Personal file photo.*

The Shapp campaign train in Milton, 1970. Between Shapp and the author is Cecily Sesler and her husband, State Senator William Sesler of Erie, the Democratic candidate for the U.S. Senate. Source: *Personal file photo.*

If I had to point to one lesson from this introduction to the legislature it would be this: Hold off on judging your colleagues by preconceived notions of what they might be like. Herbert Fineman, Adam Bower, and Clifford Jones proved to be surprisingly different than my expectations. That lesson helped me considerably in the rest of my legislative service.

5

Absentee Ballot Reform

In the mid-1960s Schuylkill County had gone without a state senator for two years, York County could not certify its senator, and Lancaster City went without a council for fourteen months. Northumberland County had no commissioners for over seven months following the 1967 election. All of these were related to disputes over the absentee ballots cast.

Absentee voting had been authorized in Pennsylvania for some time. Originally designed to permit military personnel to vote, the law was expanded to allow civilians to vote without going to their polling place. The law, however, was so broadly drafted that aggressive party organizations throughout the state could abuse it. The crux of the problem was that the rules for absentee voting lacked almost all of the safeguards that protect the votes of those voters who cast their ballots personally at a polling place. In a polling place voters must identify themselves, sign their name, and then vote behind a closed curtain, all in the presence of an election board with members of both parties. For absentee voting there was no rule on how applications for the ballot or the ballot itself was sought, delivered, or returned. There was no way to know with certainty who applied for the absentee ballot or actually voted it. This looseness provided a great opportunity for overzealous partisans of both parties in several counties to provide assured votes. When the residents of the North Umberland County nursing home all cast straight Republican votes year after year, one could only be suspicious.

The public anger at the misuse and abuse of absentee ballot created a strong force of opinion that brought Archimedes' principle of leverage to play on the issue. The Chairman of the House Elections and Reapportionment Committee, Republican Representative Guy Kistler of Cumberland

County, made absentee ballot reform a major goal for the 1967–1968 session. I thus fortuitously found myself in an unusual position for a minority party House member. The majority party was going to take up a major issue in which I had keen interest. This would provide a forum that would not be available if only the Democrats wanted to make it a legislative issue.

Chairman Kistler and his committee investigated the controversy, held hearings, and produced H.B. 1908. In advocating for the bill Kistler argued that the absentee ballot controversies in Sunbury, Lackawanna (County), Fayette (County), Pottsville, Lancaster, and York justified the legislation. Although not a member of his committee nor a participant in drafting the bill as introduced, I was pleased to see that its provisions dealt with the causes of the controversies in Northumberland County. I became an active supporter in the extended floor debates on June 19 and 24, 1968.[1] With the bill before the House for enactment on June 19, I made a somewhat lengthy speech describing in detail the absentee ballot abuse and misuse in Northumberland County. I pointed out that the County Commissioners to be elected at the November 1967 general election were still not certified or seated. I offered specific examples of abuse or misuse.

> Northumberland County Home is really a public nursing home for approximately 75 senior citizens who are indigent and unable to take care of themselves. Many of them are in pathetic condition. Some, in fact, have been declared mentally incompetent by the courts; many of them never even registered to vote before they were taken to the county home. Yet, in every general election, Northumberland County finds a large block of straight Republican votes from the county home . . . In the last election, 1967, 67 of 71 voters in the county home were "assisted" by the same individual . . . At one private nursing home . . . 30 persons applied for absentee ballots and listed "nervous" as the reason. It turned out that every one of them was fully ambulatory and many were able to go to church and other places in the community.[2]

I also offered an amendment to delete "vacations" as a reason for obtaining an absentee ballot. The word was not defined in the bill and to me opened a large loophole for further misuse and abuse. My amendment was defeated 66 to 88, with 49 not voting. Nevertheless, on the final passage vote I supported the bill, which passed on June 24, 1968, by 134–43.

As signed into law by Governor Shafer on December 11, 1968,[3] the bill contained provisions that considerably strengthened the integrity of the absentee ballot.

- Applicants have to apply for the absentee ballot in person or in writing by mail; only one application can be given to a voter.
- Copies of all applications are to be kept on record.

- Each party's county chairman is required to designate a representative for each public institution (nursing home), and the designated representatives together are required to visit each institution and provide to the county election office a list to which applications are mailed.
- Teams of three must visit each institution the Friday before election day, conduct the election, and return the ballots to the county.
- The chief clerk of each county is directed to make a list of absentee voters to be sent to each polling place, with copies to the candidates or county chairs.
- The absentee votes are to be counted in each election district after the close of the polls and the results included with the regular results.

These provisions are still part of the Pennsylvania election code.[4] Absentee ballot controversies have, as a result, been virtually eliminated in Pennsylvania.

Enactment of the absentee ballot reform clearly benefited the state's voting public, but it also helped me personally. My active involvement in House action on the bill provided considerable publicity throughout Northumberland County and enhanced my standing with the county's Democratic leaders and office holders, like Commissioners Rumberger and Kehler, as the next chapter shows.

6

Ballot Box Reform in Northumberland County

When the results for the 1967 Northumberland County row office elections were finally certified after eighteen months (as discussed in chapter 2) it marked a cataclysmic event in the county's politics. The Lark organization had been ousted from control of the courthouse, a major source of its power. Democrats William Rumberger and Oscar Kehler became the first Democrats to gain control in half a century. Lawton Shroyer, son of the co-founder of the anti-Lark Republicans but supported by Lark, won the minority commissionership.

Early in their term Kehler and Rumberger acted to eliminate the ballot box challenge agony through which they had suffered (and described in chapter 2). They realized that the traditional paper ballot was the nub of the issue.

The basic flaw in the paper ballot lay in the relative ease with which it could be tampered with after the polls closed. In each polling place the vote count began when ballots were removed from their boxes and deposited on a table. The ballots were then separated into three piles—straight Republican, straight Democratic, and split tickets. The initial count was therefore simplified. Every Republican candidate got a tally from his party's straight vote, the Democratic candidates likewise, and then the split ballots were tabulated office by office. When the tabulation had been completed, the election board signed the return sheets, put the ballots back in the box segregated by straight party ballots and split ballot, and the boxes were taken to the courthouse where they were stored in the basement to await the official count ten days later. Whoever had the keys to the courthouse basement had access to the ballot boxes.

To change the results before the official count in favor of, for example, a Republican candidate whose results were close, persons with access to the boxes could surreptitiously open them, remove the straight Democratic ballots, and place an "X" at the name of the Republican candidate needing votes to win. The ballots were then returned to the ballot box. After the official count, an appeal could be made to the court to open the boxes the appealing party knew to contain altered ballots. The boxes in question would be opened and when the recount completed, it would appear that the Republican candidate had gained votes overlooked by the polling place election board.

Another problem with paper ballots had also become apparent. It often took hours to complete the tabulations, especially if there were a lot of split tickets. Polling places frequently could not complete their work until midnight or later. Many of the election boards were senior citizens and tiredness from the lengthy counts contributed to honest errors. In the 1968 election the Third Ward of the Borough of Northumberland did not complete its tabulation until the approach of dawn the next morning. This gave

The Northumberland County special committee on ballot box reform during a hearing. Left to right, Representative Paul G. Ruane of Coal Township, the author, William J. McLaughlin of Ralpho Township, and Joseph Buchkowskie of Kulpmont. Source: Personal file photo.

Allegheny County Elections Director Will Alton (third from the right) explains voting machines to the Northumberland County voting reform committee. Left to right are William McLaughlin, Dr. Robert Yannacone, Joseph Buchkowskie, Al Santor (Northumberland County Elections Director), the author, and Alton. Source: Courtesy of the Allegheny County, Department of Public Works.

it the distinction of being the next to the last precinct in Pennsylvania to complete its work. In counties with automatic voting machines the polling places completed their work within an hour or two, and the main delay came from the count of absentee ballots.

The commissioners, led by Kehler and Rumberger, appointed a citizens' committee to study the controversy enveloping the paper ballot and make recommendations to insure the integrity of voting in the county. The commissioners appointed me to chair the committee with Representative Paul Ruane, a Republican, as co-chair. The other members included Edwin Weisbond, an optometrist from Mt. Carmel; William J. McLaughlin, a savings and loan bank officer from Elysburg; Joseph Buchkowskie, district manager of the International Ladies Garment Workers Union from Kulpmont; and Dr. Robert Yannaccone, a physician from Watsontown. Except for Ruane and me the committee members had been active in party politics.

The committee met and developed a collegial manner and a surprising sense of unity of purpose. Recognizing the basic flaws of the paper ballot, our committee decided to look for other methods of voting. The use of automated voting machines in Allegheny County, Pennsylvania, came to our attention. Our committee, accompanied by Al Santor, the county elections director, and Harry Dietz, a reporter for the Shamokin *News-Item*, traveled to Pittsburgh to see the system for ourselves. Will Alton, the Allegheny County Director of Elections, gave us a complete briefing on his experience with automatic voting machines, including a demonstration of how they worked. We were impressed.

The voting machines we saw were like oversized adding machines that record the vote every time the lever is pulled, the record being imprinted simultaneously on an original and four copy sheets. To insure the accuracy of the count, the election board checks the tabulation windows on the back of each machine just before the polls are open on election day. There should be a "0" for each candidate. When the polls close, the election board opens the machines and removes the five imprinted copies. The board signs the original and one copy and sends them to the courthouse. Each political party is given a copy and the fifth copy is posted on the polling place door. We saw at once that there was no way, short of complete cooperation between the polling place officials, that anyone could alter the results. The existence of five copies precluded that.

The machines had another advantage. They could be used to educate schoolchildren in voting procedures. Paper ballot boxes were stored in the courthouse between elections and had no other use. Automated voting machines, however, could be left at their polling place, often a school. Allegheny County allowed schools where the machines were stored to use them in conducting class elections. All the school needed was a package of blank voting paper. We raised one negative. What happened when the machine malfunctioned? Alton assured us that the machines were so simple that rarely happened. The county did have backup machines available for immediate dispatch to a polling place, as well as a trained mechanic.

When the committee met back in Sunbury to consider the voting machine, we concluded that the advantages far outweighed the possibility of machinery malfunction. Upon our return to Northumberland County we held a meeting to discuss our findings and to plan a public meeting on the automated voting machine as a replacement for the absentee ballot.[1] The public meeting was held in the main courtroom and a number of witnesses testified, including Republican County Chairman Henry Lark. County Commissioners Rumberger and Shroyer attended. Following the meeting our committee recommended that the county use the automatic voting machines in future elections. The commissioners adopted our recommendation, arranged the financing to pay for the machines, obtained the necessary approval from the State Election Bureau, and ordered the installation of the machines, which were used for the first time in 1976. Northumberland County has not had a contested election since.

In 2002, however, the Congress enacted the Help America Vote Act (HAVA)[2] that required the elimination of lever-activated voting machines, like those in Northumberland County, in federal elections throughout the country. Since there are federal elections every two years for representatives in Congress, as well as for president every four years and U.S. senator every six, it made no sense for counties to have one type of voting mechanism for federal elections and another for state and municipal elections. The counties complied by meeting the federal requirements for all elections and, as a result, there are no lever-operated voting machines anywhere in Pennsylvania today.

Although voting machines are no longer used, the method used to use them in the first place is a good model for effective reform on other issues. Although Rumberger and Kehler had the power to make the change without the minority commissioner's vote, they created a bipartisan citizens committee. The committee studied the problem, looked at alternatives, held a public hearing, and made its recommendation. When the commissioners implemented the recommendations, voting machines to replace the paper ballot were not controversial. County government reform had worked.

7

Clean Streams and the Environmental Revolution

THE HISTORICAL PERSPECTIVE

From 1966 through 1972 an environmental revolution raged through the House of Representatives that is best appreciated in the context of Pennsylvania's history. William Penn and the colonists found Penn's woods abundant with wildlife and well endowed with natural resources—water, forests, iron, and—later—coal. When the constitution writers and other founders of the state and national governments did their work, there was no apparent need to be concerned about the natural environment. They focused on the political. The result was that our state and national laws provided explicit and strong protection for our political world but were silent concerning the natural world.

As Pennsylvania developed there were no laws regulating the harvesting of our state's natural resources. In the period between the Civil War and World War II, Pennsylvania became one of the giants of the "smoke stack" economies. The mining of coal and iron deposits became the base for the railroad and steel industries. With no laws to restrain the manner in which these minerals were taken from the earth, the iron, steel, coal, and railroad interests brazenly exploited our natural endowment without any regard for their impact on the future of Pennsylvania. A good illustration is found in the Northumberland County Courthouse in a 1905 deed from the Shamokin and Pottsville Railroad to Monroe Kulp for ninety acres, upon which he built what is now the Borough of Kulpmont. The deed explicitly reserved to the company the right to discharge into the waters of Shamokin Creek the waste from its mines.¹ The results are visible to this day. Pennsylvania has large areas that are marked by culm banks, polluted streams, and scarred earth as a result of this exploitation.

Whenever legislation was enacted to protect the environment, it was done in response to a "disaster" and was limited in scope. The clean streams laws are a good example. The first was passed in 1905 in response to outbreaks of typhoid fever caused by raw sewage in the waters.² This law required some communities to stop discharging raw sewage into streams, but the coal companies were specifically exempted.³

Additional "clean streams" laws were enacted in 1923, 1937, and 1945.⁴ In each one the coal industry was exempted or given highly favorable treatment.⁵ By the mid-1960s, however, Pennsylvania had changed considerably from the days when coal, steel, and railroads were economically and politically supreme. Those industries had lost most of their political power. The people of Pennsylvania and its economy had changed. More and more children and grandchildren of the immigrants who wrested the coal and iron from the earth were educated and financially independent of the coal, steel, and railroad industries.

Television had become commonplace. Television did for the environment what it did for Martin Luther King Jr. and the civil rights movement when they were so brutally treated in Alabama. In their living rooms people saw the environmental disasters, such as the oil spill at Santa Barbara, California. Rachel Carson's *Silent Spring*, showing how commonly accepted chemicals were seriously injuring the environment, had a strong impact on our attitude to the world of nature. The public's knowledge of the environment expanded enormously as it became increasingly aware of the damage inflicted by unregulated or under-regulated use of our natural resources.

These factors came together in the Pennsylvania House of Representatives in the mid-1960s. When the 1967–1968 session began, the state's environmental laws were largely limited to protecting its fish, game, and forest resources. The state had a Fish Commission administering a fish code and a Game Commission implementing a game code. A Department of Forest and Waters managed two million acres of state forests. There were several clean streams laws and mining laws developed in bits and pieces over a period of decades. The Sanitary Water Board carried out the water protection laws and the Department of Mines and Mineral Industries looked after the coal laws. There was nothing in our state law to protect on a comprehensive basis the air, land, water, or aesthetics of our environment.

A NEW CLEAN STREAMS LAW

The environmental revolution really started in the 1965–1966 session with the enactment of House Bill 585, placing the coal industry fully under the water protection laws.⁶ But that was only a first step. In the three legislative sessions that followed, the revolution broke into full fury. The new clean streams law exemplified the force of the revolution.

While the enactment in 1965 of H.B. 585 was historically significant in that it marked the end of the coal industry's political power, I and other House Democrats, like John Laudadio, were not satisfied. We wanted a comprehensive rewriting and reform of the state's water laws. The 1967–1968 session of the legislature, however, did not deal further with the clean streams law. Under Republican control, that session focused on other environmental issues. It passed bills to give the state authority to regulate bituminous coal refuse deposits⁷ and to regulate bituminous open pit coal mining,⁸ as well as to create a Joint Legislative Air and Water Pollution Conservation Commission to study pollution.⁹ The only significant water action taken was to ratify the Susquehanna River Basin Compact with New York, Maryland, and the federal government.¹⁰ However, the main thrust of the compact was an interstate agency to better control the flow and use of the Susquehanna River. Dealing with pollution was secondary.

Stymied by being in the House minority, I spent considerable time reviewing the existing law on water pollution and in drafting a comprehensive clean streams law. On July 16, 1968, with eight co-sponsors, I introduced the bill and made a short speech outlining my objectives:

> . . . thirty years after the "Clean Streams Law" was enacted there are still at least 48 communities and four industries on the north and west branches of the Susquehanna River not in compliance with the law. As of April 1967, there were 26 communities on the Susquehanna's west branch with a population of 38,000 serviced by sewers discharging untreated sewage . . . (at the same time) . . . Watsontown, Milton, Danville, Riverside, and Northumberland, which have long been in compliance, are being required to upgrade . . . their sewage treatment . . . it is unfair to make them spend even more money for upgraded treatment while upstream communities and industries have barely taken the first steps toward compliance.
>
> One of the major purposes of this bill is to give the Sanitary Water Board increased authority to compel compliance by municipalities and industries which have failed to comply even though the law has been on the books for over three decades.¹¹

Following my introductory remarks I inserted into the House record a legal memorandum describing in detail what the bill would do if it became law.¹² I realized the bill had no chance of enactment. The bill sponsors were all Democrats in a Republican-controlled House and the fall election was less than four months away. Yet I wanted to show the seriousness of my interest in a new clean streams law, follow through on my campaign promise, and possibly lay the groundwork for such a bill when my party regained control of the House.

When the 1967–1968 session expired, H.B. 2808 died in the Conservation Committee to which it had been referred. But the Democrats gained control of the House in the 1968 election. With Herbert Fineman elected Speaker and Leroy Irvis Majority Leader we also took control of the committees. John Laudadio of Westmoreland County became chair of the Conservation Committee and I became secretary. Now we were in a position to draft and run the bills we chose, and we did it with enthusiasm.

Laudadio, a retired electrical engineer from Westinghouse Electric Corporation, from Jeannette in Westmoreland County, was the natural leader for the committee. Serving his fourth term, he had made conservation his priority. An avid outdoorsman, he was a former president of the Pennsylvania Federation of Sportsmen's Clubs. He, like Basse Beck, had been speaking out on environmental issues for several years. He was a strong advocate for H B. 585 to bring the coal companies under the water pollution laws. We got along well personally and that facilitated working together in drafting and processing of environmental bills.

A new clean streams law topped our agenda, and we went directly to work on it. Only six months into the new session, on June 24, 1969, Laudadio introduced H.B. 1353, a comprehensive rewriting of the water pollution laws. In a telling sign of the rising tide of the environmental revolution, the bill carried the strong bipartisan co-sponsorship of sixty-eight representatives. I was pleased to be one of the prime sponsors and that much of the work I did on H.B. 2808 of the prior session was utilized in drafting the new proposal. [13]

Our committee spent the rest of 1969 working on the bill, holding hearings and meetings. When H.B. 1353 was on the floor for final passage on January 27, 1970, the House had achieved a consensus that resulted in unanimous passage, 197–0. Neither Laudadio, William Wilt (the chief Republican sponsor) nor I made a speech, but simply inserted our comments into the record.[14]

The Senate passed an amended version that was unacceptable to the House because it appeared to weaken the bill. The bill was sent to a conference committee to work out the difference. Laudadio, Wilt, and I were the conferees for the House. Senators Jack McGregor, Elmer Hawbaker, and Don Oesterling represented the Senate.[15] A satisfactory compromise was reached between the houses, approved by both, and sent to Governor Shafer, who signed it into law on July 31, 1970.[16]

The new law completely revised, rewrote, and expanded Pennsylvania's control of discharges into the waters of the state. This law

- expanded the definitions of "establishment," "industrial waste," "mine," "pollution," and "waters of the Commonwealth."
- gave the Department of Health and Sanitary Water Board authority to implement the law with regulations, inspections, and orders.

- prohibited any municipality, industrial establishment or mine from discharging into the waters of the Commonwealth unless the discharge is allowed by the rules of the board or the discharger has a permit from the department.
- prohibited any person from discharging anything into the public waters any substance that pollutes.
- authorized the attorney general and county district attorneys to enforce the law with injunctions and criminal penalties of $100 to $5,000 for each offense, with each day of violation constituting a separate offense.
- authorized civil penalties of up to $10,000 plus $500 a day for each day of continuing violation.
- authorized the department to issue such orders as are necessary to enforce the act.

I took considerable satisfaction in the new law. First, I was actively involved in drafting and securing its enactment. In doing so, I had made good on the major promise of my first campaign for the House and had kept faith with Basse Beck. More than that, our House of Representatives demonstrated real leadership in a bipartisan manner in overturning a century of abuse of our state waters. We were not following other states or the federal government. In fact, the U.S. Congress did not enact a federal clean water act until two years after we did it in Pennsylvania.[17]

Today Pennsylvania's streams are considerably improved. They are largely free from pollution by sewage, industrial discharges, and discharges from active mines. I feel really good about this.

THE WIDE SWATH OF THE ENVIRONMENTAL REVOLUTION

For me, the new clean streams law was a highlight of the environmental revolution. But it was by no means the only revolutionary law enacted. In the short period of 1967–1972 the legislature enacted more environmental laws than in all of Pennsylvania history. Besides the clean stream law, they included:

- The All Surface Mining Act.[18]
- The Coal Refuse Disposal Control Act.[19]
- The Air Pollution Control Act.[20]
- The Solid Waste Management Act.[21]
- The Pennsylvania Scenic Rivers Act.[22]
- The Department of Environmental Resources creation law.[23]
- The Land and Water Conservation and Reclamation Act.[24]
- The act requiring the Department of Transportation to conduct environmental evaluations in planning highway projects.[25]
- Article I, Section 27, Natural Resources.[26]

Like a sleeping giant, the people of Pennsylvania had been aroused. Acting through their legislature, they threw the massive weight of public opinion onto the legislative levers and moved the environmental world of Pennsylvania in a new direction. The message was strong, unambiguous, and irreversible—Pennsylvania's era of environmental neglect was gone forever.

Disappointment in Restoring Migratory Fish to the Susquehanna

The legislative environmental revolution, however, failed to take decisive action to restore shad and other migratory fish to the Susquehanna. Along

At the Conowingo Dam seeking fishways for shad. Left to right are Robert Bielo, executive director of the Pennsylvania Fish Commission; William Renwick of Elk County, Chair of the House and Fish and Game Committee; and the author. Source: Personal file photo.

with clean streams, this had been one of Basse Beck's great dreams for the environment. Beck wrote about the shad in numerous "Up and Down the River" columns. He made many speeches urging installation of fish passageways on the four hydroelectric dams on the lower Susquehanna that blocked the migration—Conowingo, Holtwood, York Haven, and Safe Harbor. State law required the power companies owning the dams to install the passageways. The law, however, had no effect because the Conowingo dam, the first one coming up the river, is located in Maryland. Pennsylvania's legislature had no jurisdiction over it.

As a House member I tried to carry Beck's dream to reality. I prevailed on Representative William Renwick, chairman of the Fish and Game Committee, to take our committee for a firsthand view of Conowingo and the other dams. That visit generated interest in the problem, but the most I could do legislatively was to increase the penalties on the Pennsylvania power companies for not installing the fishways from $6,500 per year to $25,000.[27] That was only a symbiotic victory. I left the House disappointed not to have been more successful, stymied by Conowingo's location in Maryland.

Other governmental officials, however, persisted in the restoration of the shad to the Susquehanna. Ralph Abele, executive director of the Fish Commission, was particularly forceful in pursuing fishways. The Maryland Department of Natural Resources and the federal Fish and Wildlife Services were actively involved. They reached an agreement that the companies operating the three dams in Pennsylvania would install fishways as soon as Conowingo did.

Fishways came to the Conowingo because the Philadelphia Electric Company's license to operate the dam by the Federal Energy Regulatory Commission required fishways as a condition for renewal in 1988. The upstream dams followed through on their earlier agreement. By the year 2000 fish elevators had been installed in all four dams, which are now in operation. These elevators lift the shad up from the downstream side of the dam and deposit them on the upstream side. There is, ironically, no fishway in the fabridam at Sunbury, but Representative Merle Phillips, the present House member from the 108th District, has been actively pursuing funding for them for several years. He is optimistic that there will be fishways in the fabridam in late 2010 or 2011.

The results for the four hydroelectric dams have been disappointing. In 2007 only 25,464 American shad were lifted over the Conowingo dam, only 1 percent of the long-term goal of two million fish per year. That same year 10,338 shad were lifted over the Holtwood dam and 7,215 over Safe Harbor. Shad are migrating up the Susquehanna to spawn and are occasionally caught by fishermen, although they must be returned to the stream.

Nita Beck, Basse Beck's widow, shaking hands with Ralph Abele of the Pennsylvania Fish Commission at the dedication of the Basse A. Beck Environmental Education Center in the Shikellamy State Park, August 5, 1978. Between Mrs. Beck and Abele are the author, Game Commission Director Peter Duncan, and Leonard Green of the Pennsylvania Federation of Sportsmen's Clubs. Behind Mrs. Beck are Beth Kury and William Booth, Beck's son in law. Source: *Courtesy of the Sunbury* Daily Item.

The Chesapeake Bay Program (a partnership of Pennsylvania, Maryland, the District of Columbia, and the federal Environmental Protection Agency) is seeking to increase the number of shad and other migratory fish moving up the Susquehanna. It offers hope that more substantial upstream spawning runs of the shad are within reach.[28]

Basse Beck's dream for the return of the spawning shad to the upper Susquehanna has, however, been significantly realized.

8

The Environmental Amendment to the State Constitution

The idea for the environmental amendment came to me in the late summer of 1968 while reading a *New York Times* report on New York State's then proposed environmental amendment.[1] As a lawyer with a keen interest in constitutional law the idea of an amendment to Pennsylvania's constitution made a great deal of sense. Why not give our natural environment the same kind of constitutional protection that has been given to our political rights? Any student of history and politics knows that political tides rise and fall. What one legislature passes another may repeal or amend. I was well aware that the environmental tide in Pennsylvania was near its crest. This is the time, I concluded, to lock into the constitution basic environmental protections.

The New York amendment struck me as being too detailed and focused on environmental matters peculiar to that state. I therefore worked on writing two basic concepts into a single statement of broad constitutional principles: an articulation of the public's interest in the environment and the placement of the responsibility on state government to serve as trustee of the state's natural resources.

Upon my reelection to the House in 1968, I had the amendment prepared and introduced it on April 21, 1969 as H.B. 958 (P.N. 1105).

> Section 27. Natural Resources and the Public Estate. The people have a right to clean air, pure water, and to the preservation of the natural scenic, historic and esthetic values of the environment. Pennsylvania's natural resources, including the air, waters, fish, wildlife, and public lands and property of the Commonwealth, are the common propertyof all the people, including generations yet to come. As trustee of these resources, the Commonwealth shall preserve and maintain them in their natural state for the benefit of all the people.

John Laudadio joined as a prime sponsor, along with twenty-eight others of both parties, including my party leadership, Fineman and Irvis. Within days Fineman and Irvis called Laudadio and me to a meeting in the speaker's office to review the proposal. I explained the amendment and both leaders approved, except that Fineman, who practiced law in Philadelphia, expressed the fear that the state's obligation to preserve the environment "in its natural state" could be construed to prohibit urban renewal projects in Philadelphia. I agreed to delete the phrase "in its natural state." Irvis liked the title to the amendment, "Natural Resources and the Public Estate." "That's Jeffersonian, Franklin. I like it," he told me.

On April 29 the Conservation Committee met, amended the bill to delete the phrase "in their natural state," and reported the bill under Printers Number 1307 to the floor. On June 1 the bill passed the House 190–0 and went to the Senate, where it was referred to the Committee on Constitutional Changes and Federal Relations chaired by Senator Jack McGregor. McGregor's committee made three further changes. First, in the second sentence the word "public" was inserted before the phrase "natural resources" to clarify that the amendment was not to apply to purely private property rights.

Secondly, the list of natural resources to be protected (air, water, fish, wildlife, and the public land and property) was removed from the trusteeship clause so that it could not be argued that items not mentioned were not included. At the suggestion of Maurice Goddard, secretary of forests and waters, the word "conserve" was inserted in place of "preserve" in the Commonwealth's trusteeship mandate so the amendment could not be interpreted as freezing the environment in its status quo.

With these amendments the bill was reported under Printer's Number 2860 to the Senate floor on March 10, 1970. The full Senate passed it on March 17, 1970, by a vote of 39 to 0 and returned it the House for concurrence in its amendments. Laudadio and I reviewed the amendments and found them acceptable.

On April 14, 1970, the House held a special ceremony to mark the first "Earth Day—Pennsylvania."[2] Speaker Fineman invited U.S. Senator Gaylord Nelson of Wisconsin, a national environmental leader, to give the main address. Before Senator Nelson spoke I was called on by Speaker Fineman to offer the motion to concur in the Senate amendments to H.B. 958. After making the motion, which was unanimously approved, I inserted into the *House Journal* the complete text of an article entitled "The Proposed Pennsylvania Declaration of Environmental Rights" written by Robert Broughton, associate professor of law at Duquesne Law School. This analysis was done by Professor Broughton at my request and is, I believe, the only analysis of the amendment prior to its adoption.[3] Dr. Broughton's analysis is well reasoned and illuminating. I thought his article deserved to be preserved as a permanent part of the legislative history. (For the complete Broughton analysis see the 1970 *House Journal* of April 14 at page 2,272. A summary version is contained in appendix B in this book.)

On January 6, 1971, joined by ninety co-sponsors, as required of a constitutional amendment under Article XI, Section I, I introduced the bill for a second time. As H.B. 31 the bill received the necessary round of approval. It passed the House on February 3, 1971, less than a month after its introduction unanimously, 199 to 0. The Senate acted with even greater alacrity. On February 15 the Senate approved the bill 45–0 and sent it to the Secretary of the Commonwealth in time to put it on the ballot as a referendum in the primary election to be held May 18.

As Joint Resolution 3 the environmental amendment had support of organizations like the Pennsylvania Federation of Sportsmen's Clubs, the Pennsylvania Environmental Council, the League of Women Voters, and the state Bar Association. I prepared a question and answer sheet that was distributed to the news media of the state by the House Democratic Press office. (See appendix C for a copy.)

The results of the May 18 primary election were gratifying. The voters approved the amendment 1,021,342 to 259,979. This four-to-one approval margin significantly exceeded the votes given to four other proposed constitutional amendments on the same ballot, two of which were rejected.[4] With that overwhelming approval my proposal became Article I, Section 27 of the Pennsylvania Constitution.

Section 27. NATURAL RESOURCES AND THE PUBLIC ESTATE.

The people have a right to clean air, pure water, and to the preservation of the natural, scenic, historic, and esthetic values of the environment. Pennsylvania's public natural resources are the common property of all of the people, including generations yet to come. As trustee of these resources, the Commonwealth shall conserve and maintain them for the benefit of all the people.

I feel especially good about this amendment. By articulating the rights of citizens in their environment I believe we created a constitutional basis upon which the courts, on a case-by-case basis, would build a solid wall of protection for our natural estate in Pennsylvania. Prior to the enactment of Article 1, Section 27, our state's policy toward the environment was one of neglect, except as jolted out of its lethargy by occasional environmental disasters. (The legislature's bit-by-bit enactment of clean streams laws over sixty years as related in the previous chapter showed this.) By placing the Commonwealth as the trustee of our natural resources we changed forever the government's policy on the environment and natural resources.

The impact of the environmental amendment has not been as dramatic as some expected. There has been considerable litigation based on Article 1, Section 27, but few cases have blocked a project that affects the environment. A number of law review and other legal publications have analyzed the amendment's impact and they are listed in note 5 to this chapter.[5] I do not judge the effectiveness of the amendment on the litigation to date. There is always the potential for a future court to apply the amendment in ways that we cannot now imagine, just as the Bill of Rights amendments to the federal constitution has had interpretations beyond the imagination of their authors long after their demises.

Article 1, Section 27 has, however, had a broad and subtle impact. After May 18, 1971, every person sworn into public office in Pennsylvania—state or municipal—swears to uphold Article I, Section 27. Any legislative effort to weaken or repeal environmental legislation would be confronted by this constitutional hurdle. An information sheet that reveals the project's relationship to the environment must accompany all applications for Department of Environmental Protection permits for projects affecting the environment. This achieves what is truly revolutionary in Pennsylvania's history—the environmental impact of a project is considered and approved—or rejected—before work is started. Article 1, Section 27 therefore gives me the most satisfaction of any legislative initiative I undertook. I feel really good about it.

9

The Bridge at Sunbury

I remember the old toll bridge that crossed the Susquehanna from Bainbridge Street in Sunbury to Shamokin Dam. As a boy my father took me across it many times to go to Rolling Green Park in Hummel's Wharf. A two-lane structure, one lane going each way, there was a tollbooth at each end where the drivers paid the ten cent toll. By the time I left home for college, the state had stopped collecting the tolls and the collection booths had been removed. As the malls developed between Shamokin Dam and Selinsgrove the traffic load on the bridge increased to the point where there were frequent delays because the bridge was only one lane in each direction. When I returned to Sunbury after finishing law school, the need for a new bridge was evident. The Central Susquehanna Valley Chamber of Commerce and nearby municipalities began to call for a new bridge, but their efforts received no permanent commitment. While the area legislators supported the idea, getting funding for a new bridge proved elusive, possibly because the Central Susquehanna Valley had a small profile at the state level of highway planning. The state had begun to plan the project but its future was uncertain. By 1971 the project had been placed on an indefinite hold.

On the evening of Tuesday, December 28, 1971, an opportunity to move the bridge project forward came to me in a completely unexpected and surprising way. The House had before it S.B. 331 to create fifty-one new judgeships throughout the state, but twenty-five of them were slated for Philadelphia.[1] There was also to be a motion, after passage of the bill, to adjourn *sine die*, that would allow Governor Shapp to appoint the new judges and over 1,000 other interim positions for boards and commissions without Senate confirmation. S.B. 331 was, obviously, quite important to the governor. But the bill was seen by the Republican members and upstate Democrats as an unjustified boondoggle for Philadelphia.

When Speaker Fineman called for a final passage vote on the bill, the electronic voting system flashed green for those voting yes and red for no, while a total for each side was displayed. Everyone in the hall of the House could see how each member was voting and the tally. The tally showed 100 in favor, then 99, then 101, one vote short of the 102 votes required by the state constitution to pass a bill in the House. The "no" votes included virtually every Republican member, as well as some upstate Democrats. My vote showed red. I saw no reason to vote for a bill that would benefit Philadelphia and contained nothing for the Central Susquehanna Valley. The speaker directed the chief clerk to keep the voting switches open while efforts were made to find the needed vote. The overwhelming majority of House roll calls votes are taken in a matter of a minute or two, but on this occasion the voting switches were kept open for almost an hour.[2] I was talking with colleagues when a page told me that Speaker Fineman wanted to talk with me. I walked to the speaker's desk, where Fineman asked me to go to the governor's office. I knew at once what would be asked of me.

In the next few minutes I did the best extemporaneous thinking of my political career. I knew that to provide a yes vote without getting something significant in return would render me politically vulnerable in my district. In the 1968 campaign the Republican House Leader, then Speaker Kenneth Lee, made several speeches in my district accusing me of being a "tool of Philadelphia." I could not afford to give substance to that false charge. There was only one thing that I could ask for that could justify giving the governor the vote: the bridge at Sunbury.

Seated with Governor Shapp, I came right out with it. "Governor, the judges are important to Philadelphia, but they mean nothing to my district. We don't need more judges, but we do a need a new bridge at Sunbury." "Let me see what I can do," Shapp responded and called Transportation Secretary Jacob Kassab to join us. Kassab came in and the governor asked him what could be done. The project needed funding for three phases—design, right of way acquisition, and construction. I wanted funding for all three but settled for funding for design and right of way acquisition. Kassab said it was not realistic to commit to construction funding because it would be several years before the department would be ready for construction. We went back and forth on this for several minutes, and I agreed to vote for the judgeship bill in exchange for a commitment to make $20 million for engineering design and right of way acquisition a priority in the next highway bill. With Shapp's commitment I went back to the House chamber and provided the vote needed to pass the judgeship bill. I then went to the press row seats and disclosed to the reporters the agreement with the governor.

The next day's Sunbury *Daily Item* carried a banner headline that ran completely across the top of the front page: "Kury Swaps Vote for Shapp's Pledge to Push City Bypass." Under the headline the *Item* ran an Associated Press report of my agreement with the governor as well as the *Item*'s own story on the local impact, "Shapp's Pledge Welcome News in Bypass Area."[3] Private feedback from the political circuits in my district was equally encouraging. The local Republicans were stunned. What could they say about it? Nothing I did in my political endeavors had a more dramatic impact on the Republican Party of my area.

The more I thought about it the better I felt. Political "horse trading" is as old as the country. We have a U.S. Constitution because the constitution writers worked out a series of compromises. I also recalled that Republican State Senator Z. H. Confair of Williamsport gave Democratic Governor Lawrence a vote for a gas tax increase in exchange for a commitment to construct Route 80, the Keystone Shortway. Having promptly disclosed the agreement to the public, I never gave it a second thought. I had been given a lever and a fulcrum of one vote that enabled me to move the Sunbury bypass significantly closer to reality. It was a classic illustration of Archimedes' principle at work in the political arena.[4]

The follow-through from Shapp's commitment in 1971 until the bridge was actually built and open to traffic in 1986 was not as direct as I had hoped. A number of factors delayed the project—the need for an environmental impact statement under federal law, unrealistic cost estimates, inflation, and the needs of the state's 44,000 miles of highway. The delays caused such concern in my district that I arranged for Transportation Secretary William Sherlock (successor to Kassab) to meet with local leaders and the editorial board of the Sunbury *Daily Item* on Thursday, May 13, 1976. Sherlock explained the financial problems causing the delay and reasserted the administration's pledge to construct the bridge. Sherlock was killed in an airplane crash shortly after that appearance. Later the Shapp administration stopped all highway construction because of a heavy bond debt load. In 1982 the Thornburgh administration enacted an axle tax on trucks to be used to pay the bond debt and to build bridges.[5] The Sunbury bridge was reactivated and ground broken for it on July 12, 1985. Construction was completed and Governor Thornburgh dedicated the bridge on November 24, 1986. I was invited to attend and happily did so.[6]

Obtaining Governor Shapp's commitment for the Sunbury bridge was my last significant accomplishment in the House. The following year, 1972, was devoted largely to my campaign for the Senate.

To become a leader or committee chair in the House requires more time than in the Senate. After six years as a representative I was still secretary to the Conservation Committee. Becoming a leader also requires voting for the party position on issues—like legislative compensation and taxes—that could jeopardize reelection from a rural district, like the 108th.

In spite of these factors I found that a junior member of the House could be effective by having good ideas, documenting the case for them, and working with the party leadership. The most important idea I originated in my fourteen years in the legislature—the idea for the environmental amendment to the state constitution—came to me as a freshman House member. That idea became constitutional reality before I departed the House.

In retrospect, I take considerable satisfaction in what I was able to do in the House. I ran for the Senate feeling that it was "up or out" for me. I could accept either result. But I ran for the Senate feeling that my action in getting the bridge funding strengthened me by showing I could get tangible results for my district.

III
THE STATE SENATE, 1972–1980

10

Defying Gravity: Going to the Senate

I first gave thought to running for the Senate in late 1967. My first term in the House would be up in 1968, as would Senator Preston Davis's term in the Senate. But I quickly dismissed pursuing it. For starters, one term in the House is not much of a time period in which to accomplish anything, especially when your party is in the minority. Equally important, Davis was a far more formidable opponent than Bower. A respected lawyer from Milton and chairman of the Senate Education Committee, Davis showed up at events throughout the district that stretched from Berwick in Columbia County to Laurelton in Union County and from Dewart in Northumberland County to Juniata County. Davis had not cast any votes that were egregiously against the interest of his district, as Bower did in voting no on bringing the coal companies under the clean streams law. Not running for the Senate in 1968 was a "no brainer" for me.[1]

After reelection for a third House term in 1970, however, I focused again on the possibility of going for the Senate seat in 1972. I made more speeches outside of my House district, such as at the Union County Sportsmen's Club in Millmont and the Berwick Rotary Club. I added the newspapers and radio stations outside of my House district to my media distribution list. Feeling comfortable in talking with editors and other news media people, I had good relationships with Charles Johnson of the *Milton Standard*, William Weist of the *Shamokin Citizen*, Joe McGlinn of the *Danville News*, and Bob Fawcett of the Bloomsburg *Morning Press*. On the political front I increased contact with Democratic party leaders in Snyder, Union, and Columbia Counties.

In December 1971 Senator Davis announced that he would not seek reelection in 1972. With Davis not running, I realized instantly that this

The opening of a bridge at Milton. The author is on the left and Senator Preston Davis is on the right. Congressman Herman T. Schneebeli is in the center. Source: Courtesy of the Milton Standard.

was my golden opportunity to go to the Senate. The same day Davis made his announcement, Terry Abrams, a high school classmate of mine and a television personality on WGAL-TV in Lancaster, announced he was running for the seat and would campaign for it twenty-four hours a day, seven days a week. I knew the media would be calling me for a statement, so I consulted with my friend, Vincent Carocci, a press officer for the Senate Democrats. Carocci advised me to tell the media that this day belonged to Senator Davis and that any announcement of my plans would have to wait. When contacted by media, I saluted Davis for his service and declined to say anything about my own plans.

The field of candidates quickly grew. On the Republican side, Abrams never filed a petition.[2] But Dr. George Deitrick Jr., son of the former senator and leader of the anti-Lark Republicans, filed, as did Richard C. Leib, a Sunbury insurance man and a former army colonel who had served on General Eisenhower's staff. Leib became the Lark organization candidate. On the Democratic side Dr. John (Konopka) Linnet, a Shamokin dentist who ran against Davis in 1963, filed. Of course, I did too.

My primary was relatively easy. Linnet had no organization and was best known for promoting anthracite coal. He often marched in parades wearing a white suit and tie, the tie having black splotches of coal on it. Except for the area between Shamokin and Mt. Carmel, I did not see him as a formidable opponent and that proved correct. The day after the primary election, Linnet called to congratulate me and invite me to have lunch and a beer with him. I thanked him and accepted the invitation. He cooked a delicious lunch of sautéed shrimp and mushrooms, accompanied by cold beer. I found him to be delightful and gracious. I thanked him and went home with a new friend.

The results of the Democratic presidential primary in the Senate district were surprising. Senator Muskie carried Northumberland County handily; Hubert Humphrey won Montour, Snyder, and Juniata; Senator McGovern carried Union County; and Alabama Governor George Wallace carried Columbia County. I attribute McGovern's victory in Union County to the standing room only audience he addressed in Bucknell University's Davis Gymnasium. I attended and was amazed at the enthusiasm he engendered in the crowd with his anti-Vietnam War speech. Columbia County was the only county Wallace won in Pennsylvania that spring. The Civil War (as discussed in note 6 of chapter 2) had made Northumberland, Snyder, and Union Counties Republican. But it had the opposite effect in Columbia County; that was the home of the Copperhead Conspiracy that opposed the Union efforts to defeat the rebels. Columbia County has been a conservative Democratic, i.e., pre-New Deal, venue ever since.

In the Republican primary Deitrick defeated Leib, showing again that the Lark organization was losing its power. For me, it seemed a great irony that my opponent for the Senate was the son of our next-door-neighbor on Arch Street in Sunbury. I knew Dr. Deitrick Sr. from talking to him when he parked his car and walked into his home. Just as ironic, Dr. Deitrick Sr. had run for the Senate in 1956 as a Democrat, having been persuaded to run in large measure by my father, the Democratic City Chairman. Dr. Deitrick Jr. and I were well acquainted. We had a number of political "bull sessions" since my election to the House. I knew of his interest in politics, but did not foresee his interest in going for the Senate. He had not struck me as having the personality that usually marks political candidates. Nevertheless, Deitrick had three important factors going for him: his family name from his father's service as a Republican state senator and county commissioner, the Republican party label in a district where the GOP had a registration lead of 58,355 to 47,502, and President Richard Nixon leading the ticket against

Cutting the ribbon to open the Senate campaign headquarters in 1972. To the author's right are Ginny Krebs and Larry Krebs, the Democratic candidate for the State House seat. The boy in the left front is Steven Kury, the oldest son of the author and Beth, holding the scissors. Source: Personal file photo.

Senator George McGovern. Considering the geographical size of the 27th Senate District[3] Deitrick had to be taken seriously.

To win the general election, I needed to get the Democratic vote and a good portion of the Republican, as I did in seeking election to the House. To do that I would need to make full use of my position in the House and run a well-organized, aggressive campaign.

The State Senate Democratic Campaign Committee sent Neil McAuliffe to be my campaign manager, something I had not had in my House campaigns. McAuliffe proved to be exactly what I needed to pull together and coordinate my organizational effort. He was low-key, solid, and possessed a good organizational sense. We were quite compatible personally and worked well together. We became good friends.

The Senate campaign was not as narrowly focused on issues as was my first campaign for the House. I ran on a commitment to carry on the fight to protect the environment, especially the Susquehanna River; to seek better control of state spending through more effective audits; and work to reform the legislature with enactment of a lobbying disclosure law and a rewriting of the Senate confirmation process. All of our brochures contained instructions on how to vote for me by a split ticket, just as we did in the first House campaign. We made no mention of Dr. Dietrick in any of our advertising, brochures, or my speeches.

Just before the campaign got underway the Democratic National Convention in Miami nominated Senator George McGovern as the party's presidential candidate. McGovern's nomination set off a tremor of trepidation in the Democratic Party. Before leaving Miami, John Torquato, the Democratic Chairman of Cambria County, projected that McGovern's nomination would result in the defeat of several state senate candidates, including me. McAuliffe and I talked about it at length and concluded we had no choice but to keep running my campaign as we planned, with no ties to the McGovern campaign.

Working with McAuliffe, we put together a formal campaign structure that appealed to Republicans as well as Democrats. Basse Beck was confined to his home, incapacitated by the stroke. However, James T. Dildine, a Republican and respected certified public accountant from Selinsgrove, and James P. Kelley, a funeral director from Coal Township and chairman of the Northumberland County Commissioners, became chairs of the Bipartisan Citizens for Kury Campaign. William Deeter again served as treasurer and Esther Cotner, also of Montour County, was secretary. All advertising, brochures, and mailings were done in the name of the Bipartisan Committee. Mrs. Jackie Smith led the volunteers in addressing thousands of envelopes for the mailings.

The campaign worked with the county Democratic Party leaders throughout the district. McAuliffe coordinated with them so that I attended Democratic functions, but we knew that was only the beginning of building a winning vote. Our strategy thus focused on making effective contact with the several regional communities that make up the 27th Senate District—the anthracite region of eastern Northumberland and extreme southern Columbia Counties; the agricultural areas of Snyder, Union, Columbia, and Juniata Counties; and university towns like Bloomsburg, Lewisburg, and Selinsgrove.

We found and worked with leaders in each area. In the anthracite area we had two great sources of strength—Joseph Buchkowskie and the International Ladies Garment Workers Union (the ILGWU) and Commissioner James Kelley, a strong Democratic leader. The ILGWU gave me its full support. Buchkowskie arranged for me to campaign personally in two dozen garment plants between Trevorton and Mt. Carmel. Following the collapse of the coal industry the ILGWU had organized all of these plants. With the men of the region out of work or commuting to Harrisburg or Reading for work, their wives worked near home sewing clothing pieces into garments. At each plant I walked the floors and talked with each woman at her sewing machine, giving each a brochure and asking for her vote. When I had

U.S. Senator Edmund Muskie running for president in Shamokin in 1972. The author is at the left. Source: Personal file photo.

completed touring the plants I had talked personally with several hundred women.

The United Steelworkers of America local union in Milton gave me strong support. The local leader, Robert Lee, and others arranged for me to greet dozens of steelworkers at the plant gates at six o'clock in the morning on several days.

For Sundays, Kelley and McAuliffe worked out a schedule for campaigning in the coal regions at clambakes and festivals sponsored by fire companies and fraternal groups. In other areas of the Senate District campaigning on Sunday was frowned upon for religious reasons. In the coal region, however, Sunday clambakes were popular. There was no religious objection, and Sunday was a day when many of the men, who commuted out of the area to work during the week, were home. For each clambake I attended, the campaign supplied a quarter or half keg of beer.[4] With Kelley's help I campaigned at clambakes every Sunday between Labor Day and late October. On one Sunday I attended seven of them. When the clambake visits were completed, I had met hundreds of voters, many of whom worked outside of the Senate district during the week.

The campaign enlisted Mollie Lou Eyster, owner of a landscape nursery (with her husband Richard) and an independent Republican who had studied political science at Bucknell University, to organize coffee klatches throughout the district. Mrs. Eyster put together approximately forty klatches. For each one she identified a hostess, persuaded her to do it, and then guided them through the invitation, follow-up, and holding of the event. At the appointed hour I would arrive, greet everyone, say a few words, and then take questions. Following each klatch I sent a personal thank you note to the hostess and to everyone who attended. Through the coffee klatches I talked personally with several hundred women, many of whom were Republicans and all of whom were concerned about various legislative issues.

Three boys star in a 1976 campaign photo "shoot." Left to right, David, James, and Steven Kury, as their parents look on. Source: *Personal file photo.*

Michael L. Aumiller of Beavertown, Snyder County, joined the campaign as a volunteer and soon began accompanying me to agricultural fairs and fire company picnics in Snyder and Union Counties. John R. Showers, a college student from New Berlin, helped us at events in Union County. Everywhere I went I introduced myself to individuals, asked for their name, and gave them a brochure. Aumiller took notes of those I talked with. Back in the office we were then able to send follow-up letters to many of those I had met. With the cooperation of my House colleague, Kent Shelhamer, Beth and I attended numerous rural events in Columbia County.

The Senate campaign did not focus nearly as much on the door-to-door campaigning that proved so effective in the House races. The district, comprised of four House districts, was just too large. But McAuliffe did develop a schedule for knocking on doors in communities I had not previously campaigned in, such as Shamokin, Coal Township, Berwick, Bloomsburg, and Mifflinburg.

We found other venues where I could campaign effectively. Friday evenings are football nights for the high schools of the area. Although I could not campaign at football games the way I could at, say, clambakes, I did attend many of them. The campaign purchased half page ads in the football game programs. On Saturday afternoons Beth and I, with our two-year-old son, Steven, in a pushcart, attended ice cream festivals and other fund-raising events at churches. We did not pass out brochures or overtly campaign, but found that merely showing up generated a favorable reaction.

We also made a strong initiative with sportsmen and conservationists. With the help of Thomas Dunkin of Shamokin and Neil Mertz of Point Township (Northumberland County), we organized a Sportsmen and Conservationists for Kury Committee that sent out a brochure signed by twenty-four sportsmen's clubs.

Deitrick, meanwhile, conducted an unorthodox campaign. He made no speeches and showed no interest in working crowds. He traveled throughout the district with a small coterie of supporters led by John Sandri of Shamokin, an old friend. Deitrick ran a series of newspaper ads, but seemed to rely on posters and handout brochures that Sandri and the others passed out wherever Deitrick went. Deitrick's campaign was completely silent on the issues. We never met during the campaign. We did not debate.

Election day brought stunning results. Nixon defeated McGovern in the 27th Senate District more than two to one, 60,177 to 27,402, but I had defeated Deitrick by 3,757 votes, 46,535 to 42,778. A county-by-county review of the votes proved quite revealing. In Snyder, Union, and Juniata Counties Deitrick received 11,214 votes to my 8,979. But I carried Northumberland, Montour, and Columbia Counties by a plurality of 5,992, giving me a net plurality for the whole district of 3,758. The Republicans of the 27th Senate District had demonstrated that they knew how to split their tickets and were willing to do so. I never forgot that.

The 27th Senatorial District election should have been relatively easy for the Republican candidate, particularly with Nixon swamping McGovern by a two to one margin in the district. My campaign succeeded in spite of the perceived odds against it for several reasons. First, the Republican voters of the district had become comfortable in ticket splitting. My campaign gave them a reason to split. My six years in the House were critical to this. I had a record of following through on my campaign promises, such as clean streams, and also showing effectiveness in getting funding for the bridge at Sunbury. Beyond that, we ran a well organized "on the ground" campaign that placed me in every section of the district. We worked well with the local Democratic leaders, and we received enthusiastic support from volunteers for coffee klatches, envelope addressing, and telephone calls. We had a clear message of continued reform efforts in the legislature. All of this came together and brought the victory.

11

The Senate Is Not the House

Upon my arrival in the Senate in January 1973 I quickly found substantial differences from the House, as well as from the Senate George Leader described to me that he entered in 1951. Twenty-eight of the fifty senators were Democrats, giving our party clear control. I also found that the freshman Democrats received considerably more personal attention from our leadership than had been received previously in the House. For one thing, in the face of the McGovern disaster we weren't supposed to be there. More importantly, by winning we had kept the Democrats in control of the Senate, for which twenty-six votes, the constitutional majority needed to pass bills, is required. When the Democrats won twenty-six seats in 1970 they obtained control for the first time since the Roosevelt landslide in 1936. Except for that election, the Democrats had not previously elected a majority to the Senate in the twentieth century. (During the 1961–1962 session the Senate was evenly divided between the parties, 25–25. The Democratic Lt. Governor, John Moran Davis, broke the tie votes.) With only a two-seat majority over the Republicans, every Democratic senator became even more important. Our party leaders, Senate President Martin Murray of Wilkes-Barre and Majority Leader Thomas Lamb of Pittsburgh, took substantial time to talk with us individually and to develop a personal rapport. With the Senate having only one-fourth as many members as the House, a senator's relationship with his leadership was far more personal than in the House, where it was more a matter of party loyalty.

The Senate had the earmarks of a club. To the rear of the chamber was a private dining room, reserved for senators. A Senate staffer who was also a licensed barber was available to provide barbering services. In contrast to

Celebrating the author's swearing in as a senator in January 1973. Left to right are Leonard Kurlowicz (uncle) and his wife, Marie Kurlowicz; Stephanie Kurlowicz (aunt); the author; Helen Kury and Dr. William Heazlett, Beth's father. Beth is seated. Source: Personal file photo.

the small support staff provided for House members in groups, I was given a private office, a secretary, executive assistant, and other staff.

The ornate decorations of the Senate added to the aura, as did the almost plodding pace of the daily calendar. The House is a very difficult place in which to speak and be heard by your colleagues. House members commonly read papers or converse with colleagues while a member is speaking. Only a few House members, like Leroy Irvis, commanded the attention of the full House when they rose to talk. But in the Senate every speaker was heard. There was no conversation and no obvious newspaper reading.

The Senate also had a significant perquisite that came with the office. Every senator had twenty full tuition scholarships to be awarded at his discretion at each of five state-aided universities—Pennsylvania, Temple, Lincoln, Pittsburgh, and Penn State. John Mazur, chairman of the Northumberland County Democratic Committee, saw the scholarships as patronage and asked me to let him award the scholarships. I declined. From my own family's experience I felt a special interest in scholarships and decided to award them on financial need and academic ability. I established a citizens' scholarship committee of five or six to receive and evaluate applications that included a copy of the parents' federal tax returns and a high school academic transcript. My staff prepared guidelines for the application process, sent them to the high schools of the district, and coordinated the applications for the committee. The committee treated the tax returns and grades as confidential, evaluated, and ranked the applicants. I awarded the scholarships based on that ranking.

The "club" aspect of the Senate was, however, misleading. When the freshman senators arrived in January 1973 we found the Senate in the throes of being radically changed. Like the Democratic Commissioners who finally took control of the Northumberland County courthouse, the Senate Democratic leaders were determined to make changes. Prior to the Democrats taking control in the 1970 election, lobbyists had free access to the Senate floor, as former Governor George Leader told me. (See the prologue.) The seats near the majority leader's seat, reserved for lobbyists from Sun Oil (Harry Davis) and the Pennsylvania Railroad (William Reiter),[1] had been removed and all lobbyists were denied floor access. Upon being elected president of the Senate, Senator Murray had promptly ordered all lobbyists barred from the floor.[2] In 1973 Murray also removed the press corps from their seats in the front of the chamber on the Republican side and required them to sit in the front row balcony at the rear.[3]

Harvey Taylor, the patronage boss and long-time Senate president, was gone, defeated in the Republican primary election of 1964 by William Lentz of Millersburg. Over lunch with Senator Lentz after I was sworn in I asked him how he defeated the powerful Taylor. He told me.

> I was interested in running for the House of Representatives and went to Taylor to talk about it. He kept me waiting in the reception room of his office. I waited and waited, but he refused to see me. I was angry, so angry that I might as well run against him I thought. That's just what I did. Taylor's arrogance . . . he had lost touch with the voters—that's what did him in.

Democrat Martin L. Murray of Luzerne County was now the president of the Senate and he conducted that office in a manner far different from Taylor. Taylor ran the Senate from his base of power as the patronage dispenser. Murray ran it through his considerable skills as a listener and conciliator. Taylor saw the Senate as a Republican domain. Murray, while an avid Democrat, saw the Senate as an institution of two parties.

Murray held court in his office after every session day. Any senator, Democrat or Republican, could stop by to have a drink with him and talk about whatever was of concern. Occasionally Murray would call to his office two or more senators who had been having personal difficulties between them. Murray listened and usually worked out the problem. Known as "Marty's Bar and Grill" or "Father Murray's Confessional," these sessions were more

The Senate staff. Left to right, Michael Aumiller, administrative assistant; Jean Brannon, secretary; and Joseph R. Powers, legislative assistant. Source: Personal file photo.

than social. They had a salutary effect on the Senate as a body because of the manner in which Murray dealt with each member.

When the 1973 session began, Murray and Lamb decided to overhaul the constitutional system for confirming the governor's nominations. In discussions Lamb had with Vincent Carocci, then a staff assistant to the majority leader, Carocci suggested me to lead the effort, pointing out that I was both a lawyer and reform minded. About two weeks later Senator Lamb asked me if I would chair a special committee to review the confirmation system and make recommendations to reform it. The request to me as a brand new senator showed that, indeed, the Senate was not the House, where after six years I was a committee secretary and never a chairman. It also underscored that luck has a great deal to do with what one is able to accomplish in public office. I was fortunate to enter the Senate at a time when my party was in control and under the leadership of Senator Martin Murray and Thomas Lamb, senators determined to make reforms. I recognized that my charge was of importance to improving the checks and balances of the state constitution and enthusiastically welcomed the opportunity to take it on.

The exhilaration I felt upon joining the Senate soon receded to the realization that I had serious work to do. My experience in chairing the paper ballot reform committee in Northumberland County would prove to be a good model from which to work. We moved quickly to the task.

12

Senate Confirmation of the Governor's Appointments

THE CONSTITUTIONAL PERSPECTIVE

American constitutional law is based on the separation of powers between the executive, legislative, and judicial branches so that no branch acquires excessive power. Several checks and balances enforce the allocation of power between the branches. In Pennsylvania, for example, the legislature makes the laws but the governor may veto them. The executive makes the appointments to executive positions but his choices are kept in check by statutes requiring the consent of the Senate for policy-making positions. (The vast majority of state employees do not need Senate confirmation.) In the federal constitution and every other state but Texas the "check" on executive appointments was a majority vote of the Senate. For Pennsylvania in 1973 Article IV, Section 8 of the Constitution provided:

> [The Governor] shall nominate and, by and with the advice and consent of two-thirds of all the members of the Senate, appoint . . . such (other) officers of the commonwealth as he may or may be authorized by the Constitution or by law to appoint; he shall have power to fill all vacancies that may happen, in offices to which he may appoint, during the recess of the Senate, by granting commissions which shall expire of the end of their next session.

The 1968 Constitutional Convention did not address this provision and it remained in effect on paper, but of no practical use in the Senate's constitutional power to serve as a check on executive nominations.

In the winter of 1973, when the new legislative session began, the Pennsylvania system for Senate confirmation of the governor's appointments to

1,914 positions had become, like the appendix, a vestigial remnant that served no usual function but could cause considerable pain. The two-thirds vote requirement had brought the confirmation process to a virtual halt. When the Senate was in recess, the governor was authorized to make interim appointments that expired at the end of the legislative session. Since neither political party had thirty-four votes either one could block a nomination. Without a viable confirmation process, interim appointments made when the Senate recessed for the Christmas holidays filled the overwhelming majority of the executive positions requiring confirmation.

During the 1972 session, for example, Governor Shapp submitted 887 nominations and the Senate confirmed only 41. During the first ten months of the session, the governor sent only 58 nominations, and the Senate confirmed 36 of them. In the last eighteen days of the session, however (between election day and the end of the session on November 30), 829 nominations were sent to the Senate, and the Senate confirmed 5. But when the Senate adjourned on November 30, Governor Shapp made 1,047 interim appointments.

Senate Rule XXX compounded the problem by mandating that all information on nominees be kept secret, a holdover from the patronage era in the Senate. Hearings on the qualifications of nominees were never held and even senators, except the one from whose district the nominee hailed, were kept largely in the dark. Clearly, any constitutional check on the governor's appointment had rusted into uselessness. As Ralph Tive, Governor Shapp's legislative secretary put it, "gubernatorial appointments gather dust (in the Senate) for confirmation that never comes."

TACKLING THE PROBLEM

On January 27, 1973, three weeks after taking the oath of office, I offered Senate Resolution Serial Number 11 to create a Special Senate Committee to Study Confirmation Procedure. Murray and Lamb joined as co-sponsors, as did the Republican floor leader, Richard Frame, and Democrat Joseph Ammerman. The resolution was adopted February 6, and our committee promptly went to work.[1]

The first priority was to get agreement that the committee would work in a bipartisan, cooperative manner, and keep our deliberations private until we had a report to make public. Considering the incendiary nature of nominations, I feared that making our meeting public would create a major obstacle to success. The committee quickly reached agreement. We would operate with the ground rule that all discussions and recommendations would not apply to current office holders and personalities. Any new procedures would be effective after the next governor's election in 1974.

To maintain confidentiality of our deliberations, the Republican floor leader Senator Frame and I agreed to take turns hosting the committee to working dinners at local restaurants, such as Alfred's Victorian in Middletown, where we could be served in a private room. Except for the public hearing, all of our meetings were held that way. The senators and support staff from both sides discussed and argued, without rancor, while enjoying dinner. We developed a good rapport and came to trust each other.

As a background for our work, we requested and received from the Joint State Government Commission a detailed staff report on the history and experience with the confirmation system. It provided politically neutral raw information and made no recommendations. This staff report was placed in appendix A to the Report of our Senate Committee. It describes the then current confirmation requirements and practices, as well as the federal and state historical background of Senate confirmations.

One point in the staff report was particularly startling.

> Texas is the only other state that requires the advice and consent of two-thirds of the Senate to confirm gubernatorial nominees . . . there are certain limitations and party alignments in Texas not prevailing in Pennsylvania . . . in the 1971 session the Texas Senate was composed of 31 members—29 Democrats and 2 Republicans.[2]

That staff report provided a sound basis on which to move forward.

On May 3, 1973, we held a public hearing at which we heard from nine witnesses: Ralph D. Tive, legislative secretary to Governor Shapp; Lt. Gov. Ernest P. Kline; Jack R. Weinrauch, chief counsel to Senator Lamb; Roberta Ehrenberg, chair of the Legislative Study for the Pennsylvania League of Women Voters; Dr. Daniel J. Elazar, professor of political science at Temple University; Helene Wohlgemuth, secretary of public welfare; John C. Pittenger, secretary of education; and Joseph Gallagher, chair of the Pennsylvania Bar Association's Judiciary Committee, who was accompanied by Frederick H. Bolton, executive secretary of the Pennsylvania Bar Association.

The committee met privately over dinner on several occasions to discuss the testimony and the staff report prepared by the Joint State Government Commission. We reached several conclusions:

1. There were too many nominations requiring Senate confirmation—1,914 positions, many of which did not involve significant administrative responsibility and all of which required a two-thirds vote. We would recommend that 473 positions be eliminated from confirmation all together but add sixty deputy secretaries of departments.

2. The two-thirds vote requirement should be limited to 196 positions—the governor's cabinet and the members of forty-four boards and commissions.
3. The remaining 1,312 positions on twenty-seven boards and commissions (including approximately sixty departmental deputy secretaries) should be subject to a majority vote.
4. Article IV, Section 8 should be amended so that the positions requiring two-thirds, a majority, or no confirmation would be determined by statute.
5. Article IV, Section 8 provided no time limits for the governor in submitting nominations or the Senate in acting on them. There was nothing to prevent a rejected nominee from continuing in office. We would recommend an amendment to Article IV, Section 8 to require the governor to send nominations within ninety days of a vacancy and the Senate to act within twenty-five legislative days of receiving the nomination. If the Senate failed to act, the nominee would take office as if confirmed. Rejected nominees would be prohibited from serving.
6. Senate Rule XXX precluded an open, thorough, and expeditious handling of the nominations. The nominations were cloaked in secrecy and public hearings on qualifications were never held. At that time all nominations were handled by the Rules and Executive Nominations Committee. We would recommend changing Rule XXX to refer nominations to the committee most knowledgeable on the nominee's position, e.g., the nomination for Secretary of Agriculture would go to the Agriculture Committee. We would also recommend that each nominee be required to complete a questionnaire on qualifications which would be available to all senators and the public, a confidential state police report be prepared on each nominee, and authorizing any three members of the Rules and Executive Nominations Committee to demand a committee chair to hold a meeting on nominations held by the committee for more than fifteen calendar days.

The conclusions and recommendations were unanimously agreed to. All five members of the committee signed the report submitted to the Senate.[3] (See appendix D for the report and signatures.)

S.B. 1408, a proposed constitutional amendment to change the two-thirds vote requirement of Article 4, Section 8 took four amendments in the 1973–1974 session before winning the approval of both houses.[4] The second round of legislative approval, in the 1975–1976 session, occurred with record speed. As S.B. 22 sponsored by the leadership of both parties it passed the Senate 46–2 and the House 164–0 three weeks after introduction. The electorate approved it at the May 20, 1975 primary 937,249 to 209,026, thereby giving Pennsylvania a new Article IV, Section 8 and a new breath of life for the incapacitated confirmation system. (See appendix E for the text of Article IV, Section 8 as amended in 1975.)

Under the new Article IV, Section 8 nominations are approved by a two-thirds or majority vote as determined by statute, the governor must submit nominations within ninety days of a vacancy, and the Senate is required to act within twenty-five legislative days. If the Senate has not acted within fifteen legislative days, any five senators can request a vote by the full Senate. If the Senate does not act within the twenty-five legislative days, the nominee takes office as if confirmed. The new obligation on the governor to submit nominations within eighty days and the Senate to act within twenty-five days terminated the old practice of interim appointments.

The change in Article 4, Section 8 of the Constitution was not enough to carry out our committee's recommendations. We also needed a statutory provision to determine which gubernatorial appointments required a two-thirds vote and those which needed only a majority. And I soon learned that getting the Senate as a whole and the House to enact the necessary implementing legislation for the report would be a difficult and intricate challenge. The two-thirds rule, in spite of the committee's agreement, provided an obstacle that brought our initiative close to failure.

REFORM WOBBLES TOWARD SUCCESS

I introduced legislation to implement the statutory portion of the committee's report on January 21, 1974, well before the constitutional amendment could be adopted but confident it would be. S.B. 1410 contained the committee's recommendations: 196 positions under the two-thirds vote, 1,312 under the majority vote, and at least 473 with no confirmation requirement. The Senate passed the bill quickly by a vote of 46-1. The House, however, loaded the bill with several amendments that were at best marginal to the confirmation process. These amendments provided consumer advocates for liquor control board, milk marketing board, and the public utility commission, as well as creating a consumer service agency. The Senate rejected the House version, sending it to a conference committee, where it expired at the end of the session.

On January 27, 1975, I reintroduced the Senate version of S.B. 1410 as S.B. 21, joined in co-sponsorship by six Democrats and seven Republicans, including the leadership from both parties. When S.B. 21 came before the full Senate the two-thirds vote provision became a lively issue. Senator James Kelley of Westmoreland offered an amendment to make all of the governor's appointments, except vacancies in state treasurer and auditor general, subject to a majority vote. Kelley's amendment failed, 21-26. I voted for it. Then Senator Thomas Nolan of Allegheny County, the new Democratic floor leader, proposed to remove the governor's cabinet from the two-thirds requirement and make it subject to a majority vote. Nolan's amendment passed 26–23, revealing a party line differences on the two-thirds issue. Senator Frame then proposed to require by statute (not a rule change as the report recommended) that the governor send with each nomination an information sheet on each nominee, including whether there was any criminal record. That was approved 37–11. With those amendments the bill was sent to the House by a 44–3 vote.[5]

The House, however, amended the bill to make all of the governor's appointments, except judges and state elected official vacancies, subject to a majority Senate vote. That set the stage for a confrontation on the two-thirds issue that threatened to derail the confirmation process reform. The Senate sent the bill to a conference committee of myself and Senators Messinger and Frame, joined from the House by the Majority (Democratic) Whip, James Manderino; Norman Berson of Philadelphia; and Matthew Ryan, the Republican floor whip.

The conference committee quickly divided on party line over the two-thirds vote requirement. The Republicans, Frame and Ryan, wanted to use the two-thirds requirement as recommended in the Senate Committee report. They distrusted Governor Shapp and viewed a two-thirds vote as necessary to preserving legislative power. The House Democrats, Manderino and Berson, insisted on making all positions, except vacancies in elected state offices, subject to a majority vote. My Democratic colleague, Henry Messinger, and I decided to compromise with the House and apply the two-thirds requirement to the Milk Marketing Board, the Fish Commission, the Game Commission, the Liquor Control Board, the Public Utility Commission, the Turnpike Commission, judges, and vacancies in state treasurer and auditor general. Manderino and Berson agreed. We four Democrats signed a conference report in this version and sent it to both houses for approval. Republicans Frame and Ryan issued a minority report asserting that the S.B. 21 conference report had turned "a badly needed governmental reform proposal into a dangerous and iniquitous measure which would permit the invasion of partisan cronyism and political corruption into some of the most vital areas of Commonwealth responsibilities."

On the Senate floor for final approval the S.B. 21 conference report even drew fire from Democratic Senator Joseph Ammerman, a member of the original confirmation study committee, and known for his streak of independence. He declared that approval "is surrendering to the Executive Branch nearly all of the voice that it (the Senate) has in matters of confirmation." The Republican leadership weighed in heavily against approval. Senator Frame argued that approval would eliminate needed checks on procedural abuses. Senator Henry Hager of Lycoming County suggested I had broken a commitment to the deceased Senator Stroup to support the two-thirds provisions recommended by the original committee report.

> Senator Stroup . . . went to numerous meetings with . . . Senator Kury, and came back with the commitment of . . . Senator Kury that the enabling legislation, if we would allow the constitutional change to take place, would state two-thirds . . . We feel that a serious breach of faith has taken place here with our departed colleague, Senator Stroup.

I saw it differently. Politics is the art of the possible. For me the choice was a compromise with the House or no bill, a large piece of the "loaf" or no bread at all, so to speak. I rose to respond.

> I want to reply (to Senator Hager) . . . the five of us on the study committee (including Senator Stroup) agreed that (we would like to see the recommendations enacted.). We then passed a constitutional amendment saying the confirmation shall be two-thirds or a majority as the legislature would dictate and that the plan would be what our recommendation would be for allocation of the two-thirds or majority. We passed it in the Senate, but (the) bill ran into very difficult problems in the House of Representatives and with the Governor. I thought we had a choice between seeing the bill (passed) or sticking to the letter of the that (report) totally(and losing it altogether), and, faced with that choice, I made the decision that if we had to make some compromises to pass the bill, that was the most important thing to do. So in my view, Mr. President, I do not feel there has been a breach of faith with anybody.[6]

The Senate then passed the S.B. 21 Conference Committee report by 26–23, the narrowest of majorities, without a vote to spare. Two Democrats, Senator Ammerman (who served on the original study committee) and Senator Jeannette Reibman of Northampton County, joined all of the Republicans in opposition.

Having barely skimmed over the reef of the two-thirds vote in the Senate, the legislative vessel carrying confirmation reform headed for an even stormier passage in the House. On the first vote, the House rejected it, 100–65, a constitutional vote of 102 being necessary. Six weeks later the House reconsidered the bill and passed it 102–74, again without a vote to spare and along straight party lines. Thus reform of the confirmation process, born in a vibrant exercise of bipartisan collaboration, limped to the governor, having survived defeat by the narrowest possible margin in both houses. Governor Shapp signed the bill into law on November 8, 1976, and gave me the pen he used to sign it. Framed with a copy of the bill's front page the pen hangs on my home office wall, a hard-earned trophy. A moribund constitutional check on executive power had been given a new chance at life.

I believe the Senate confirmation process as revised has worked reasonably well, but imperfectly. The information sheet required by Senator

Frame's amendment accompanies the governor's nominations, public committee hearings on the nominations are held as a matter of routine, and Senate votes are taken. Interim appointments are no longer made. The only positions now subject to a two-thirds vote are the Turnpike Commission and the Liquor Control Board, as well as judges and vacancies in elected state officials.

After the Republicans took control of the Senate in 1980 they methodically removed the two-thirds requirement from most of the remaining "two-thirds" vote positions, possibly because the governor was Republican. The spirit of the revisions, however, is violated from time to time and the intent of the changes is occasionally evaded. Governors who have not chosen a nominee within ninety days of the vacancy have resorted to sending "placeholder" names, usually a gubernatorial staff member that shows technical compliance with the law. Before the twenty-five days in the Senate have expired the governor recalls the bogus nominee and then resubmits it or sends a genuine nomination.

Although S.B. 21 forbids a rejected nominee from serving, in the case of departmental secretaries, governors can use a loophole to get around the prohibition. The loophole is that acting secretaries can serve indefinitely. Governor Rendell, for example, sent to the Senate the name of John Hanger to be the Secretary of Environmental Protection. But considering that Hanger might be rejected, Rendell at the same time designated him as the acting Secretary of the Department. (Hanger was eventually confirmed as full secretary.) If confirmed the nominee resigns the deputy position. If not confirmed, the nominee can continue to run the department as the executive deputy, as allowed under Section 207.1 of the administrative code. This is a loophole that was not foreseen during the reform of the confirmation process. In spite of my disappointment in these misuses of the system, I believe the effort made to restore vitality to the confirmation process has worked fairly well. The Senate check on the executive's appointment power is very much alive.

13

The "Bloodless Coup" Bill and the Governor's Disability

Saturday, June 14, 1993, Governor Robert Casey sent an extraordinary letter to the House and Senate.

> Pursuant to 71 P.S. section 784.1, hereby declare that effective 5:00 A.M., June 14, 1993, I will be temporarily unable to discharge the powers and duties of the office of Governor, and that in accordance with Article IV, section 13 of the Pennsylvania such powers and duties shall be discharged by Lieutenant Governor Mark S. Singel, until such time as I transmit to the General Assembly a declaration to the contrary.
> Sincerely,
> /s/ Robert P. Casey
> Governor

At about 6:00 A.M. that day the governor underwent surgery for a dual transplant for a new heart and a new liver, a perilous procedure from which his survival, let alone a full recovery, was in doubt. Bishop Donald Wuerl of the Pittsburgh Diocese offered the last rites of his church before the operation began, but Casey declined. By sending that letter, Governor Casey transferred the powers and duties of his office to Lieutenant Governor Mark Singel. This had never been done before. Singel served as Acting Governor for six months and a week, until 12:01 a.m., December 21, 1993, when Casey certified his own recovery.[1]

Besides being one of Casey's multitude of friends rooting for his recovery, I was more than a casual observer. As a senator twenty years earlier I had drafted and guided to enactment a bill that provided the procedure for determining the disability of the governor and the lieutenant governor. Now I would see how the procedure would work.

Article IV, Section 13 of the State Constitution since 1874 had provided that "in the case of the disability of the Governor, the powers, duties and emoluments of the officer shall devolve upon the Lieutenant Governor until the disability is removed." This simple provision raised a number of questions. Who determines if the governor is disabled? If the disability has been removed? If there is disagreement, who resolves it? These are the kind of questions I hoped to answer by introducing S.B. 803 on May 21, 1973.

My interest in the question of executive disability began in 1964, a year after my admission to law practice in Northumberland County. I joined the Young Lawyers Section of the Pennsylvania Bar Association and was asked to chair its committee on Presidential Inabililty and Vice-presidential Vacancy, the subject of an evolving amendment to the U.S. Constitution that became the 25th Amendment. I found the subject fascinating, read several books on the presidency, and worked with John D. Feerick, the national chair of the project for the American Bar Association.

The inability of presidents had been a serious, but not widely appreciated problem throughout our history. President Garfield lay disabled for eighty days before his death following the assassin's attempt on his life and Vice President Chester Arthur remained on the sidelines. Woodrow Wilson had been felled by a stroke and lay incapacitated for 280 days while his wife decided who would see him. President Eisenhower had three disabling health problems: a heart attack in 1955, an ileitis attack in 1956, and a stroke in 1957. In these cases the authority of anyone to act in place of the president was clouded in doubt. The assassination of President Kennedy brought the issue back to the fore in Congress. President Johnson had a serious heart attack in 1955 and his successor was John McCormack, the 72-year-old Speaker of the House. As a former president, Eisenhower supported an effort to clarify the constitutional provisions on successions.[2]

Congress sent to the state legislatures for ratification in 1965 a proposed amendment to the U.S. Constitution that provided for the president to appoint a vice president when there is a vacancy, for the president to certify his disability or the Cabinet to do so in the event of his disability, and for the president to resume power on his own declaration. In periods of presidential disability, the vice president would serve as acting president. The Cabinet and Congress would resolve any disputes.

About the time the proposed federal amendment was sent to the state legislatures for ratification, C. Brewster Rhoads, the president of the Pennsylvania Bar Association, asked if my committee and I would serve as the committee for the full state bar association. We agreed. Our committee worked with the bar association's headquarters staff to inform the public and persuade the state legislature. As part of that effort I wrote an article, "The Crisis in the Law of Presidential Succession," published in the March 1965 issue of the *Pennsylvania Bar Quarterly*.[3]

The 25th Amendment was ratified in Pennsylvania and other states and became part of the U.S. Constitution on February 10, 1967.

I paid little attention to the 25th Amendment after its adoption until I was elected to the Senate. Reading Article IV, Section 13, it was then obvious that Pennsylvania's constitutional provision on executive inability had the same weaknesses as the U.S. Constitution did prior to the adoption of the 25th Amendment in 1967. Drawing on my work for the Bar Association on the federal amendment, I drafted and introduced S.B. 803 as a parallel proposal. A major difference between the 25th Amendment and my proposal was that S.B. 803 did not address the question of a vacancy in the lieutenant governor's office. Senator Stanley Stroup, a senior Republican and solid conservative, joined me as the chief co-sponsor, along with my own party leadership, Senators Lamb and Murray, as well as Republican Senator R. Budd Dwyer. As a courtesy I called Governor Shapp and told him of the bill and what it intended to do. He had no particular reaction.

S.B. 803 turned out to be one of the easiest bills to pass I ever sponsored. No opposition was expressed in either house and the bill received only one amendment challenge. Senator Richard Tilghman offered an amendment to remove the lieutenant governor from the decision-making process in determining if the governor was disabled or if a disability has been removed. Senator Richard Snyder of Lancaster supported him.

> Senator SNYDER: It seems to me rather fundamental that the one person, who should not participate . . . is the man who would succeed him . . . Either he will be accused by some persons of an attempt to replace the governor, or he will, if overly conscientious lean over backwards to avoid doing, perhaps, what he ought to do. At any rate, the decision ought to be left to a third party.

I responded.

> Senator KURY: . . . (that) the lieutenant governor is the next in line and the one to step in and act is the exact reason why he should have some involvement in the determination . . . he is the one who must bear the responsibility for acting. This bill is drafted in such a way that, with the cabinet being involved, the onus will not rest on him (the Lt. Governor). He is not the one to make the decision, it is the cabinet in consultation with him and I, therefore, think that he is amply protected.[4]

The amendment was defeated 24–26 and then the bill was sent to the House by a vote of 44–6. The House approved it November 20, 1974, by 165–0 and sent the bill to the governor's desk.

Soon I took a call from Governor Shapp, upset that he didn't know about the bill and called it the "bloodless coup" bill. I explained how the bill worked and that the participation of the cabinet in the disability determination gave ample protection to the governor. I also reminded him that I had called him and discussed the bill when it was introduced. The governor was mollified sufficiently to sign it into law on December 30, 1974.[5] As Act 347, S.B. 803 collected dust in the state statutes for almost twenty years, until Governor Casey invoked it and put it to its intended use.[6]

14

Righting a Listing Ship by Rewriting the Utility Law

By the time Milton Shapp made his second run for governor in 1970, consumer protection, "consumerism," had become a strong political issue, just as environmental protection had a few years earlier. Shapp made consumer protection a major theme in his successful campaign.

A NEW SENATE COMMITTEE IS BORN

At the beginning of the 1975-1956 session, the Senate Democratic leadership created a new committee, the Committee on Consumer Affairs, of six Democrats and four Republicans. I was appointed chairman and Senator John Sweeney of Delaware County Vice Chairman. The Republican minority named Senator Wayne Ewing of Allegheny County as its ranking member. In establishing a Consumer Affairs Committee, the Senate responded to a rising crescendo of public opinion on behalf of consumers. The ever-increasing price of electricity had become a hot political issue. Governor Shapp's election relied significantly on his criticisms of the Public Utility Commission (PUC) and its perceived failure to protect the consuming public. In the House, C. L. Schmitt, Democrat from Westmoreland County and Chair of the House Consumer Protection Committee, had already introduced H.B.175 to create a Department of Consumer Advocate to protect the public's interest in rate making cases. "Mr. Consumer," as he was called, Schmitt was as much the leader of the consumer movement in the House as John Laudadio was for the environment.

The chairmanship of this new Senate committee offered an uncommon opportunity to generate and advance significant legislation. The more thought I gave it, the more it made sense that our first mission should be a complete investigation of the Public Utility Commission and its operations. After creating it in 1937, the legislature pretty much ignored it for the thirty-eight ensuing years. The law of utility regulation by the PUC had become sanctified, as if it was beyond the competence of the legislature to understand sufficiently the utility law to make changes. Bills amending the PUC law were not drafted by senators or their staff, but by David Dunlap, the lawyer and lobbyist for the electric industry trade group. I do not attribute this to improper motive on Dunlap's part, but to the political patronage system of the Taylor era in the Senate, as well to the belief that the subject was too technical for anyone but insiders to understand.

I discussed the question of a PUC investigation with Senator Murray, the Senate president, and Senator Thomas Nolan, the new majority leader, as well as the committee. They agreed to it. I then made several decisions on how the investigation would be conducted.

First, the committee would hire lawyers and staff so that we could conduct a thorough investigation and write whatever legislation we deemed appropriate. We would not ask Dunlap to do it for us. We would do our own drafting and then ask Dunlap, as well as other interested parties, for their comments. I felt strongly about this. The integrity of the Senate required it. In addition, I did not see the PUC law as an inscrutable text.[1] There was nothing in the PUC law that the senators and staff could not deal with competently. Consequently, I hired James H. Cawley as the committee's chief counsel and the Republicans employed Susan Shanaman and Frederick Taylor.

I knew from chairing the Committee of Senate Confirmations that we could not legislate on the basis of current personalities if we were to get a lasting result. The investigation, I was determined, would not get bogged down in the swamp of party politics. George I. Bloom, a distinguished old guard Republican of the patronage era, had served as PUC chairman before the Shapp administration and was the frequent subject of Democratic attacks. Herbert Denenberg, a younger consumer activist, had become Shapp's point person on PUC issues. Either could easily become lightning rods for criticism. Senator Ewing and I agreed that the committee investigation would not be used as a forum to attack either Bloom or Denenberg. We would invite both as witnesses.[2] In addition to keeping party politics outside of the committee room, we would conduct a balanced investigation of the PUC itself, representatives of the regulated industries, the consuming public, and government regulators from other states and the federal government.

The Senate Consumer Affairs Committee working on the Public Utility Commission investigation. Speaking at right is James H. Cawley, Committee Counsel. To his right are Senators Wayne Ewing, the author, Robert Myers, and Paul McKinney. Next to McKinney in the light suit is Frederick Taylor, Republican counsel. Source: Personal file photo.

THE INVESTIGATION AND REPORT

On that basis my committee and its staff then developed a comprehensive investigation that resulted in six public hearings with twenty-five witnesses, supplemented by fact-finding trips to Wisconsin and California, two states with progressive utility regulation considered possible models for other states. The lead witnesses were four current or past PUC commissioners—Louis Carter, James McGirr Kelly, Robert Bloom, and George I. Bloom (not related). We also heard from five current PUC bureau directors and staff, five electric industry executives (including Dunlap), two telephone company executives, three consumer groups, the chief administrative law judge of the Federal Power Commission, the chairman of the Wisconsin Public Service Commission, and a utility industry specialist from Wall Street. In California we had extensive meetings with three commissioners and six top staff members, and in Wisconsin we talked with four senior staff members.

(For a complete list of the witnesses and persons interviewed in Wisconsin and California, see appendix F.)

The trip to California provided me with a valuable insight into dealing with the press. Several weeks before our scheduled trip, a committee led by Senator Nolan had gone to California ostensibly to study the Bay Area Rapid Transit System. Reporters found that Nolan and his colleagues had spent little time on their expressed mission, but on dining and sightseeing. The Nolan trip was widely criticized. To avoid this kind of press reaction I went to the newsroom several days before our departure, at the suggestion of Vincent Carocci, who was working with our committee, and personally distributed a copy of our itinerary to each reporter. I offered to brief them on our findings when we returned. During our first meeting with the California Public Utility Commission, one of the Harrisburg reporters called the office to ask if my colleagues and I were there. There was no further follow-up or negative press reports when we returned to Harrisburg. The lesson from this is: If something you (as a public official) plan to do has the possibility of being controversial, disclose it yourself in advance and then do it as promised.

We completed our investigation in seven months, prepared a ninety-one-page report with forty-nine recommendations for change and submitted it to the Senate.[3] All of the committee members, except Senator Clarence Bell, signed the report. Bell filed his own report of recommendations, saying that he neither concurred nor dissented from the committee report. The minority members did add their own supplement to the report in which they noted their concurrence in the "overwhelming majority" of the matters considered by the committee. The minority, however, found "significant differences" on twelve of the forty-nine recommendations.

The report received a good reception. William Ecenbarger of the Philadelphia *Inquirer* reported:

> The Kury Report . . . probably is the best piece of work turned out by a legislative committee in at least a generation. There is no magic involved here. It was accomplished by hard work and a staff appointed on the basis of professional competence rather than party persuasion.[4]

With our investigation done, I concluded that the PUC was a ship that had been to sea for thirty-eight years without coming to port or drydock for maintenance and an overhaul. We found that the PUC was a ship listing heavily to one side, in favor of the utilities it was supposed to regulate and against the consumers it was supposed to protect. The challenge for the committee was to implement the report with legislation that would restore balance to the decks of the PUC and relaunch it.

THE IMPLEMENTING LEGISLATION

To draft such legislation we had to understand what created the heavy tilt. Our investigation had done this by, in effect, closely examining the PUC's officers and crew, the operations room, the engine room, and the navigation room. Our findings made it clear that, as then structured and staffed, the PUC was incapable of the needed balance, regardless of the effort made by the commission.

We found, for example, that the Bureau of Rates and Research, which had the job of reviewing and analyzing rate increase applications, had only sixty persons, paid $14,000 to $15,000 each, with no chance of increasing their compensation. Pennsylvania's electric utilities, on the other hand, had virtually unlimited resources to prepare and pursue rate increases. In one case, the Philadelphia Electric Company (PECO) spent $636,000 to prepare its case, while the PUC spent $106,000 to respond to it. The regulated industries outspent the regulator by six to one in the preparation, submission, review, hearings, and final order on a multi-million dollar rate application. This is why I frequently said that the crew of the PUC was "outmanned" and "outgunned" in rate proceedings.

Other findings proved equally startling:

- The PUC lacked the funds to hire outside consultants to assist in analyzing rate increase applications, but the regulated utilities did it routinely.
- The utilities filed rate applications in stages, thereby putting the rate increases into effect over an extended time period.
- Rates could be increased without a public hearing. The existing law allowed a rate increase to take effect unless suspended by a unanimous vote of the commission. One commissioner had the power to insure automatic approval.
- The regulated utilities could have conversations with the commissioners without other parties being present that became known as *"ex parte* communications."
- The manner in which PUC hearing examiners conducted hearings was particularly outrageous. The committee's report speaks to the point.

> a cadre of 20 hearing examiners are on fulltime payroll . . . at scattered locations throughout the state with salaries ranging anywhere from $18,000 to $22,000 annually . . . the only requirement for their employment is that they be members of the bar in good standing for a period of three years. The only condition for hiring is securing the affirmative votes of at least three . . . commissioners. They do little more at a hearing than serve as traffic officers in so far as what is permitted into the record and what is not. They write no decisions. Nor do they analyze the testimony for the benefit of the Commission . . . The hearing examiner system as

it now functions is nothing less than a deplorable sham on the hearing process. There is absolutely no justification for it. It must be terminated immediately.[5]

The PUC had no staffing or legislative direction to plan for the long-range energy needs of the state and often resorted to asking the utilities to make studies for them.

- While the regulated utilities employed lawyers from the state's largest law firm to prepare and present their cases, there was no one to represent and speak for the consumer. The public interest required an advocate who was not part of the PUC, but independent of it. We recommended a Consumer Advocate in the Attorney General's office.

While these findings focused on a short-term response, for improving the performance of the commission, we also saw a need for a "long run response" on such relatively esoteric topics as original cost versus fair market value for utility assets, whether construction work in progress should be included in the rate base, a forward looking test year, the automatic fuel adjustment charge, and natural gas allocation and curtailment procedures.

The three committee counsel, led by Cawley but working collaboratively, proceeded to draft the necessary legislation. When they reached disagreement on a particular point, Senator Ewing and I would review it and try to work out a mutually satisfactory version. After several weeks of sustained effort the counsel had drafted a package of five bills that was introduced on November 25, 1975, under the sponsorship of ten Democrats and seven Republicans. Majority Counsel Cawley and Minority Counsel Taylor and Shanaman later prepared a "Final Report of Counsel" of the committee's lawyers that provided an overview of the drafting intent.[6]

S.B. 1216 clarified the PUC's jurisdiction, limited the automatic fuel adjustments to actual cost, suspended rate increases for six months, allowed a future test year, regulated billing procedures, required personal contact with consumers before a service shut off, provided for depreciation schedules, regulated affiliated interests, and established fees by the commission.

S.B. 1217 dealt with the commission itself by providing for:

- raising the salaries of the commissioners from $24,000 to $30,000;
- requiring Senate confirmation in accord with the recent amendment to Article IV, Section 8 of the state constitution;
- requiring commissioners to be full time and to disclose and divest themselves of stock interests in any utility. Commissioners were also prohibited from employment with a utility for a year after leaving office;

- a judicial code of ethics for the commissioners;
- a strong administrative director for the commission;
- creation of the Office of Administrative Law Judge to replace the discredited hearing examiner system, all administrative law judges to be full-time commission employees;
- the commission to appoint its counsel, rather than the governor.

S.B. 1219 created a new commission bureau, the Bureau of Conservation, Economics, and Energy Planning, so that the commission could make its own determinations of long-run energy needs.

S.B. 1223 authorized the commission staff to cross-examine witnesses at the discretion of the commission counsel and with the consent of the presiding officer.

S.B. 1224 eliminated the thirty-year-old age requirement for commissioners and set aside $50,000 for the commission for educational study by its employees in utility regulation.

THE CONSUMER ADVOCATE

We did not draft a consumer advocate bill because Representative Schmitt's bill had already passed the House and was in my committee. We added H.B. 175 to our Senate package.

While the entire package of six bills was, in my view, essential to restoring a balanced deck to the PUC, I think the single most important step was the creation of the consumer advocate. It is impossible for the commission to be both a judge of the rate increase application before it and an advocate for the rate payers at the same time. The ratepayers needed an independent lawyer to represent them. By establishing a consumer advocate, we ensured that for the first time a lawyer knowledgable in utility law, with the support of a good staff, would confront the utility lawyers and make them prove their case for an increase.

The initiative for the consumer advocate came from the House in H.B. 175 that received House approval on March 27, 1975, by a vote of 155–20. H.B. 175 arrived in the Senate in broad form. It called for the creation of a Department of Consumer Advocate with the authority to represent the public's interest in proceedings before the Milk Marketing Board, the PUC, and the Insurance Department. Moreover, the consumer advocate would serve at the pleasure of the governor without any Senate confirmation requirement. The consumer advocate would, under the House bill, have a wide range of investigation powers, including the power to issue subpoenas.

H.B. 175 could not pass the Senate in such broad form. Phillip Kalodner, an imminent Shapp nominee to the PUC, came to my office to seek our approval of the House version. I had to disappoint him. The Senate was by nature more conservative than the House, and there was more distrust of the Shapp Administration in the Senate. A conversation with Senator Murray confirmed that. Murray felt sure we could pass the bill confined to a consumer advocate at the PUC, but not for other state agencies as provided for in the House bill. I called Representative Schmitt.

> "Schmitty, I can get your bill through over here, but only if it is limited to the PUC. Can you live with that? The votes aren't here for anything beyond the PUC."
>
> "Franklin, if that's the way it is, I'll take it," Schmitt replied.

My committee then amended H.B. 175 to provide for a consumer advocate in the Department of Justice to be appointed with the approval of two-thirds of the Senate. At that time the attorney general was appointed by the governor, not elected, so that the Department of Justice was under the governor's control. In addition, we proposed to give the consumer advocate statutory standing to intervene in all rate increase cases.

As so amended in my committee, H.B.175 still received spirited opposition. Senator James Kelley of Westmoreland offered an amendment to allow the consumer advocate's decision to intervene in a case to be subject to review by the Commonwealth Court. This amendment was defeated on a voice vote.

Senator Henry Hager, a Republican from Lycoming County and a rising force on the Republican side, rose to oppose the bill outright.

> Senator HAGER: . . . (with this bill) we create an entirely new agency, an entirely new bureaucracy, as voracious as the others have proved to be. Today the PUC, tomorrow all of state government; new offices, new jobs, new forms, new supplies, new government red tape, miring the productive economy and all paid for by the unsuspecting consumer.[7]

Senator Clarence Bell, a Republican member of my committee, rejoined by pointing out that the purpose of the bill was to make the PUC an impartial, quasi-judicial body. Even though he had not signed the committee report, Bell described the bill as "a great step forward." The bill then passed 34 to 13, the 13 being all Republicans except for Senator Kelley.

The House did not approve the Senate version and sent it to a conference committee of Representatives Schmitt, Manderino, and Geesey and Senators Sweeney, Ewing, and me. The conference committee quickly worked out a compromise that reduced the Senate confirmation requirement from two-thirds to a majority, prohibited the consumer advocate from having any interests or employment by a utility for two years after leaving office, authorized the appointment of assistant consumer advocates, and delineated the powers of the consumer advocate.

A small but vocal band of Republicans again rose in opposition when the conference committee report came to a vote. Senator Ewing, the ranking Republican on my committee and a signer of the conference committee report, changed his mind. He argued that, since the Senate had spent considerable time in fashioning PUC reform legislation that was now before the House, we should hold off on the consumer advocate until the Senate bills had passed and been given a chance to work.

I responded.

> Senator KURY: . . . (there is a misconception) that the PUC can be both the judge and advocate before the commission, (that) the PUC can be both impartial in reviewing the application and still represent, in effect, a party to the case (the consuming public) . . . the public which is not ordinarily represented before the PUC ought to have somebody there in an adversary capacity on its behalf.
>
> Let me tell you what we are up against, Mr. President . . . when the Philadelphia Electric (Company) went before the PUC for its last increase, . . . they were represented by the blue chip Philadelphia law firm of Morgan, Lewis & Bockius, one of the finest law firms . . . of Pennsylvania. They were paid $200,000 to prepare their case and argue it . . . Who was there for the residential user, for the small businessman or the farmer? How many of those people can afford Morgan, Lewis & Bockius, or any other lawyer, to . . . question the case presented on behalf of Philadelphia Electric?
>
> Mr. President, that is one of the fundamental things wrong with the PUC. For thirty years they have been listening to utility lawyers argue . . . and have nobody there on behalf of the residential user, the small businessman, or the farmers. The big corporations can afford counsel, but nobody else can.[8]

Senator Ewing replied to me by again arguing that the Senate passed bills should be enacted and given a trial work out before enacting a consumer advocate. Senator Jubelirer followed by objecting to the reduction of the Senate confirmation approval from two-thirds to a majority. He reiterated Senator Ewing's argument that S.B. 1216 and S.B. 1217 should be enacted first. Ewing's and Jubelirer's arguments were to no avail. The Senate approved the Conference Committee Report 41 to 9, with all 9 negative votes coming from the Republican side. Governor Shapp signed the consumer advocate bill, H.B. 175, into law on July 9, 1976, making it Act No. 161 of the 1975–1976 session.

REFORMING THE PUC STRUCTURE

The two major Senate proposals, S.B. 1216 and S.B. 1217, were passed by the House on June 29, 1976, the day the Senate adopted the Conference Committee Report on H.B. 175. Both bills had, however, been strenuously debated and substantially amended. The Senate non-concurred in

Governor Shapp has just signed the Public Utility Commission reform bills and has given one of the signing pens to Representative C. L. Schmitt and the author. Source: Courtesy of AP/Worldwide Photos.

the House amendments and sent the bills to a conference committee of Senators Sweeney, Jubelirer, and me and Representatives Schmitt, William Shane, and Frank O'Connell.[9]

When the legislature returned for the fall session in September, the committee had worked out compromises on both bills, which I believed did not significantly impair the goals stated in our report on the PUC. Both houses quickly approved the conference committee reports with relative ease and without debate. S.B. 1216 received unanimous approval in both houses. S.B. 1217 received House approval by 147–41 and Senate approval 45–5. The governor signed them into law on October 7, 1976, making them Acts 215 and 216 of the 1975–1976 session.

With the enactment of the House Consumer Advocate bill and the Senate PUC reform bills now law, I felt that the initial mission of my Consumer Affairs Committee had been successfully completed. We had drastically overhauled and refitted the structure of the commission and sent it back to sea, so to speak, with a balanced deck.

Under the new laws:

- The PUC Commissioners were established as a full-time judicial body with judge's salaries and a judicial code of ethics. *Ex parte* communications between utilities with pending rate increase applications and the

commissioners and their staff were prohibited. (*Ex parte* communications are those made to the commission or its staff in a contested proceeding without opposing parties present. This rule has long existed in state and federal courts.) The staff of the commission was restructured to give it the duty and power to fully investigate all applications for rate increases. This included the employment of lawyers, accountants, and consultants as needed to properly evaluate the requested increases.
- Three new bureaus—Consumer Services, Law, Administrative Law Judge, and that of Conservation, Economic, and Energy Planning—were created to give the commission a full set of tools to do its job.
- Future rate increase applications were suspended for seven months upon filing and could not take effect without the approval of the commission within that time.
- The hearing examiner system was replaced by an administrative law judge (ALJ) system based on that used by the Federal Power Commission. The ALJ's were required to be full-time PUC staff and empowered and directed to conduct the initial hearings under a stringent set of judicial-type guidelines. The ALJs were, however, given substantial independence through a provision that they could be discharged only "for cause."
- Contracts between the regulated utilities and their subsidiaries or other "affiliated interests" were subjected to PUC review and approval.

Beyond this legislation, the Senate Consumer Affairs Committee's Report on the investigation of the PUC concluded with admonitions for the three parties affected by the PUC—consumers, the commission itself, and the regulated utilities. The report told the consumers that, while our recommendations could produce a fair and open regulatory process, electricity was no longer a cheap energy.

> ... (consumers) bear a heavy role to play ... the best answer ... may rest in energy conservation ... that will require rather dramatic alterations and limitations on the life-style we now experience. Without it (conservation) this battle may prove to be winless.

The report then admonished the commission that, while our recommendations would provide the tools to do the job, it would be expected to provide leadership. "The old way of doing business is no longer adequate to the demands and challenges of the day."

Then our report said to the utilities that, while, our proposals offered a fair and professional regulatory process, the exploding growth in energy usage must be managed.

Energy conservation and planning must be the new order of the day. We expect you to cooperate and to participate in the established of this new order.

Our committee report concluded with a point from one of our committee's witnesses, Richard Cudahy of the Wisconsin Public Service Commission.

> The habits of a half century are hard to break. But having stood at the . . . precipice for several years now . . . both utility and customer should be more than ready to kick the . . . habit in favor of a new, and sound idea . . . we must go forward.[10]

Looking at this legislation a third of a century later, I feel good about it. The commission became an active regulatory body that makes the utilities seeking a rate increase prove their cases through a rigorous examination process. No longer a passive recipient of utility filings, the commission provides leadership in consumer education on energy conservation and heating for low-income families during the winter months.

From the time of its first consumer advocate, Mark Widoff,[11] to the present, the Office of Consumer Advocate has been particularly successful in representing consumer interests. The Supreme Court of the United States demonstrated this in 1989 in a unanimous decision written by then Chief Justice William Rehnquist in *Duquesne Light Co. v. Barasch*.[12] In this case Duquesne Light and the Pennsylvania Power Company joined a venture to build seven nuclear electric generating plants.

In 1980 the utilities cancelled plans for the construction of the plants. At the time of the cancellation Duquesne's share of preliminary work for the four plants was $34,697,389 and Penn Power's share was $9,569,665, a total of $44,267.054. Duquesne and Penn Power asked the PUC to let them recoup the $44,267,054 from their ratepayers even though the plants were not constructed. The administrative law judge assigned to the case recommended approval of the utility application, and the PUC granted it, allowing Duquesne and Penn Power to recoup their expenditure over ten years. David Barasch, then consumer advocate, appealed the commission's decision to the Commonwealth Court, which upheld the PUC's decision to allow recoupment.[13] Barasch again appealed, this time to the State Supreme Court, which reversed the PUC and upheld the consumer advocate's position. The State Supreme Court held that, without a generation plant that is used and useful in providing electricity, the PUC law prohibited recovery of the costs incurred prior to cancellation from being included in the company rate base or being collected by amortization of the costs in rates.

The utilities, represented by Peter Buscemi, of the Washington office of Morgan, Lewis, and Bockius, appealed to the Supreme Court of the United States and argued the case before it. Irwin Popowsky, then the senior assistant consumer advocate, argued for the consumers.[14] The court ruled unanimously in favor of the consumer advocate's position and thereby saved Pennsylvania consumers $44,267,054 they otherwise would have had to pay.

This result would not have happened without the consumer advocate. The consuming public does not have standing to appeal PUC decisions. The PUC could not (and would not) appeal a Commonwealth Court decision in its favor. But the consumer advocate has authority to appeal the PUC and Commonwealth court decisions, as well as to defend the Pennsylvania Supreme Court's decision before the U.S. Supreme Court. As Representative Schmitt and the rest of us contemplated, a consumer advocate could face off with the utility lawyers and give the consuming public representation that protected its interests.

In recent years the PUC has sailed through increasingly turbulent waters. Times have changed and so has the law. In 1978 the legislature codified the two laws my committee developed and enacted in 1976, thus creating a Public Utility Code.[15] There have been amendments since but by far the most important was the Electric Generation Customer Choice and Competition Act signed into law by Governor Ridge in 1996.[16] In the name of competition, this bill removed electric generation from PUC jurisdiction. The distribution portion of electric service remained under PUC regulation but generation and transmission were removed from PUC jurisdiction under a scheme which placed a cap on rate increases for most utilities until 2010. With two exceptions, the electric distribution companies are predicting substantial rate increases when these caps are gone, as much as 60 percent. The prospect of such a steep rate increase has engendered a stormy and complex debate over what the legislature should do about it.

In partial response, the legislature enacted and the governor signed on October 15, 2008, a bill to require energy conservation measures, allow electric distribution companies more latitude in how they purchase electricity from the generators, and to provide "smart" electric meters to consumers.[17] Written at the behest of the current PUC, another section of the bill amended the PUC structure created by our 1976 legislation to give the commission the authority to restructure the Office of Trial Staff, the Office of Special Assistants, and the Bureau of Conservation, Economics, and Energy Planning.

The day after the legislation to manage electric power when the caps came off went to the governor, PUC Chairman James Cawley, who served as counsel to the Consumer Affairs Committee that drafted our legislation in 1976, explained the commission intended to do the restructuring authorized by the bill.

> The Commission asked for this flexibility, not with the intent of . . . (of eliminating) any people or bureaus.

What we are looking to do is to have the statutory flexibility to realign our staff to meet the needs of this century.

I personally was involved in drafting the legislation which gave us our present structure and specifically names the bureaus. But, over the passage of the last 25 years, a number of those bureaus have changed in their functions and their responsibilities, while new bureaus and offices were created, and new obligations needed to be addressed.

All this legislation does is give us the flexibility to realign.

I agree with Cawley. Legislation as important as a PUC code should not be allowed to continue indefinitely without revision to fit changed circumstances. The legislature's failure to revisit the public utility law enacted in 1937 enabled the PUC to slide into the badly tilted position we found when we looked at in the 1976–1977 session. Considering the serious energy problems confronting Pennsylvania, continued legislative surveillance of the PUC Code and its effectiveness is in order.

15

Our Rendezvous with Flood Disasters

The highlight of my Senate tenure was the enactment of the flood plain and storm water management laws. The track leading to those laws began inauspiciously on Sunday afternoon June 20, 1972, when I participated in the dedication of a state water recreation marina on the island between Sunbury and Northumberland. Dr. Maurice Goddard, Secretary of Environmental Resources, was the principal speaker. As Goddard began his remarks, a rain commenced and became increasingly heavy. The rain did not stop for four days. When it did, the Susquehanna River (as well as other rivers in the state, except for the Conemaugh at Johnstown) became a flood that made it the most costly and damaging natural disaster in Pennsylvania history. Tropical Storm Agnes, as it was called, inflicted $2.1 billion dollars in damages and took forty-eight lives.

The Senate district I was seeking to represent in the election that fall was particularly hard hit. The entire town of Watsontown on the west branch had to be evacuated. Large portions of Milton and West Chillisquaque Township to its south were inundated. Mobile homes that had been assembled in a park near the Lewisburg bridge lay scattered throughout the cornfields toward Chillisquaque Creek. In Lewisburg, Bull Run Creek that flows through the center of the borough had inundated a large section of the town. On the north branch, Bloomsburg, Danville, and Riverside had large stretches of their communities under water. At Sunbury, a high school classmate, Robert Hepler, drowned in the swirling waters of Shamokin Creek which runs into the Susquehanna south of the city. But Sunbury itself was spared, barely, because of an eight-foot-high flood wall that Congressman Fenton had obtained following the 1936 flood that had inundated the center of the city. At the crest of the flood the Sunbury *Daily Item* published

The Sunbury Daily Item *photograph of the Sunbury flood wall at the height of Tropical Storm Agnes. The distance to the ground from the top of the wall is eight feet. The author used an enlarged copy of his photograph on an easel on the Senate floor during the detates on the flood plain bills. Source: Courtesy of the Sunbury* Daily Item.

a photograph taken from the top of the flood wall showing the Susquehanna on the left side of the wall two inches from the top, and on the right the eight-foot drop to Front Street. Downstream from Sunbury, from Selinsgrove to Harrisburg and beyond the flood waters of Hurricane Agnes left a heavy toll of damage and destruction.

Governor Shapp responded with alacrity to provide state resources for the clean-up and recovery. I accompanied him on his visits to places in my area, such as Milton, where we saw firsthand the extensive damage that flooding inflicts. Agnes had delivered a heavy blow to the lives and property of the 27th Senatorial District. I shall never forget the sights of its aftermath.

Back in Harrisburg that summer the legislature also responded. Among other things we redirected to flood relief $150 million from a revenue surplus that had been scheduled for refund to the taxpayers.

Governor Shapp talking with a reporter while touring the flood damage in Milton from Tropical Storm Agnes in June 1972 while the author looks on. Source: Courtesy of the Milton Standard.

THE LESSONS OF HISTORY

After the election I went to work to find a way to do something about averting another Agnes. The first step was to do a study of flooding in Pennsylvania to see what history had to teach us. To do this I asked John Showers of Union County, a college student working in my office, to make the study. Showers was studying American government at American University in Washington, D.C., and had a good academic bent. He spent several months reviewing newspapers, magazines, and books, as well as talking with state and federal officials involved in flood control work.

When Showers had completed his study, I read it carefully and discussed it with him and others at length. Based on the study and subsequent conversations I came to several conclusions about flooding, the overflow of water from the normal stream course onto the adjacent land.

Pennsylvania ranks as the most flood-prone state because 2,418 of its 2,800 communities are situated along a river or stream in flood zones.

Pennsylvania's towns and cities developed as a matter of convenience along the major transportation corridors of the day, its waterways. No thought was given to the dangers involved.

Those who live in a flood plain live there at the mercy of the river. To live in a flood plain is to defy the immutable law of nature, a law—unlike those of the state legislature—that cannot be amended or repealed. The river will occupy the flood plain during floods. The flood plains belong to the rivers.

Flood control projects and engineering projects, regardless of their cost, can never provide more than partial protection. The waters of Tropical Storm Agnes overwhelmed much of the $3 billion in engineering spent on the Susquehanna since 1936, sparing the Sunbury wall by two inches. In 1993 another great flood completely overwhelmed $25 billion in dams and 10,000 miles of levees constructed on the Missouri and Mississippi Rivers by the U.S. Corps of Engineers in the preceding seventy-five years.[1]

Flooding is a normal and inevitable act of nature that has occurred throughout recorded history and will continue to into the future as long as there is snow and rain. Flooding is not a freak event. Future floods are a certainty, the only question being the date of their happening and the level of destruction. There is, therefore, no way to prevent floods. All we can do is seek to alleviate their impact. The first step is to stop building homes in the flood zones. In the many discussions of the flood plain bill I often put it this way. If I gave you $150,000 for a new house, would you build it on a railroad track? Then why would you build in the flood plain?

Flood insurance, available through the federal government, is only a small part of any answer to the flooding problem. Flood insurance pays only for property damages. It pays nothing—zero—for loss of life, or the sheer agony and misery that follows floods as victims try to reconstruct their lives. Humanitarian assistance to flood victims must be the immediate priority for government and private relief organizations in the aftermath of flooding. But we should not stop with that. We need to learn from experience. Otherwise we will be blindly repeating the development patterns which lay the groundwork for flood disasters.

In my view, management of the flood plains should not be left to the discretion of each municipality on the river, any more than we leave treatment of sewage discharges to the discretion of each local government. The rivers must be considered as a whole system, as a surgeon deals with veins and arteries in the body as a single system. If each municipality were left to its own on flood plain management and control, those downstream, as well as those living in the flood plain, would be adversely affected if ineffectual action is taken.

Archimedes is famous for another natural law, the law of water displacement. He demonstrated this by stepping into his bathtub and seeing the water rise as displaced by his body. This law of nature applies to levees, walls, and other engineering projects on rivers, as well as by the construction of new buildings in flood zones. Every new brick in a flood plain displaces the equivalent quantity of water. Thus construction in the flood plain forces the flooding water to rise as it goes downstream. This led me to ask this question: How much more construction in flood zones upstream from Sunbury will it take to make a future flood top Sunbury's flood wall?

THE LOGIC OF HISTORY CONFRONTS POLITICAL REALITY

Based on this logic and historical information I offered S.B. 1122 on September 18, 1973, co-sponsored by three Democrats, including Senator Martin Murray, the president of the Senate and a resident of Agnes-devastated Luzerne County, and three Republicans. Titled "The Pennsylvania Flood Disaster Prevention Act," the bill contained a lengthy declaration of legislative findings reflecting the conclusions described above and the following basic provisions: (1) the Environmental Quality Board was directed to adopt regulations to insure comprehensive flood area management, including criteria, standards and flood proofing requirements; (2) municipalities with flood areas were directed to develop and administer a flood area management plan in accord with state regulations; (3) the Department of Environmental Resources was directed to coordinate and supervise the management of flood areas; (4) municipalities were prohibited from issuing permits for construction in flood zones unless the permit applicant had approval in conformity with the law; (5) the Department of Environmental Resources and municipalities were given the authority to investigate complaints, conduct educational programs, initiate legal proceedings and prosecutions, and conduct inspections; and (6) violations of the law and regulations were subjected to enforcement orders, abatement and civil penalties of up to $10,000 and $500 per day for each day of continued violation.

I thought, considering the magnitude of damage inflicted by Tropical Storm Agnes, that S.B. 1122 could be enacted with relative ease. How wrong I was! Flood plain legislation proved to be the most contentious and fiercely contested issue of my legislative experience. Enacting it took three legislative sessions over five years that put my debating and political skills to an extended test. Success required drafting and reintroducing three bills other than S.B. 1122, responding on the Senate floor to dozens of interrogatories from my colleagues about the legislation, drafting or opposing dozens of amendments, and devoting dozens of hours to negotiations and conferences with supporters and opponents.

Equally important was the strong, determined support of my party leadership, especially Senator Murray and Representative Manderino. But success also occurred because of the unforeseen intervention of the Third

Johnstown flood in 1977 and the presence in the House of Johnstown's Democratic State Representative Adam Bittinger, who provided effective rebuttal to amendments offered to defeat the bill.

The central issue presented by S.B. 1122 and its successor bills is simple: Should the government of Pennsylvania extend its use of the "police power" to require municipalities to regulate new development in flood prone areas? The "police power" is an inherent constitutional authority of the state government that it uses to carry out one of state government's most important obligations—protecting the lives and property of its citizens. Examples of the "police power" are the Fire and Panic Act, which requires nursing homes to have fire detection and escape devices, and the clean streams laws requiring municipalities to treat sewage before discharging it into the waters of the state.

I believed then and now that the state should apply the "police power" to require municipal governments to control new building in flood zones and on high ground out of flood zones that can add new water to floods by faster runoffs. What I failed to appreciate at the time was the depth of emotional opposition that would arise because of the traditional resentment of state government regulations by local governments, as well as from property owners who believed they should be allowed to build without more government interference. I also did not realize that the DER, led by such an esteemed conservationist as Dr. Goddard, would become the object of fierce animosity. Residents of the rural areas had been living free of government regulation. They resented the seeming avalanche of pesky regulations that now befell them from the Department of Environmental Resources. The benefit to them and the public at large was lost in an outburst of irritation at the new government intrusion. The opposition was eventually overcome.

When S.B. 1122 came before the Senate for final passage consideration I inserted into the Senate record three documents to explain and justify the bill: a question and answer explanation, a copy of my testimony on the bill before the Senate Environmental Resources Committee, and a copy of the Report on Flood Disaster Prevention in Pennsylvania prepared with the help of John Showers.[2] The report is also in appendix H.

Before the vote was taken, however, Senator John Stauffer of Chester County offered three amendments—to provide 50 percent state funding for the municipal costs, to remove the state's authority to have the county government take over responsibility when a municipality failed to act, and to make the Department of Community Affairs the lead state agency instead of the DER. These amendments were defeated.

Senator Hager asked whether the bill could be construed to give the DER the power of eminent domain. I replied that it could not.

Senator Stroup rose to question the bill and urge a negative vote.

Senator STROUP: ". . . (I want to point out) the impact of this bill on local government and the basic property rights of our citizens . . . the object of the bill is splendid but the means we are using to attain that objective . . . are erroneous in many ways.

First, . . . the enforcement and regulatory power conferred by this bill is given to the Department of Environmental Resources, despite the fact that the Department of Community Affairs has been dealing with this problem of floods under the Federal Flood Insurance Program . . .

Another weakness is . . . the marked failure to provide reimbursement to the municipalities for the money they have to expend . . . for the development of their (flood plain) plans.

Another fault in this bill is that the system . . . embodied in the bill is, in essence, a state-wide zoning system. Historically, zoning has been a local problem . . .

. . . this bill allows lawsuits to enforce the provisions of the bill by any person without the necessity of showing . . . that he or she has suffered, or will suffer, any personal loss or damage . . .

. . . (under the bill) the Environmental Quality Board . . . can go well beyond the best technology (in promulgating minimum design and construction standards) . . . We pass legislation and we leave it to the agencies to devise rules and regulations, and we wake up to find that the rules and regulations have gone far beyond what the intent of the legislature may be . . . (the means this bill uses in) attaining (its) objectives are open to considerable question."[3]

I responded:

Senator KURY: ". . . as we approach the second anniversary of the (Hurricane Agnes) disaster, . . . one thing is clear from that experience . . . the Commonwealth of Pennsylvania has a legitimate interest, a proper interest, in regulating what is constructed in the flood plains . . . for two reasons: One, because . . . all of the taxpayers of Pennsylvania, whether they reside on the highest mountain or in the midst of the flood plain . . . pay for the damages when floods . . . occur.

. . . We also have an interest because what happens upstream can affect what happens downstream . . . the picture (of the flood wall at Sunbury) says it more vividly than any speech . . . why we need a flood plain bill . . . what happens up the river is going to affect what happens downstream at Sunbury and Harrisburg and all the way to the Chesapeake. Who know how much unregulated construction upstream would make the difference to send the water over the walls?

. . . (this bill) will not eliminate (Hurricane Agnes) kind of damage in the future, but it can do a great deal to minimize it when the next flood comes, and surely one will come."

Senator Stroup's concern about giving the DER the lead in implementing the act was a hint of growing resentment against the agency of which I was unaware. Senator Duffield of Fayette County said it directly.

Senator DUFFIELD: ". . . it has almost come to rebellion in Fayette County, the actions of the DER in coming in there, and regardless of the views of the people, say, 'We know best. You only own a house that is worth $500, but put in this sewage, and it is going to cost you $2000. If you do not do it, you are going to be cited at $50 a day.' . . . those are some of the dictatorial actions I have seen over the past few years."

It took until the end of the next legislative session for me to realize fully that the animosity against DER was so great that flood plain legislation would not pass as long as DER was given the main responsibility for implementing it.

S.B. 1122 passed 38 to 9 and was sent to the House, where it was referred to the local government committee, and where it died at the end of the 1973–1974 session.

When the 1975–1976 session convened, S.B. 1122 was reintroduced, and thanks to the support of Senator Murray given the number S.B. 1. The bill came to the Senate floor for final passage on June 9, 1975. Eighteen amendments were offered but only three, offered by Senator Austin Murphy of Washington County, were adopted.[4] Murphy's amendments provided that state funding could be used by municipalities for administrative as well as planning purposes, that a municipality need zone only the flood plain (and not other land), and for property owners to be allowed to file grievances before a flood plain ordinance was adopted. These amendments, which I opposed as unnecessary, did no significant damage to the bill. On the fifteen defeated amendments, only one that would have significantly impaired the bill came close to enactment. This amendment, also from Senator Murphy, would have removed the authority of DER to require regional planning of flood plain management by changing the word "require" to "encourage." That one word change would have impaired the point of having every municipality managing its flood plain. The hammer of state police power to force compliance would have been removed. Fortunately, the amendment lost, 23 to 24.[5] The Senate then sent the bill to the House with overwhelming approval, 44–3.

The treatment S.B.1 received on the Senate floor was mild and restrained compared to the hostile reception given on the floor of the House. The House subjected S.B. 1 to the ordeal of a stiff gauntlet of twenty-three amendments, a challenge to its constitutionality, and a motion to recommit (or kill).[6] The first speaker when S.B. 1 reached final consideration on October 1, 1975, was the Democratic Majority Whip, James Manderino, a forceful and articulate debater. Manderino said the bill could be the most important piece of legislation to be considered in the session, described the bill's contents, and urged its approval without further amendments. The House had other views of S.B.1, and ironically several of the most potentially damaging came from Representative George O. Wagner, a Republican lawyer from Danville, who held the seat for the 108th legislative district I had held.[7]

Wagner first raised the issue of the constitutionality of the bill, forcing the House to vote on the question. If Wagner had prevailed, the bill would have died on the spot.

> Mr. WAGNER: ". . . the basic unconstitutionality . . . is appropriating private property without due process of law, for a public purpose . . . If an owner is prevented from developing his land, he is deprived of a use . . . it is confiscatory if most of the value of a person's property has been sacrificed so that the community welfare may be served . . . It is a fraudulent and economic taking if you leave a man with title to his property, but not the use, and that is exactly what we are doing here. We are saying, you own it; it is your land, but you cannot use it."

Majority Leader Manderino responded:

> Mr. MANDERINO: "Floodplain zoning is nothing more than that; it is zoning. It has been held to be constitutional, not a confiscation of property without compensation. Is has been held to be a reasonable regulation of property . . . the Assembly should sustain the constitutionality of this measure which is so drastically needed in Pennsylvania."

The House upheld the constitutionality of S.B. 1 by 115 to 79.

Wagner later offered an amendment which he described as "really (coming) to heart of the issue . . . an amendment that is contrary to the whole thrust of S.B. 1." As Wagner explained the amendment,

> . . . it mandates that municipalities adopt flood plain maps and it mandates that those maps be put on record so landowners know where they are. But it stops there. It does not go any further. It does not require any sort of flood permits, regulations, prohibitions, and so forth as contained in S.B. 1. That is really where one of the problems is that people have with S.B. 1. There is no need for S.B.1.
>
> I think that government ought to let the individual make the decision (to build or not build in a flood plain) for himself . . . I call your attention to the last section of the amendment . . . "No person who . . . constructs any building, or resides, or has property within a flood area as delineated on the official map shall be eligible for future state financial aid."
>
> . . . it (serves) no legitimate purpose to require that a man get off a floodplain if he wants to go there . . . Man has always had to fight with nature, and, to my knowledge, the government has never come in and said that is not good for you, so get out. This is really what the guts of the matter is . . .

Manderino replied:

> Mr. MANDERINO: "What one community does in a floodplain, in a watershed, affects communities downstream. The amount of debris that comes downstream in many floods in the smallest waterways is what does the damage. I can envision the communities downstream who have complied, who have done everything they can to protect themselves who are going to suffer devastating effects of these types of disasters because somebody upstream did not comply. The is what we are aiming at here in S.B. 1
>
> The Wagner Amendment . . . does nothing towards this end. It does nothing for the community that complies and must suffer the ravages of the disaster because of communities upstream who did not comply."[8]

Manderino prevailed, and the Wagner amendment lost 82 to 115. However, Manderino was unable to beat down several other amendments that were aimed at weakening the bill. Representative Richard McClatchy's amendment to provide that Pennsylvania's flood plain regulations may not exceed the federal standards passed 113–81. This amendment would prevent municipalities wishing to exceed federal standards to deal with local conditions from doing so. It placed, in my view, an unnecessary manacle on the hands of local government. A more serious problem was in McClatchy's amendment to require an economic impact statement be prepared before state regulations could become effective. If this provision became part of the law the implementation of flood plain management would have been considerably delayed. The economic impact statement required under this amendment was detailed, complex, and applied to the statewide regulations. It would take years to complete. This amendment received approval by 109 to 89.

Skepticism toward the bill was not a party line matter. Representative Galen Dreibelbis, a Democrat from Centre County, successfully added an amendment to delay municipal flood plain management until the state provided its full 50 percent share of the costs. Another Democrat House member (from my Senate district), Kent Shelhamer of Columbia County, secured an amendment that no municipality shall be required to expend more than 10 percent of the costs of a comprehensive flood plain management plan. As Representative Manderino pointed out in opposing these amendments, the federal government had set a deadline for municipalities seeking flood insurance to adopt flood plain management plans. These amendments did nothing to help municipalities meet that deadline; they provided an excuse to delay.

The most ironic amendment, seen in retrospect, came from Representative Pat Gleason, whose hometown was Johnstown. Gleason proposed that communities, like Johnstown, which has the protection of federal flood control projects (as Sunbury did) shall have those projects considered by the state in developing and promulgating flood plain regulations.

Mr. GLEASON: "My city, of course, is probably the most afflicted city in the Commonwealth in terms of floods over the last 100 years . . . We were very fortunately blessed when in the 1930s when President Roosevelt inserted a flood control project through the Army Corps of Engineers in our city. This has saved us over the past 40 years. And I can remember during the Agnes flood of 1972 . . . Johnstown, because of its flood control projects, escaped all damage because of that flood . . . my city should (not) be treated exactly the same way as another city without the blessing of a flood control project . . ."

Manderino had no objection to the Gleason amendment, which was accepted without a vote, even though it could continue leaving cities with flood control projects, like Sunbury (with its wall) vulnerable to increased flood heights caused by unregulated construction upstream.

With these and several less consequential amendments, S.B. 1 received House approval on October 1, 1975, by 147–50. As sent back to us in the Senate, S.B. 1 was significantly impaired by the McClatchy, Dreibelbis, Gleason, and Shelhamer amendments. If the House version became law, Pennsylvania's government, like a well-hobbled horse, could move forward against future flood disasters only haltingly and with great difficulty.

The Senate rejected the House version and sent it to a conference committee chaired by me and including Senators Mellow and Holl and Representatives Manderino, Laudadio, and O'Connell. Our committee reached a compromise that required eighteen amendments but was agreeable to everyone but O'Connell. The committee report dealt with the major House amendments in several ways.

The Gleason amendment giving special consideration for exclusion to cities like Johnstown and Sunbury was left intact. McClatchy's economic impact statement amendment was rewritten as an economic study to be done by the Department of Community Affairs that would not prevent municipal compliance while it was being done. A Wagner amendment requiring that appeals from municipal flood plain ordinances be taken to the county court of common pleas, rather than the Commonwealth court, was deleted. McClatchy's amendment that the regulations adopted by the DER shall not exceed federal standards remained in the bill. Dreibelbis's amendment that allowed municipalities to delay action until they received the full 50 percent share of state funding was rewritten so that municipalities not receiving full funding of the state's share would receive it as part of a deficiency appropriation in the next state budget. The Shelhamer provision limiting a municipality's share to 10 percent of the costs was deleted.

The underlying criticisms of S.B. 1 continued to fester and grow to the point that the conference committee report was twice recommitted to the Conference Committee rather than voted. The House did not have the votes to approve it. Unrelenting opposition from local government had taken its toll.

On November 25, 1975, sensing the difficulties confronting it in the House, the Senate approved the report by 31 to 18. Senator Holl took the floor to explain.

> I am a sponsor of this bill, and I have served on the Committee of Conference. I feel that great harm has been done to this fine piece of legislation because of a great deal of misinformation which has been disseminated to the various boroughs and the first class townships. This has been a volatile issue, and it was created essentially by individuals who either misunderstood or, by design, have attempted to cause the defeat of this legislation.
>
> In my opinion, the local government officials who are now opposing this legislation just do not know what is contained in Senate Bill No. 1.[9]

The House did not act on the conference committee report for six months. On June 3, 1976, the House rejected the Report by 44 to 123 and thereby killed the bill for the 1975–1976 session. If I wanted to try again it would have to be in the 1977–1978 session.

THE THIRD JOHNSTOWN FLOOD

In early 1977 Margot Hunt, president of the state League of Women Voters that had been a strong supporter of S.B. 1, came to my office and asked whether the flood plain issue should be given a rest for the new session. I had been thinking about that since the House had killed S.B. 1 and was determined to move forward. The effort invested so far had resulted in a fairly good understanding of the issue by both the legislators and the newspapers. I told President Hunt that we would try again. But before introducing a third flood plain bill I evaluated what we had learned from the first two unsuccessful efforts. Senator Murray and others who shared the desire to act on flooding agreed that a new approach was needed. A reintroduction of S.B. 1 would not do any better. The local government organizations would continue in adamant opposition for two reasons. They did not like the state telling them how to manage land development in their municipalities and they were intensely hostile to the Department of Environmental Resources. The DER, as the department became known, created the hostility through its implementation of the environmental laws enacted during the environmental revolution described in chapter 7 above. The anger toward DER expressed by Senator Duffield in Fayette County had spread throughout the state.

To overcome the municipal opposition we decided to offer two bills, rather than one, and to take from DER the responsibility for flood plain management. I introduced S.B. 743 and S.B. 744 on April 18, 1977. Titled the Flood Plain Management Act, S.B. 743 required every municipality that received notice from the federal government that it had a flood plain to adopt a plan to manage development in flood plains through zoning. The plan had to meet the requirements of flood plain zoning to qualify for federal flood insurance. The Department of Community Affairs (DCA) would review and approve the municipal plans. The federal regulations were designated as minimum standards and municipalities were not required to exceed those standards, although free to do so. The DCA regulations prohibited subdivisions, certain constructions, and the utilization of earthen fill in the flood areas. Hospitals, nursing homes, jails, and new mobile home parks were expressly forbidden in the flood areas. To sweeten this new law on municipalities, the bill called for state grants of up to 50 percent to assist in the implementation costs.

While S.B. 743 focused on minimizing future flood damage by stopping new construction in flood areas, S.B. 744 provided for regulation of new construction outside of the flood areas that could contribute to heightened flood levels by increased rainwater runoff. Titled "the Storm Water Management Act," S.B. 744 directed each county to prepare and adopt a storm water management for each watershed in the county in accord with guidelines promulgated by the DER. After the county plan was adopted, all development and construction in each watershed that could result in greater storm water runoff had to be done consistent with the plan. For example, a new housing development might be required to install a storm water detention basin to hold back and slow storm water discharges. A hundred-acre cornfield, I argued, absorbs rain like a huge sponge, so that the water is absorbed into the ground and slowly runs off. Turn that cornfield into a mall, with large asphalt parking space, and it is now acts like a turtle shell when the rain hits, causing flash runoffs.

I also decided to take the case for floodplain and storm water management legislation directly to the opposition. The Pennsylvania State Association of Township Supervisors, a leading critic, graciously published my views in the May 1977 issue of its monthly magazine. Titled "Rendezvous with Disaster," the opening paragraph contained a prediction.

> Pennsylvania has a rendezvous with disaster. It is only a matter of time until another major flood devastates Pennsylvania as Agnes and other great storms have devastated our state in the past. Floods are a permanent threat to Pennsylvania.[10] (The full article is found in appendix G.)

Making this prediction did not require unusual prescience or daring on my part. It was the safest prediction I would ever make. All I did was look at the history of flooding and draw the obvious conclusion. When the article was published, however, I had no idea the prediction would be fulfilled by the third Johnstown flood, only two months later.

Despite the new approaches in these two bills, they—especially the flood plain management proposal—went through another volley of heavy criticism. I had prepared by doing my "homework" on the proposals and flooding. As an extra measure, I brought to the floor with me Timothy Weston, a knowledgable water lawyer in the Department of Environmental Protection loaned to me by Dr. Goddard.[11]

When final consideration came before the Senate on February 28, 1978, Senator Hager began the debate by questioning why the definition of "person" in S.B. 744 included shareholders of corporations, not contained in S.B. 743, and whether shelters for farm animals would be regulated. Senator Tilghman opposed the bills because they authorized fines for municipalities and their officials that did not comply. Then Senator Michael Schaefer questioned the impact of the legislation on the expansion of existing industrial facilities in flood zones, after which Senator Gekas moved to recommit S.B. 743 to committee. The motion lost 14 to 31.

Senator Duffield argued that the legislation would not prevent another Agnes and therefore would do no good.

> ... my feeling is ... that the (federal) flood insurance program is available to the municipalities today and the only thing this bill does ... is to force compliance all over the Commonwealth by those municipalities who see fit not to follow the federal plan.

To respond I walked to the center of the Senate floor where the enlarged photograph of the Sunbury flood wall at the height of the Agnes flood had been placed on an easel.

> This ... photograph (shows that) ... the City of Sunbury has done what it could to protect itself; it built a wall. You see how close it came to losing it? Two inches. (This wall) is worthless if there is higher water coming from upstream ... that is the problem. What they do upstream can send higher water downstream and over the top of the dike ... that is why no community is an island unto itself ...
>
> We cannot stop the water. Of course, we can not stop the flooding, but we can stop this senseless pattern of building and building in a floodplain where they will be washed away by the next flood.[12]

Senators George Gekas and Edward Howard voiced objections to the penalties on municipalities for noncompliance. Gekas offered an amendment to reduce the maximum fines against noncomplying municipalities and officials from $10,000 to $500 and the $500 per day for each continuing violation to $50. The amendment failed by 19 to 27.

The flood plain management bill was to put to the final passage vote. To my chagrin and surprise it was defeated 19 to 26, 9 Democrats and 14 Republicans voting no. Was the bill dead, all of the work on it and its predecessors in vain? Fortunately, Senator Mellow moved that the vote by which S.B. 743 was defeated be reconsidered. The motion was agreed to and the bill given a reprieve.

Shortly after that the Republican whip, Senator John Stauffer, walked over to me and said, "Frank, if you can give me a couple of amendments, I can get you half a dozen Republican votes."

"Jack, let's talk. What do you have in mind?" I replied.

Stauffer's requests were relatively simple—allow the use of fill material in flood plains to elevate the expansion of existing industrial plants and add the costs of enforcement and implementation to those for which state funding would apply. He also suggested an amendment by Senator William Moore of Perry County that would replace fines on non-complying municipalities and their officials with a withholding by the state treasurer of all state funds for the violating municipality. Moore's amendment struck me as a responsible way to keep the state pressure on for compliance but avoid personal penalties for officials.

I agreed to Stauffer's requests.

On March 6 Senator Moore offered his amendment to both the flood plain and storm water bills as an agreed-to amendment, and I did the same with the other Stauffer suggestions. The next day S.B. 743, as amended, passed the Senate 31 to 16. Senator Stauffer kept his word. Six Republicans switched their votes from nay to yea. And with effective work by Senator Murray, four Democrats did the same, a total of ten changed votes. Murray, the president of the Senate, had written a note to every Philadelphia senator saying that he would appreciate their vote for the flood bills as a personal favor to him.

Much less controversial, S.B. 744 received Senate approval on April 4 by 48 to 1 without debate.[13]

The flood plain and storm water bills arrived in a House that had changed significantly since it had defeated S.B. 1. The opposition to the legislation had become concentrated almost entirely on Frank O'Connell of Luzerne County. He took on the leadership of defeating the bills with as much zeal as I possessed in advocating them. He made numerous speeches, issued many press releases, and appeared on radio and television with frequency. We held several debates, including one on Johnstown television. The House supporters of the bills, however, had also grown more resolute in their determination to pass them.

Another change in the political climate was produced by the third Johnstown flood, which ravaged that city in the summer of 1977 only two months after my prediction in the *Township Magazine* that it was only a matter of time until we suffered another flood disaster. After the second Johnstown flood, in 1936, the U.S. Army Corps of Engineers had built so many flood protection projects there that Johnstown began to call itself the "flood-proof city." That claim was obliterated by the flood of July 1977 when 84 people lost their lives and $300 million in damages incurred. The 1977 flood gave a new sense of purpose to the Democratic leadership and also to the new representative from Johnstown, Adam Bittinger.

As a result of these developments, the only amendments put into the bills were added in the Conservation Committee, chaired by Representative Thomas Fee of Lawrence County, who became chairman upon John Laudadio's death on June 7, 1977. Fee checked with me before offering the amendments. Yet the legislation did not have an easy ride through the House. The amendments were offered and debate took several hours and occupied 46 pages of the *House Journal*.[14]

When S.B. 743 came to the House floor for final passage, O'Connell offered an omnibus amendment to eviscerate the bill, the first of fifteen amendments he would offer. Representative Fee quickly opposed it.

> Mr. FEE: ". . . Any further amendments to this bill will undoubtedly cause a great change in the bill in a fashion that be totally unacceptable or will cause the bill to be less effective than the current federal regulations now require . . . This bill was substantially amended in committee, and, I might add, was acceptable to the entire committee on both sides of the aisle.
>
> Section 207, dealing with prohibitions of subdivisions in the floodplain area, has been deleted. Section 208, which prohibited construction in the flood hazard area where alternatives exist, has been amended out of the bill . . . (as has) Section 209, which prohibits the use of fill for expansion purposes . . . Any further amendments will accomplish absolutely nothing other than to water down this bill and to (make) it worthless."

O'Connell made no substantive reply to Fee, but Representative Bittinger rose in opposition to O'Connell's amendment, as did Representative Ronald Cowell of Allegheny County. Bittinger argued that local governments have had several years to act on flood since Hurricane Agnes and the 1977 Johnstown flood but have done nothing. Cowell suggested that the bill struck a proper balance between meaningful state action and the traditional role of local government.

Representative Fred Noye of Juniata County sounded an alarm.

> . . . if we pass these bills in their present form, without the O'Connell amendments, we are about to create a monster that we will never be able to control . . . Without these amendments we are going to have our local governments being faced with dictation from the Department of Environmental Resources and the Department of Community Affairs.

The O'Connell omnibus amendment failed 79 to 114. Not deterred, O'Connell offered fourteen more amendments, all of which were defeated. On every amendment opposition was forcefully expressed by the Conservation Committee Chairman Thomas Fee, Majority Leader Manderino, or Adam Bittinger. Bittinger was especially direct and acerbic and drew on the experience of Johnstown in its third major flood. In response to one O'Connell amendment he declared that "O'Connell is trying to do to S.B. 743 . . . what the flood waters of July 27, 1977 did to the residents of Tannersville and Salmon Run (in Bittinger's district)."

On another amendment Bittinger again pointed to Johnstown.

> In 1977, 77 lives were lost; about 10 are still missing and presumed dead. There were $300 million in damages . . . This state, including the bond issue that we just passed last week, has appropriated something on the order of $75 million to $80 million in flood-recovery money.
>
> . . . (to get away from the emotional flood issue here in Pennsylvania) discuss a house that a fellow builds in the swamp in Louisiana and that house sinks out of sight. He comes to you...and says, I want money to rebuild my house on the same spot. (Is there any member in this House) who would hand over the money without saying, what precautions have you taken that it is not going to happen again? And yet that is precisely what Mr. O'Connell would have us do.
>
> The question simply is this: Which is going to prevail in the State of Pennsylvania, common sense or the emotion and rhetoric that has prevailed to date? . . . I urge defeat of the O'Connell amendment.

Manderino reenforced the point:

> If you are going to come to the Commonwealth and to the Federal Government from time to time and ask for moneys for relief, for building dams, for rebuilding roads, for rebuilding your homes, then you ought to allow reasonable restrictions to be placed upon future building—and we are talking about future building—in the floodplains. That is all we are doing.

None of O'Connell's fifteen amendments to S.B. 743 survived that kind of rebuttal. The House voted its approval 118 to 61 and sent it back to the Senate, where we agreed to the House amendments the next day by 49 to 0, without debate. S.B. 743 was on its way to the governor.

The House took up consideration of S.B. 744, the storm water management bill, following its passage of S.B. 743. Again O'Connell went on the attack in an effort to stop the bill. He offered six amendments. Each time Adam Bittinger went "toe to toe" with O'Connell and argued for rejection. All of the O'Connell amendments went down by a thirty-vote margin. Following his defeat on the sixth amendment, O'Connell admitted to the House that further amendments would be an exercise in futility and withdrew further amendments.

Representative Wagner, however, was undeterred. He offered three amendments to weaken the bill, such as to eliminate the authority of the

Department to order storm water planning. Bittinger responded firmly to each amendment. Wagner's amendments went down by a margin of thirty or more votes. With no other amendments to be considered the House was ready to act finally on the storm water bill.

O'Connell, Michael Fisher of Allegheny County, and Fred Noye of Juniata made closing remarks against S.B. 744. They argued that the financial costs of implementing the bill would be overwhelming, that there were not sufficient funds to pay for it, and that local governments would lose tax revenue because of reduced land values in the flood areas. Bittinger had the final argument, and he delivered it with unmatchable poignancy.

> (This bill) is needed very badly. We had the big flood in Johnstown last year. We have had a number of flooding situations since then from storm water run-offs. We have learned the hard way that with rare exception local governments and individuals simply will not cooperate and/or finance proper handling of storm water. They have screwed up beyond belief, and there is absolutely no reason to think that the situation will improve without a two-by-four between the eyes, to get their attention.
>
> ... The bottom line is this: I support most strongly S.B. 744 because I am convinced that it is far cheaper to prevent damage than to repair or replace. It is a whole lot less painful to be a bit limited sensibly in where and how we build than to dig through the muddy remains afterward trying to salvage a little bit of our lives or, worse, looking for the bodies of friends and loved ones.
>
> ... Hiding our heads in the mud will not make the problem go away, and we have been hiding our heads in the mud for the last 40 years. This legislation should have been passed after the storms of 1972. It was not. It should have been passed every session since. It was not. It is time we had the guts to do what is right. I urge passage of S.B. 744.

The House then gave final approval 124 to 66. The Senate agreed to the House amendments (made in the Conservation Committee with my agreement) without debate, 49 to 0.

Governor Shapp held a reception on October 4 for the supporters of the flood plain and storm water bills in the governor's residence and signed the bills into law. Senator Murray, Representatives Manderino, Fee, and Bittinger, and other legislators attended, as did leaders of organizations like Margot Hunt of the League of Women Voters and Curt Winsor of the Pennsylvania Environmental Council. Of course Beth and I were there, savoring every minute of it. The governor and others, including DER Secretary Goddard and DCA Secretary William Wilcox, made complimentary remarks about the bills and my persistence in pursuing their enactment. It was the high point of my legislative career. After the governor signed the bills and handed me a pen for each, I leaned over to Beth and asked her, "What do I do for an encore?" I knew it was time for me to leave the Senate.

Governor Shapp signing the flood plain and storm water management bills. From left to right at the table are Department of Community Affairs Deputy Secretary Al Hydeman, the author, Governor Shapp, Senate President Martin Murray and Representative James Manderino. Standing are Don Oesterling, deputy Secretary of Environmental Resources (behind Hydeman); Beth Kury (in the stole); Representative Ted Stuban (behind Mrs. Kury); Margot Hunt, president of the League of Women Voters; Representative Adam Bittinger (wearing dark glasses); Representative Paul Yahner; Representative Tom Fee (behind Murray); Environmental Secretary Maurice Goddard (over Manderino's left shoulder). William Wilcox, Secretary of Community Affairs, is in the third row, over Bittinger's left shoulder. Curtin Winsor, president of the Pennsylvania Environmental Council, stands in the third row between Representatives Yahner and Fee. Source: Personal file photo.

UNFINISHED BUSINESS

Looking at the flood plain and storm water management laws thirty-two years later, I am disappointed that they have fallen short of their intended purposes. Of the two, the flood plain law has been, on paper at least, the more successful. As this is written, 2,450 of the state's 2,562 municipalities with flood zones qualify for federal flood insurance. They have enacted a

The author shows Governor Shapp the photo used on the Senate floor during the flood plain and storm water management debates as Beth looks on. Source: Personal file photo.

flood plain management program limiting new construction in flood zones and requiring a permit for projects that are allowed. This record of 99 percent municipal compliance is, however, probably misleading.

Enforcement by the complying municipalities is uneven. Some have appeared to forget they have a flood plain management plan and others are lethargic in carrying out their plans. Some, like many in southeastern Pennsylvania, are aggressive in carrying out the law.

Since the law was enacted in 1978 Pennsylvania has suffered many so-called one hundred year floods, floods that in theory are estimated to have a 1 percent chance of occurring in any given year. However, even the Department of Community and Economic Development, which now administers the flood plain management law, has difficulty in finding out the extent of flooding, damage caused, or flood insurance paid. The state has no program for accumulating flood damage assessment or even the number of floods, many of which are local. It is therefore almost impossible to obtain a good estimate of what floods are now costing Pennsylvania taxpayers.

Two new developments should strengthen the program. The Federal Emergency Management Agency (FEMA) is preparing updated maps of the flood plain in each municipality. When the new maps are received the municipality must change its plans to match the new maps. Only a third of the maps have been completed, and the remainder are expected within the next two to three years. As part of this updating process, the state's Department of Community and Economic Development is obligated to help 1,900 municipalities modernize their flood plain zoning ordinances in harmony with the new maps. The department's funding to assist municipalities with updating their ordinances comes from the Federal Emergency Management Agency, not the state. However, the state must provide the funding to reimburse municipalities for their 50 percent share of the updated ordinance enactment costs The department's ability to obtain the ordinance updates depends in part on the level of funding provided in the state budget.

The Delaware River Basin Compact Commission is working to bring uniformity to flood plain management in the states of the Delaware River Basin—New York, New Jersey, and Pennsylvania. These may strengthen the law, but only in that portion of Pennsylvania occupied by the Delaware River basin.

Implementing the storm water management law has been frustrating. Thirty-two years after the law took effect only Northampton County is fully covered for storm water management. Lehigh County is virtually covered, and Lycoming County is expected to be so within the year. As of June 2009, forty-eight other counties were in various stages of progress toward coverage and eight more counties had requested funding to proceed, but then the state legislature deleted the funding for the program from the 2009–2010 budget. In prior budgets the department had received about $2 million a year. With the state funding eliminated, the eight other counties that had requested a grant to comply were unable to proceed. Of the counties that have not been progressing toward compliance only two—Indiana and Armstrong—have expressed outright refusal. Almost all counties have difficulty in raising the 25 percent of the planning costs they must bear, so this tends to extend the time it takes counties to complete their initial storm water management plans. The state's share is 75 percent.[15] There is a lot more work to be done to make the storm water management law fully effective. Legislative efforts to strengthen the program have failed.[16] The most immediate need is for funding of the program by the General Assembly. Without such funding, it will be very difficult, if not impossible, to make the law effective.

It is obvious that lack of full implementation of the flood plain and storm water management laws is leaving the state seriously at risk for future flood damage. This is an appropriate time for the legislature to do an investigation of the enforcement of these acts like the one my committee did on the public utility commission in 1975. These laws have been in effect for thirty years and have not fulfilled their purpose. Pennsylvania has more rendezvous with flood disaster awaiting it. The time to act is now.

16

The Thornburgh Administration and Farewell

A month after Governor Shapp signed the flood plain and storm water management bills, Republican Richard Thornburgh, the former U.S. attorney for Western Pennsylvania, defeated the Democratic nominee, Pete Flaherty, to become the next governor of Pennsylvania. Thornburgh focused his campaign on a single issue—he would clean out the corruption that tainted the second term of Milton Shapp. He aimed much of his criticism at the patronage system that continued in each county highway shed and cabinet officials who misused their offices. There was no indication that Governor Shapp himself was involved in unlawful activity, but some of his appointees were, and the governor found it hard to fire them. Even though he was the mayor of Pittsburgh and not part of the Shapp administration, Flaherty ran as far from Shapp as he could.

At the inauguration in January 1978, as an incumbent senator, I—along with Beth—had a seat on the capitol steps right behind the podium where the new chief executive would be sworn in. The capitol steps and walkways, as well as State Street and Third Street, were brimming with spectators. Just before noon, Governor Shapp walked down the steps from the capitol on the arm of Michael McLaughlin, his press secretary. Shapp took his seat right behind the podium. Thornburgh was seated to the right of Shapp, only a few feet away. What followed left an indelible imprint on me.

Thornburgh did not shake hands with Shapp. He did not acknowledge him. He did not look at him. He did not mention him in his inaugural address. When the swearing in and speech were done, Thornburgh turned his back and walked away, as if Shapp were invisible or did not exist, an egregious breach of good manners. This was the most egregious case of bad manners I have ever seen in politics. If Thornburgh had ever heard of Churchill's admonition that political victors should show magnanimity, there was no indication of it that day. Thornburgh's personal behavior toward Shapp provided a clear sign that his administration would indeed be quite different than that of his predecessor.

The organizational structure created by Thornburgh reinforced that view. The new governor operated behind a tightly-closed personal staff to which access was strictly guarded. The secretaries of the administrative departments and their staffs were placed on firm control from the governor's office, so much so that departmental speeches and press releases had to be cleared there in advance. Cabinet members were forbidden to contact members of Congress without advance approval from the governor's office. Access to Thornburgh was so tight that Thornburgh's governing style seemed more appropriate to a military command than to a political office. The new governor showed no inclination to take the ship of state into new directions. He was there to "clean house," overhaul some of the departments, and administer well.

Fortunately the new governor put into his cabinet a number of able and dedicated public servants, such as Clifford Jones, whom he asked to be Secretary of Environmental Resources; James Bodine, Secretary of DCA; James Scheiner as Revenue Secretary; Walter Baran at General Services; and Thomas Larson at the Department of Transportation. They were accessible and cooperative with legislators.

As put off as I was by the new governor's management style, I did find the better side of his personality. When my oldest son, Steven, was at the capitol with me we encountered the governor, and I introduced Steven to him. He was gracious and charming, a complete contrast with his inaugural.

I also found myself in agreement with some of Thornburgh's new policies, particularly his decision to abolish the county highway shed patronage system. To get to the House, I had to overcome the Lark organization that relied heavily on the county highway shed for its patronage. When Governor Shapp took office, I wanted no part of patronage and was not involved with it. I left Democratic patronage to the Democratic county chairs of my district.

In Thornburgh's view,

> PennDOT had long been a patronage dump. For example, the maintenance manager in each of the state's sixty-seven counties traditionally had been chosen by the local party chairman, more to strengthen the party apparatus than to maintain the highways (in 1979, only one of the sixty-seven was a professional engineer). Many of the managers, in turn, essentially sold highway jobs for political contributions.[1]

Steven Kury meets Governor Thornburgh while his father looks on. Source: *Personal file photo.*

Within a month of taking office, the new governor announced that the county highway superintendents would now be chosen by a merit selection system using nonpartisan screening committees. Transportation Secretary Larson issued a directive that the criteria for selecting the new superintendents would be his or her highway engineering or maintenance qualifications. I was asked to serve on the committee for Northumberland County and did so with enthusiasm. We interviewed half dozen applicants and then unanimously recommended David Winters, an engineering graduate of the U.S. Military Academy at West Point with no political experience. I went home that evening thinking that hell had just frozen in Northumberland County and relishing what Henry Lark and Harvey Taylor would think of this, coming from a Republican governor. Thornburgh took a lot of criticism from the Republican Party for this reform, but I thought he did the right thing.

As the Thornburgh administration moved forward, I increasingly realized that the good fortune I had of serving in the Senate while my party controlled all three branches of government was over. My successes as a

Opening of the new bridge at Northumberland over the West Branch in early 1978. Left to right are Mrs. Charles Lewis, wife of Northumberland mayor Charles Lewis; Robert Lauf, editor of the Sunbury Daily Item; John Dagle, Sunbury merchant; Kenneth C. Larson (in the fur cap), District PennDOT engineer; Mayor Donald Morgan of Sunbury; the author; and Beth Kury's station wagon, which took the first drive across the bridge. The man in the hard hat, center, is not identified. Source: Courtesy of the Sunbury Daily Item.

senator needed—and received—the support of the Democratic leadership in the Senate and the House, as well as Governor Shapp.

I did make several legislative initiatives. For example, I worked with Senator Richard Snyder, the conservative Republican from Lancaster, on a proposal to require that candidates for governor designate a running mate for lieutenant governor with whom he or she would run as a pair in the primary election. We were concerned that a governor could be saddled with a lieutenant governor with whom he was incompatible. This was possible because, while candidates for governor and lieutenant governor run separately in the primary election, they must run as a pair in the general election. We believed that the choice of a second in command should be a governor's choice, as vice-presidents are for presidential candidates. Our effort was in vain. We did not find significant support.

Apart from my run for auditor general in the 1980 primary (described in the next chapter), the time remaining before my term expired on November 30, 1980, was routine and desultory, the least enjoyable of my fourteen years. I knew I would not run for a third term. There were no issues I wanted to tackle the way I did clean streams, the environmental amendment, the PUC law rewriting, or the flood plain and storm water issues. I

At the British House of Commons, London, with John Stokes, a conservative member of Parliament, after a tour of the Commons and the Lords, 1970. When asked his party affiliation, Stokes replied, "Tory! Can't you tell by looking?" Source: Photo by Elizabeth Kury.

knew I could make significantly more income in law practice than in the legislature. Most important, my family was waiting for me. When I came to the Senate, we had one son—Steven, age ten. We had two more sons, David, age eight, and James, age six. It was time for me to be home with them. I had no qualms about leaving.

On the last day of the Senate session before my term expired, November 19, 1980, I made my farewell speech.

> . . . this Legislature is better than the public perception of it, but it is not as good as it can become. The great challenge before this body is to close the gap between the public perception and the reality. The goal for every legislator must be to achieve a greatness in this General Assembly which is truly worthy of the people of Pennsylvania, . . . everyone who serves here has a special responsibility in this regard, because we are the trustees of a legislative system which is a hallmark of western civilization.
>
> . . . in the past two years, I have been to the Tien a Mien Square in Peking, a vast monument to the communist revolution in China. I have been to the Kremlin in Moscow and seen the memorials to the Soviet Revolution of 1917. I have also been to the British House of Commons, a monument to the evolution of legislative government in the English-speaking world.
>
> . . . it is our great fortune as Pennsylvanians and Americans to trace the beginnings of this Legislature through the American Revolution and the British House of Commons to the Magna Carta of 1215. The Chinese and Russian Revolutions saw one dictatorship replaced with another . . . our revolution took the best of the old system, conserved it, and adapted it to meet our country's special needs . . . The legislative bodies (that exist in fifty states and Congress) are the results of over seven centuries of evolution that has expanded and protected the rights of free men. The measure of our good fortune is that less than one quarter of the world enjoys the freely elected legislative bodies we prize so highly
>
> . . . (we must act for the) care and protection of this beautiful but fragile plant of legislative government. We must nourish and guard the environment in which it lives. We must act to strengthen the spirit of compromise . . . the U.S. Constitution, declared by Gladstone to be the greatest document ever written by the hand of man, is a series of compromises.
>
> . . . as trustees of legislative government, those who serve here will always, I hope, "strive to seek, to find, and not to yield" in their determination to make this body a more effective instrument of the public interest. To do less is to betray those who came before us. To do less is to deprive and cheat those who will come after us.
>
> Mr. President, the time has come for me to leave. I do not know where the path of life will take me, but I do know that my thoughts will never be far from this house or the other. My heart will always be here.
>
> Thank you and farewell.[2]

With that, I left the Senate and went home.

IV

POLITICAL LIFE AFTER THE LEGISLATURE AND REFLECTIONS, 1981–2010

17
Political Life after the Legislature

Having left the legislature, politics still attracted me, although I found nothing to compare with the sense of excitement and satisfaction experienced in the House and Senate. I made two unsuccessful runs for statewide office—auditor general in 1980 and state treasurer in 1996—but found them frustrating and disappointing efforts. My legislative record and the campaigns I waged for the House and the Senate were of almost no help; it was virtually impossible to get the attention of the news media.

The kinds of issues that I articulated in legislative campaigns were hard to come by. I learned the hard way that running statewide office requires at least one of several things I did not have—a well-known name, a large political base, or several million dollars to spend. Of these, name recognition proved to be the most important. As Al Neri, a veteran Harrisburg political reporter, observed ten years later, in statewide elections "name recognition trumps public records, issues, financial advantage, message, campaign staff, organization support or voter base or party."[1] These campaigns did, however, give me a great deal of insight into Pennsylvania statewide elections that enabled me to help other candidates.

Two years after I left the Senate, my friend Allen Ertel, the former district attorney of Lycoming County and the congressman from our district, became the Democratic nominee for governor. The state party had had a difficult time finding a credible candidate to go against Thornburgh for his second term. Although the FBI investigation had not yet caught him, Auditor General Al Benedict declined to run. Others declined, but Ertel saw an opportunity and took it, even though it was an uphill struggle. As an incumbent governor, Thornburgh had a relatively easy time raising funds. Ertel couldn't find a fund-raiser, so I volunteered.

The first thing Ertel did after I agreed to take on fund-raising was to arrange for me to get educated on the subject by visiting with Senator Edward Kennedy's chief of fund-raising in Washington. He made points I have never forgotten. First, identify prospective donors you know can afford the contribution you seek. When you talk with that person, don't just ask for a contribution. Ask for a specific amount. He told me that his great accomplishment with Kennedy was to get him to say, "Will you send me a check for a $1,000?" Kennedy had previously been reluctant to ask for money at all, often asking "will you help me?"[2]

I spent August and September making telephone calls for money and giving the candidate names he should call. The results were meager. Thornburgh was well up in the polls. Ertel was considered a sacrificial lamb until late September, when the national economic recession hit Pennsylvania. Thornburgh, a supporter of President Reagan's economic policies, began to slip significantly in the polls. Suddenly we had a real race. Ertel became a possible winner and contributions began to flow in, almost without being solicited. Now some of the state party fund-raisers, who had previously remained aloof from the campaign, became involved. They made personal contributions and began to gather more from their colleagues. The smell of victory had infused life into the Democratic Party of Pennsylvania.

Ertel and his running mate, Senator James Lloyd of Philadelphia, went to the finish line within winning distance, but did not quite make it. The national television networks early in the evening projected Thornburgh the winner, but then withdrew the projection as the results tightened. Thornburgh finally won, 1,872,784 to 1,772,353, a margin of only 100,431.

A year later I took a telephone call from Mike Berman of the Walter Mondale for President Campaign. He asked if I would be willing to help Mondale in Pennsylvania. I said yes. Berman invited Beth and me to a dinner in Washington to be followed by a day of campaign planning. When Beth and I arrived at the dinner, I was seated in the rear of the room, but Beth was escorted to the front and given a seat next to Mondale himself. When she rejoined me afterward Beth had been thoroughly captivated by the candidate. The next morning the state volunteers gathered in a large conference room. On the platform at the front were Mondale and several staff, including Berman, Robert Beckel, and Robert Reich, future Secretary of Labor for President Clinton. Reich briefed us on the campaign issues, and Berman walked us through the campaign structure, fund-raising, and delegate section. Berman closed his remarks by asking everyone to write a check "on the spot" to the campaign for $1,000. Virtually everyone, including me, did so.

The meeting closed with Mondale thanking everyone and giving a forceful pep talk. Before he left the room Mondale talked individually to every volunteer present.

I returned to Harrisburg excited to be part of the Mondale team. In the following months I worked enthusiastically on fund-raising and delegate selection. The national campaign office assigned me thirteen congressional districts in the midstate. In these districts I was to identify the best candidates to be Mondale delegates and then ensure that their names appeared on the ballot. I spent late November and December of 1983 talking with county chairs, legislators, and other party leaders seeking suggestions. I then talked personally with the prospective delegate candidates.

After the list of delegate candidates was compiled and approved by the national campaign office, we sent candidate petitions, along with complete instructions, to each candidate. Rules for petitions to be a candidate for public positions in Pennsylvania are technical, and a petition can be rejected if not properly executed. The persons signing the petition must be registered to vote, be of the same party as the candidate, and reside in the same county. The circulator's affidavit must be properly completed.

Our goal was to see that all of Mondale's petitions were valid and not subject to a challenge. We directed that every Mondale delegate's candidate

Democratic presidential candidate Walter Mondale speaking in Harrisburg after having been introduced by the author, one of the organizers of Mondale's 1984 primary election campaign in Pennsylvania. Source: *Personal file photo.*

The author talking to a television reporter at the Northumberland Bridge opening. Source: Personal file photo.

petitions be sent to one address in Harrisburg at least a week before the filing deadline. When the petitions were received, volunteer women in the AFL-CIO offices, using a checklist, reviewed each for correctness of execution. If there was any question the petition was brought to me, and I decided its validity. The system worked. Several petitions were returned to the candidate for correcting and returned to us by the filing deadline.

The day before the filing deadline I hand-carried Mondale's delegate petitions, as well as his personal petition to appear on the ballot as a presidential candidate, to the Bureau of Elections in the Commonwealth's Department of State. There were no challenges, and Mondale carried Pennsylvania in the primary election. His slate of district delegates won as well.

After the primary it became time for Mondale to select delegates at large to the national convention. These delegates are not elected but designated by the state party in conjunction with the presidential candidate. Mondale put me near the top of his delegate at large choices for Pennsylvania and said my designation was not negotiable. So Beth and I went to San Francisco that summer, participated in the state meetings, and enjoyed the convention floor. Mondale lost that fall to President Reagan, but I have always felt he was the best candidate to work for I have ever helped. He made direct personal contact, always expressed appreciation, and showed it by making me a delegate at large to the national convention.

In subsequent elections I helped with fund-raising for Harris Wofford in his successful campaign for the U.S. Senate against Thornburgh in 1995, Bob Casey Jr. for the U.S. Senate in 2006, and Jack Wagner for auditor general in 2008.

In 2008 Beth and I also worked for Barack Obama's campaign by providing "bed and breakfast" for out-of-state campaign workers who came to Harrisburg for training and campaign work. We were greatly impressed by the quality of these campaign workers—in their twenties, recent college graduates, energetic, bright, and highly motivated. The public has not yet heard of David Glickman of New York, Elliott Wilkes of Texas, Hanna Chatalas of Oregon, or Meredith Segal of Maine, but Beth and I have. They were among the Obama campaign workers who stayed with us while being trained for the campaign. We got to know them well enough to believe that, if young people like they are getting involved in politics, the future of the United States will be in good hands.

I hope that they, and others like them in both parties, will take the next step in their political careers by doing what George Washington, James Madison, Abraham Lincoln, Theodore Roosevelt, Franklin Roosevelt, Jimmy Carter, and Barack Obama did—run for the state legislature.

18

Reflections

> Your representative owes you, not his industry only, but his judgment, and he betrays instead of serving you if he sacrifices it to your opinion.
>
> —Edmund Burke, from his Bristol Constituency Speech November 3, 1774

MY EXPERIENCE

I found politics exciting, endlessly challenging, occasionally distressing and disappointing, but ultimately rewarding well beyond any expectations held during my first campaign for the House. In reflecting on how this came to be, several things come to mind.

An organized effort by issue-motivated volunteers can defeat an entrenched patronage-based organization. Winning the House and Senate seats away from the Lark organization clearly demonstrated it. By winning those elections we underscored a political principle enunciated by President Kennedy—an enthusiastic volunteer patriot is worth a dozen hired Hessians. Certainly the patronage politics of that day has vanished, having been given its interment by Governor Thornburgh's order to select county highway shed superintendents on merit. Job patronage has been replaced by "pinstripe" patronage for contracts in which bond lawyers, financial consultants, and other service vendors who give large campaign contributions are rewarded with state contracts, but that is another story. Yet the principle holds true: Citizens, when motivated and organized, can have a dramatic impact on elections and the government that follows from those elections. None of my legislative accomplishments described in this book would have happened without the dedicated work of volunteers like Harriet Klingman, Jackie Smith, Mollie Eyster, Esther Cotner, and the many others who freely gave countless hours to addressing envelopes, making telephone calls, arranging coffee klatches, and related campaign work.

Enacting significant reform legislation on major issues is possible. As my experience shows, it is not easy but it can be done. Several conditions must be present. Foremost, the legislators advocating the legislation must provide persistent leadership while maintaining willingness to compromise. The House and the Senate are, in effect, two large committees. It is impossible to get agreement from a majority of either body on major proposals without compromise. I had the good fortune to serve with Republican senators like Stanley Stroup and Jack Stauffer who were willing to work out compromises needed to pass important legislation.

The legislature can create and develop significant legislation on its own. I take some pride in the fact none of the major legislation I was involved with was originated by the governor's office or an outside organization. My legislative colleagues and I originated all of this legislation.

Working with members of the minority party early in the legislative process is essential. Reform of the confirmation procedure demonstrated this. Senate confirmation was and is a controversial matter. We would not have had significant Republican support if the three Democrats and two Republicans on the committee had not spent so much time dining together while discussing and working out the report. That all five committee members signed the report is, I believe, a significant achievement. While the bipartisan harmony of the report became strained in the debate on the implementing legislation, the reform effort would not have gone as far as it did if I had not worked closely with Senators Frame and Stroup from the very inception of the project.

Strong support from my party's legislative leadership was essential. Speaker Fineman, Majority Leaders Irvis and Manderino in the House, and Senate President Martin Murray and Majority Leader Thomas Lamb in the Senate provided indispensable backing.

Another vital ingredient is doing the "homework" necessary to document and justify the proposed legislation. The Consumer Affairs Committee Reports, from the committee itself and the legal counsel's report, fully documented the changes we made in the PUC law. Other examples, such as Professor Broughton's analysis of the proposed environmental amendment and the flood disaster prevention report, are found in the appendices to this book.

The remaining element in legislative enactment is luck, an ingredient out of the legislator's control but, fortunately, not always necessary. This was demonstrated by the House passage of the flood plain and storm water management proposals in 1978. I am convinced that it took an "act of

God" in the third Johnstown flood, to give the bills the momentum needed after failure in the prior legislative sessions.

Participation in politics and the legislature provided another satisfaction I did not foresee when I first ran for office. In my campaigns and in the legislature I met and worked with truly outstanding individuals in both political parties, persons who would be considered outstanding in any line of work. I think, as examples, of Northumberland County Commissioner James Kelley; House members Leroy Irvis, Herbert Fineman, James Manderino, John Pittenger, James Goodman, Robert Butera, and William Hutchinson; of Senators Martin Murray, Thomas Lamb, Stanley Stroup, and John Stauffer; of executive branch officials Ronald Lench, Clifford Jones, Maurice Goddard, James Scheiner, and Walter Baran. There are many others, but these illustrate that politics and government has had—and continues to have—conscientious and able persons in both political parties who avidly pursue the public interest.

My legislative efforts were incredibly blessed by the caliber of the professional staff that worked with me. They gave outstanding service to me and have gone on to success in their own careers. Michael Aumiller, my executive assistant in the Senate for my two terms, went back to Snyder County to perform his own political magic. In 1983 he was elected a commissioner of Snyder County as a Democrat by winning more votes than both Republicans, who came in second and third to hold the majority. This impressive vote performance by a Democrat had never happened in Snyder County. After two terms as commissioner Aumiller made an unsuccessful run for the House of Representatives and returned to Harrisburg, where he served as a deputy secretary for administration of the Departments of Labor and Industry, Agriculture, and State. He is now a deputy auditor general for Jack Wagner.

Neil McAuliffe, manager of my 1972 Senate campaign, became executive assistant to Senator (and, for a term) Congressman Joseph Ammerman of Clearfield County. He then worked for Senator James Romanelli for eight years and Senator Michael O'Pake. He retired in 2008.

Vincent Carocci, who worked on the Senate Confirmation Special Committee and Consumer Protection Committee, went on to join the administration of Governor Casey. Carocci capped his public service career by serving as Casey's press secretary.

John Showers, who researched the flood report, also performed political magic. He was elected to the House of Representatives in 1980 by defeating Republican Reno Thomas, a five term incumbent, while Ronald Reagan was sweeping the area over President Carter. Showers is the only Democrat in the history of Snyder and Union Counties to represent them in the House. He served four terms, ran unsuccessfully for the State Senate, and then became Economic Adviser for Rural Affairs to Governor Casey. He was appointed to fill a Union County commissionership in 2005 and has since been reelected.

Joseph Powers, my Senate legislative assistant, became executive assistant to Lt. Governor Mark Singel for eight years and then executive deputy secretary of the Department of Environmental Protection. He retired in 2009.

James H. Cawley, my counsel for the Senate Consumer Affairs Committee, was appointed to the PUC, along with Republican counsel Susan Shanaman, by Governor Thornburgh, before going into private law practice as a utility law lawyer. He was reappointed to the PUC by Governor Rendell and is now its chairman.

Thomas Seaman, who worked in my district office, is now an adult education teacher at the State Correctional Institution at Camp Hill and an author of books on the history of railroads in Pennsylvania, including *Trackside Harrisburg*.

Jean Brannon, my personal secretary, served in the same capacity for Lt. Governor Singel and Senate Democratic Leader Mellow and is now retired.

Peggy Chamberlain, who managed my district office, was news director for Radio Station WFYY in Selinsgrove until March 2010, when the judges of Snyder County appointed her as a county commissioner to fill a vacancy.

THEN AND NOW

The immense changes in politics and the legislature amaze me. In my 1966 House campaign I spent only $7,500, all personal money, and relied on volunteers that hand-addressed envelopes, manually dialed telephone calls, and relied on 3" × 5" file cards for organization information. The advertising was done through newspapers, radio, mailings, and handouts. There were no computers. Secretaries made carbon copies. We did not advertise on television.

Now contested House campaigns typically cost several hundred thousand dollars and have gone as high as a million. Today's campaigns rely on electronically addressed mailings, Internet mailings, robot delivered phone calls, and lots of television. The Senate is fairly comparable. My 1976 Senate campaign cost $75,000, and included television. The mailings were still hand-addressed and the advertising emphasis was on radio and newspaper. The computer and Internet were still several years off.

When I left the Senate in 1980, my salary was less than $20,000, and I had a staff of six, including two in one district office in Sunbury. Beginning December 1, 2008, the base salary for House and Senate members became $78,315, plus a defined benefit pension program and health care benefits. The leaders of both houses receive additional salary, topping out at $122,254, for the Speaker and Senate president. Legislative salaries now receive an automatic increase based on the Federal Consumer Price Index.

The increase in staff and technological support is particularly impressive. In October 2008 the four House members from the 27th Senate District had a total of twenty-two on staff at a cost totaling $879,000.[1] At the same time two senators representing the 27th and 29th Districts had twenty-one staff at the annual cost of $1 million.[2]

In 1966 House members had no office in the capitol or in their district. Now every House member has at least one district office and senators have several. Each House and Senate office is equipped with computers and access to the Internet. House members have laptop computers with them on the House floor. Those senators who want them have laptops as well.

One of the more troubling changes is in the level of partisan animosity. Legislative bodies, whether American or British, should be party based, but the partisanship should be held in balance with the need to serve the public good. I have the impression that the kind of willingness to work "across the aisle" by Senators Stroup and Stauffer, for example, is harder to find now. The trust between the parties seems to have deteriorated that far.[3]

Speaker Herbert Fineman initiated the movement toward a modern legislature. He believed that improved compensation and staff support services were necessary for the House to serve as a check and balance on the executive branch. By 2010, however, the legislative support system had grown well beyond Fineman's contemplation. For one example, an entire new wing was added to the new capital building in the 1980s to provide modern offices for legislators.

Fineman had a meritorious idea in pushing the House into the modern age. The growth in staff support and technological assistance are appropriate for the twenty-first century. If the legislature is to fulfill its constitutional obligation to serve as a check and balance on the executive branch and state budgets approaching $30 billion, it needs the staffing and support system it has. The legislature has never been better staffed and equipped to do research, conduct investigations, and produce legislation.

THE FUTURE

Events of recent years have given the public reason to question whether the size and cost of the legislature is excessive. Is the legislature "under performing"? Are the citizens of Pennsylvania getting their money's worth? What the public has seen is a General Assembly that surreptitiously asserted itself for pay raises and related compensation benefits, used public funds for bonuses to state employees for campaign work, used the legislative district reapportionment system to exclude competition, and allowed partisan excess to preclude effective action on major problems. These are serious matters. Fairly or unfairly, the House and Senate, as institutions, have been seriously damaged in the eye of the body politic. This is regrettable. The legislature is better than its public image, but not nearly as good as it can be. The great majority of members in both political parties are hard working, conscientious public servants. They have it within their power to rise to the occasion, put their houses in order, and restore the respect the House and Senate ought to have.

This book is not the place for me to prescribe the changes that the legislature ought to take. But I do exhort its members to act in the context of the legislature's historical legacy. The Pennsylvania General Assembly, and the fifty other legislative bodies in the United States, trace their roots back 900 years to the time following William the Conqueror's successful invasion and occupation of England. William rewarded the military leaders who supported him by giving them large English land holdings. This was more than a reward for past services. It was also done with the expectation that the sovereign could, as needed, call on them to supply the soldiers, horses, weapons, and other supplies for the defense of the kingdom. The king's barons realized before long that the relationship with the sovereign worked two ways. The king could govern only with the support and cooperation of the landed gentry. This realization led to centuries of confrontation.

In 1215 the nobles of the kingdom met with King John and forced him to sign the Magna Carta. In signing it the barons renewed their loyalty to the sovereign, but the king's signature agreed to limitations on his royal power, including a provision that he could not levy taxes without the approval of the barons. This "contract" between the governor and the governed, so to speak, is the seed from which constitutional law and the parliamentary system spouted and grew. In the centuries following—through the English civil war, numerous confrontations, and endless plotting—the concept of a "parliament" developed, took form, and evolved into a vibrant and effective instrument of public representation.

By the time of the American Revolution, the two-house parliament held great—but not complete—power to check the conduct of the crown. The power to tax, to raise armed forces, and enact a budget resided in the Parliament. In the American colonies, however, the king was still seen as a powerful autocrat whose government abused them. The American constitution writers therefore took the best part of the British system—a two-house Parliament and revised it to be an equal, but separate, branch. In place of a king they created a chief executive stripped of royal attributes, limited to enumerated powers, and subject to checks and balances from a two-house legislature and judiciary. The chief executive would manage the government, but only the legislature would have the power to pay for it, as well as have the authority to review critically the executive's conduct. Of course, in 1776 Pennsylvania already had three quarters of a century of experience with an elected legislature, thanks to William Penn's Charter of Privileges.

I make this historical reference for a practical reason. Freely elected legislatures as part of a constitutional government of checks and balances are among the great accomplishments of the Western world. Everyone elected to the General Assembly has, during his or her tenure, a trustee's duty to maintain and nourish the institution in which they serve. Taking the oath of office means more than agreeing to the mechanical rules of government provided in the state constitution; it is also, I believe, an oath to guard and strengthen one of our democracy's great bodies. An enhanced appreciation of the historical heritage from which the legislature has grown and the purposes for which it exists can bring out the highest ideals of the legislature. Armed with those ideals the House and Senate can forge the collective resolve needed to lift the General Assembly to the heights of achievement and integrity that will restore the public confidence it should have. As institutions they have what it takes to do this. They have ample ability to research, analyze, investigate, and determine what needs to be done. They have able and honorable members. And then there is Archimedes's lever and fulcrum—they have them too.

I wish them well.

APPENDICES

Appendix A

A Sampling of Basse Beck's "Up and Down the River" Columns

BASSE A. BECK, "COMMONWEALTH LEADS NATION—IN MILES OF POLLUTED STREAMS," *THE DAILY ITEM*, SUNBURY, PENNSYLVANIA, SEPTEMBER 25, 1964

As if we did not know it! A good half of the rivers and streams in the United States polluted by mine acids are located in Pennsylvania. And Sunbury is situated at the junction point of the two most mine acid loaded streams in the Keystone state.

Want the authority for this? The United States Department of Interior has just published Fish and Wildlife Circular 191 entitled "Extent of Acid Mine Pollution in the United States Affecting Fish and Wildlife."

Thirty states reported no pollution problems from coal mining run offs. Eight states were bothered by copper, zinc, silver, and aluminum seepages. But of the dozen states affected by bituminous and anthracite spillage into their streams, Pennsylvania is the highest on the list.

The overall picture in the nation shows 5,890 miles of streams which are mine acid polluted. Of this total Pennsylvania alone counts for 2,906 miles of lost clean water. In the Susquehanna River basin alone, 1,031 miles of water are poisoned by the mine acids from anthracite workings which drain into the North Branch and the main river and from the countless bituminous workings which use the West Branch for their discharges.

Even West Virginia, which wears the badge of poverty in current Congressional debates, has less than half the destroyed river and tributary bottoms destroyed by mine acid pollution than does prosperous Pennsylvania. The survey shows West Virginia with 1,150 miles of ruined streams; Kentucky with 580 and Ohio follows with 278 black streams.

Uncle Sam Surveys Mine Acid Fish Kills

Picture used in Department of the Interior booklet on Acid Mine Pollution in the United States. It was taken between October 9-14, 1961 along the North Branch of the Susquehanna River near Sunbury after pumping from Glen Alden mines in South Wilkes-Barre poisoned the river destroying more than a million fish.

If ever a government report revealed what is the matter with Pennsylvania this one does the trick. Here is a quote:

> Pennsylvania reported that about 2,900 miles of streams and 10,100 surface acres of reservoir are seriously affected by acid mine pollution. The data apply to streams ranging from those which have had substantial decreases in aquatic life to those which are practically devoid of life.

Every mile of active fishing waters lost to anglers because a nearby stream has been polluted by mine waters is reflected in a drop off in fishing license sales by the State Fish Commission. Every one knows a fisherman who has given up buying licenses. Nothing cramps his angling urge more quickly than to watch his favorite fishing holes blotted out by acid from uncontrolled mining operations. He has the right to be sore when he comes on the banks of his favored stream to find it strewn with dead and dying fish and flaked with destroyed minnows—his future crop of fun.

This is a serious matter to the sportsmen because the Pennsylvania Fish Commission operates directly from fishing license sales. It is not a tax supported body. The Fish Commission faces the problem of meeting high fishing pressures from increasing populations at the same time its fishable waters are diminishing by reason of acid mine water pollution. In 1956, there were 714,000 fishing licenses sold in this state whereas this year the total will barely reach 500,000. Thus when you see, hear, or read about the

Fish Commission stocking streams with fish, it is not taxpayers' money that is being distributed, it is money from the sale of fishing licenses doing the job.

However, in 1956 when over 700,000 fishermen bought licenses about 2,000 miles of polluted streams existed in Pennsylvania. Today, better than 2,900 miles of dirty streams can be tabulated. Year by year, more than 100 miles of clean waters are abolished. In July, 30 miles of Slippery Rock Creek in Butler county were wiped out by the advancing tide of uncontrolled mine acids and the pleasures of a State Park at McConnell's Mills were ruined by the destruction of clean water.

But to get back to the importance of adding additional fishing waters as stressed in the Federal report by quote:

> The six States presently having the greatest pollution loads caused by mine acid drainage—Pennsylvania, West Virginia, Kentucky, Ohio, Illinois and Missouri—have about 4,646,000 fishermen. Of these, 1,471,432 have indicated a preference for stream fishing. Significantly enough, only Missouri in this group has had an increase in fishing license sales during the past 10 years. . . .When the average annual fishing license sales of the 1951–1953 period are compared with those of the 1961–1963 period, a decrease is noted of 317,094 licenses sold in the six States named. This is in contrast to the picture generally found over the United States.

Creeping Communism may or may not be taking over the world, according to which group of national leaders you may listen to, but this much is dead certain, creeping acid mine waters from the hard and soft coal regions are taking over the pure waters of Pennsylvania.

While Pennsylvania's taxpayers pour millions of dollars into the construction of municipal disposal plants, and nonmining industries millions more into water cleansing devices, the mining groups in this State claim and use rights of way to dispose of destructive effluents which are denied to the rest of the Commonwealth.

The State Sanitary Water Board must start saying no, No! and NO! and mean it. The world cannot accommodate Communism—and Pennsylvania cannot play patty-cake with pollution!

BASSE A. BECK, "STUDY SHOWS STATE STREAMS WORST ACID CARRIERS IN THE NATION," *THE DAILY ITEM*, SUNBURY, PENNYSLVANIA, JULY 19, 1966

Of deep interest to Pennsylvanians as the result of passage in this state of Clean Streams Laws coming into enforcement in both the soft and hard coal areas is the study of the "Stream Quality in Appalachia As Related to

Coal Mine Drainage 1965" as published in Geological Survey Circular 526 now available at the U.S. Department of the Interior, Washington, D.C.

The study was made in connection with the Appalachian program to relieve the poverty in mine acid swept stream states of Pennsylvania, Ohio, Kentucky, Maryland, West Virginia, Tennessee, Georgia, and Alabama. Two of these states lead the Appalachian field in coal production, Pennsylvania with 39.7 percent and [sic] could be expected both these states, their residents, rivers and streams suffer the most damage from acid mine waters.

During an intensive study in May 1965, eleven two men teams of hydrologists and chemists visited 318 stream sites from northeastern Pennsylvania to central Alabama covering an area of 160,000 square miles. They made field measurements including water discharge, pH, specific conductance, water temperature, dissolved oxygen concentration, and acidity.

They found streams in the coal regions that are unaffected by mine drainage to be excellent in quality. But the study proved what conservationists who forced adoption of the Clean Streams laws have long held to be true—that free mineral acidity in the streams of northern Appalachia damages the chemical quality of waters more than in the southern sections of the mine state afflicted regions. Free mineral acidity was found in rivers as large as the West Branch Susquehanna River, Kiskiminetas River, Casselman River, North Branch Potomac River, Monongahela River, and Raccoon Creek.

Some of the pH readings taken by the hydrologists in creeks and streams in the Susquehanna Basin are of interest to local lovers of clean water. Fish start to die when alkaline water turns to acid and the turning point between neutral water and aquatic life is about pH 5.5.

The West Branch of the Susquehanna River is stricken several times each year by run-off from the soft coal fields in Clearfield, Centre and Clinton counties. When heavy rainfalls cover the soft coal regions an inordinate flush out of mine acid takes place, changing the water in the stream from alkaline to acid content. Fish kills from this cause have occurred which extended down to Selinsgrove. These kills happen most often in periods of low water flow when the water quality is changed rapidly from neutral to acid and the fish have no chance to escape the acid flood waters.

The Appalachian study reveals the constant threat hanging over the West Branch from the coal regions. Here are some readings: Clearfield Creek at Dimeling pH 3.50; Moshannon Creek pH 2.85; Sinnemahoning Creek (Bennett Branch) pH 3.65; Renovo pH 4.25; Beach Creek pH 4.20. Bald Eagle Creek is a limestone stream with a pH of 6.6 near Mill Hall. Water from this creek usually holds the West Branch in balance except when overcome by huge storm waters from the acid streams.

Up the North Branch conditions show a normal alkaline river from about Berwick downstream to Sunbury. The field report was taken at Wilkes-Barre and showed a pH 7.4 reading. How the study failed to encompass the Glen

Alden mine discharges at South Wilkes-Barre leaves much to the imagination. These discharge points are the worst along the river and the Sanitary Water Board admits this to be the case. A chemical analysis of a sample taken from the Covell Street discharge pipe, as recently as May 16, 1966 showed a pH 3.7 heavily acid reading. Also the spillage was loaded with 2800 parts per million sulfates, 400 ppm iron; 352 ppm ferrous iron and 20 ppm manganese. When will the Sanitary Water Board require treatment of this discharge by the Blue Coal Company which has now bought out Glen Alden?

This is the worst spot on the North Branch. In second place is the Old Forge Borehole which tests pH 4.7 but throws out little sulfates and irons compared to the former Glen Alden mines. The gravity outfall at Duryea which drains the flow from the dying Lackawanna coal fields tested pH 5.4 recently.

Outside of the pumped mine acid drainage spots near Ashley, the North Branch of the Susquehanna River seems to have no trouble retaining its alkalinity. Nescopeck Creek with a pH 3.60 and Catawissa Creek pH 4.25 do not seem to upset the water quality at Bloomsburg and Danville which showed readings of pH 6.4 at both towns on the same dates the creek readings were collected. Other local stream readings made by the Appalachian hydrologists were: Shamokin Creek at Weigh Scales pH 4.7; Mahoney Creek (near mouth) Dornsife pH 6.4 and East Mahantango Creek near Dalmatia pH 6.8.

BASSE A. BECK, "OF TIME, THE RIVER, AND PURE WATER FAIRPLAY," *THE DAILY ITEM*, SUNBURY, PENNSYLVANIA, DECEMBER 30, 1965

This will be a rambling column. It is written to comfort and encourage the citizens of Central Pennsylvania who are being conned into accepting the belief that laws and court decisions against the public interest and welfare are immutable and not subject to change for the common good.

It is induced by thoughts which came to mind after reading a sparkling column written by Vermont Royster, editor of the Wall Street Journal who quotes the philosopher Thomas Aquinas who observed that laws not serving the common weal could be changed.

It is particularly applicable to the people of Central Pennsylvania now undergoing misery in their attempts to solve the problem of clean water due to conflicting laws and legal interpretations of the same. It offers a ray of hope.

Way back in the Middle Ages Saint Aquinas wrote:

> Nothing can be absolutely unchangeable in things that are subject to change, and therefore human law cannot be altogether unchangeable.

> For those who first endeavoured to discover something useful for the human community, not being able by themselves to take everything into consideration, set up certain institutions which were deficient in many ways; and these were changed by subsequent lawgivers who made institutions that might prove less frequently deficient in respect of the common weal.

In Pennsylvania the time has clearly come to correct the deficiencies in the Clean Streams Law. Loopholes granting special privileges to the mining interests are destroying public rights to pure water and devaluating property prices along our streams. There was a time when mine acid dumping into these streams could be held to be economically justifiable in a young and growing country. That time is long past. Correction is overdue.

There are some who say it cannot be done. The coal barons arrogantly take this position. However, on such issues of public right things can be done. Memory serves to point out a local issue started by this newspaper to free the Bainbridge Street toll bridge. This was accomplished and expanded meanwhile to free all the toll bridges in the state.

Twenty years ago Pennsylvania had ten toll bridges within its borders. State highways led directly to the entrances and exits of most of these privately owned stream crossings. Sunbury, Amity Hall and bridges at Harrisburg were the closest structures to this city. This newspaper, convinced that public ownership of all such bridges was a necessity, launched a campaign to have them taken over by the Department of Highways.

Toll bridge owners and lobbyists fought back. During this campaign one state court held that "toll bridges are not a contiguous part of the state highway system." Try telling that one to your ten-year-old son as an intelligence test. Well, contrary legal opinions notwithstanding and to shorten the story—the cause snowballed aided by public pressure. In 1949, the Highway Department took over the toll bridges and eight years later the bridges were paid off and freed largely from their own collections.

Result? Today motorists may travel everywhere in internal Pennsylvania without paying toll charges.

Now about clean streams. This newspaper firmly believes public rights are paramount. Mining interests and their lobbyists hold otherwise. They stand on an archaic state law which they hold gives them the right to pollute almost as they please. In the case of the Susquehanna River, which drains two-thirds of the Commonwealth, they claim exemption from the civic duty required of every municipality, town, factory, individual, farm and processing plant in this state.

In the Susquehanna River basin alone, this last named discriminated against group has spent more than $50 million to keep the river pure. Where is the equity in this situation? In the face of such injustice, coal lawyers and courts muddle their lengthy ways to conflicting decisions. One court opines you cannot increase acid mine pollution in an already acid mine drainage stream while another court takes the opposite point of view. Something has got to give. Pure water must be preserved. The question must again be asked: "Who owns this river?"

BASSE A. BECK, "SOMETIMES THE WEIGHT OF PUBLIC OPINION WINS OUT," *THE DAILY ITEM*, SUNBURY, PENNSYLVANIA, AUGUST 23, 1965

Passage of Clean Streams Bill 585 this week in the Pennsylvania Senate marks a distinct victory for the common people of our Commonwealth. For more than three years the clean streams issue stood unfaced, delayed by conflicting court decisions and crippling amendments to proposed legislation, all of which evaded the bald fact that certain interests in this State were privileged to despoil our waters for nothing while the general public was forced to pay sewage treatment processing costs.

Pennsylvania, which in the last United States survey of streams polluted with mine drainage, led all the States in the nation with 2,906 miles counted and losing about 100 miles more to mine acid run-offs every year, can now look forward happily to January 1, 1966 the effective date of the new law.

Do not look for miracles. Results will not come in days, weeks or months. But with untreated mine acid discharges shut off, Pennsylvanians year by year will witness a slow reversal of the depressing trend of contamination they have watched in the past. Streams and rivers do have recuperative and regenerating forces of their own as they work their ways twenty-four hours daily to the seas. Now given this chance, Nature may prove itself a surprising comeback artist.

Passage of the Clean Streams Law is a brilliant victory for the cause of conservation in the Keystone State. It could never have taken place here had not the combined common sense of our citizens demanded that it be done.

It is true the sportsmen of Pennsylvania took the lead in spearheading the cause, led by Representative John F. Laudadio, of Westmoreland County, who introduced the bill in the House after securing 116 cosponsors to his bill. Another strong asset in the legislative battle, was Representative Thomas J. Foerster, of Allegheny County. As Chairman of the House Fisheries Committee, Mr. Foerster toured the State, holding hearings at which people were allowed to speak their feelings. Many citizens resident in the Susquehanna River basin attended these hearings. They now enjoy the satisfaction of having done their worthy parts.

House Bill 585, passed the Legislative House May 11, 1965 by a vote of 195–6. This took place after an effort to have the bill re-committed was defeated on May 5, 1965 by a vote of 140 to 62. Then came the long wait for the bill to reach the Senate floor. When it did appear there, the important words "mine drainage" were missing from the printed context. A linotype operator and a proof reader accepted responsibility for the error. After all the buck passing and time consuming delay, the Senate finally passed the new law 41 to 4 on August 18, 1965.

You may wish to know who the four Senators were who opposed the Clean Streams strengthening law? And where they are from? Senator George N. Wade was the only opponent directly from the Susquehanna River basin. Senator Wade represents the 31st Senatorial District comprising Juniata, Perry, Mifflin and Cumberland Counties. The other three "aginners" were Senator Daniel A. Bailey, of Centre County; Senator Thomas J. Kalman, of Lafayette County; and Senator William J. Lane, of Washington County.

It was a glorious victory for the people who love Pennsylvania—those who truly believe the days of special privilege are over in this Commonwealth.

Appendix B

Robert Broughton's Analysis of the Environmental Amendment

"CONSTITUTIONAL AMENDMENT COVERS ENVIRONMENT: LEGISLATURE MUST PASS BILL IN TWO SESSIONS."*

The Pennsylvania legislature has under consideration a House bill (HB 958) which would amend Article I of the state Constitution to provide for the preservation and restoration of our natural resources. If it is adopted, the bill would expand the base for citizens' legal action to protect our environment against air, water and land pollution.

This bill is one of the most important bills presented so far in the fight to save the environment. The bill passed the House (190–0) and is currently before the Senate Committee on Constitutional Changes, of which Jack F. McGregor, Pittsburgh Republican, is chairman.

"Section 27. Natural Resources and the Public Estate.—The People have a right to clean air, pure water, and to the preservation of the natural scenic, historic and aesthetic values of the environment. Pennsylvania's natural resources, including the air, waters, fish, wildlife, and the public lands and property of the Commonwealth, are the common property of all the people, including generations yet to come. As trustee of these resources, the Commonwealth shall preserve and maintain them for the benefit of all the people."

The state Department of Forests and Waters has suggested that the word conserve be substituted for preserve, in the last sentence.

---

*This is a summary version of the article by Dr. Broughton published in the *Pennsylvania Law Quarterly* and inserted in the *House Journal* on April 14, 1970. Robert Broughton was an associate professor of law at Duquesne University Law School.

As with any proposed constitutional amendment, it will have to be passed by the legislature twice—the second time in the 1971–1972 legislative session—and submitted to the electorate in a statewide referendum, before becoming effective.

As Franklin L. Kury, Representative from Sunbury, and the initial sponsor of H.B. 958 has said in a statement to the House of Delegates of the Pennsylvania Bar Association:

> When our original constitutions were drafted in the 18th Century, the issue was preserving man's political environment, not his natural environment. Our natural resources then were so great, our population so small and our technology so undeveloped that the future of the environment and our natural resources was taken for granted. Because our political environment was imperiled our Constitution makers added Bills of Rights to our federal and state Constitutions. No mention was made of protecting our natural environment because there was no need to; the future of our natural resources was taken for granted.
>
> Now that situation has altered. Our political environment is strongly protected by vigilant courts and an alert press, but population and technology have run amok through our environment and natural resources. If we are to save our natural environment we must therefore give it the same Constitutional protection we give to our political environment.

As citizens interested in environmental quality, we may be pleased to see a statement of policy with which we agree placed in the Constitution of Pennsylvania. We can hardly get very excited about it, however, if it is only to be a statement of policy: Will it, as hoped, give citizens a weapon which may be used in the courts, in litigation, to protect and enhance the quality of our environment?

I think it will in many areas; and in those cases where the proposed amendment would not, itself, create a legal right, it may be used as a basis for building or expanding common law rights, and as a basis for giving added effectiveness to political force applied in favor of environmental quality.

Governmental Actions

One can distinguish at least three different categories of governmental actions, and two categories of private actions, to which we might expect an amendment such as H.B. 958 to be relevant: (1) Action by government (state, municipal, or an authority) which itself causes environmental harm (e.g. the Department of Highway's Sinnamahoning Creek decision). (2) Failure or refusal of government to act (a) to correct environmental damage which has already taken place (e.g. failure to back-fill strip mines on state lands), or (b) to prevent environmental harm (e.g. failure to enforce air or water pollution control laws). (3) Governmental licensing of others to engage in acts which will harm the environment (e.g. the grant of a license to construct and operate an electric power plant, with the knowledge that the air pollution control equipment proposed for the electric power plant is inadequate).

Private Actions

Private action might include: (1) Acts by a private person or corporation subject to licensing or regulation by government (e.g. location of an overhead electric transmission line through a scenic area). (2) Acts by a private person or corporation that is not directly subject to governmental licensing or control (e.g. strip mining, without land reclamation, of limestone, gravel, or any mineral other than coal).

Now, there is no legal right to contest any of the types of acts listed, if a harm falls short of being a private nuisance. (Private nuisance is defined as an unreasonable interference with a person's use of his property—e.g. air pollutants emitted which kill the trees in his apple orchard.) And even if the harm is serious enough to be a private nuisance, the courts traditionally tend to favor productive economic interests over environmental or aesthetic interests.

The amendment may or may not, in and of itself, create a right to challenge any of the described acts. To the extent that it does confer such a right, the legal basis or bases for that right may differ. Let us examine the legal techniques for invoking the protection of the proposed amendment in each of the listed situations.

Legal Techniques

If a governmental agency proposed to do something which directly damaged the environment, then affected citizens would have standing (would be recognized by a court as having a sufficient legal interest) to bring an action to enjoin (prevent) the agency from doing it. Violation of a constitutional right would give someone standing, even aside from the fact that Pennsylvania allows taxpayer's suits to prevent the illegal, or unconstitutional, expenditure of public lands.

Governmental inaction is now, and would remain almost impossible to litigate. If the legislature refuses to appropriate money for pollution control, that is, and will remain a political problem, not a legal one. Similarly, if an enforcement agency refuses to prosecute antipollution laws, it will not be compelled by the courts to do so—any more than a district attorney will be compelled to prosecute every breach of every criminal statute (e.g., adultery, which is commonly ignored). But the existence of a constitutional mandate can materially strengthen political efforts to deal with all forms of governmental inaction. Legislatures, public officials, and citizens all seem to take constitutional mandates seriously; therefore, political pressure applied in the context of a constitutional command is likely to be more effective than political pressure applied in its absence. The amendment will also make more certain the constitutional basis for legislative action.

Legal Rights

As applied to administrative agency rulings, the proposed amendment would probably create legal rights to appeal to the courts any agency ruling that had the effect of damaging the environment, but under the Pennsylvania Administrative Agency Law as now interpreted, that is not certain. Suppose an administrative agency disregarded the constitutional amendment (this in itself might be unlikely), and authorized a regulated industry to do something which damaged the environment. Under current law, the agency would probably allow any person reasonably interested to intervene and participate in the agency's proceedings. To have a right to appeal the agency's decision to a court, however, a person must be not only aggrieved, but "directly affected." This language has been interpreted restrictively, one decision even going so far as to assert that the interest must be "immediate and pecuniary." Even with a restrictive interpretation of the statutory language, however, it seems probable that someone whose constitutional rights were violated by an administrative agency ruling would be held to have a "direct interest" in that ruling, even if his interest were not "pecuniary." Unfortunately, this must remain an argument, only until it is tested in the courts. To be certain that such appeals could be taken, the Administrative Agency Law should be amended to make clear a legislative intent that any reasonably affected party, including associations or organizations representing those whose interests particular agencies are intended to protect, "shall" have a right to appeal agency rulings to the courts. Such an amendment would help to make Pennsylvania law in this area consistent with a growing body of federal law.

Regulated Industries

Where acts of regulated industries are complained of, and the acts in question are within the regulating power of the government, then individual citizens cannot enforce the law themselves. They must depend on the regulating agency to act. This would probably not change, under the proposed amendment. Under Pennsylvania law, a statutory remedy for a problem is regarded as exclusive: no other remedy can be invoked. The only way to overcome this rule is for the legislature to specifically preserve other remedies, or provides additional ones. This is commonly done, in antipollution laws, but is quite rare in more general regulatory statutes.

Similarly, the amendment would not, in and of itself, provide a right to challenge in court the acts of unregulated private persons or corporations. It might, however, become the nucleus of an enlargement of the common law action of private nuisance. And it could substantially change the weight given to various factors when a court, in deciding whether to enjoin particular acts, balances the benefits and burdens of granting an injunction.

Conclusion

I conclude that the proposed amendment, while it would not solve all the environmental problems of Pennsylvanians (no single legal document would), will, if passed, effectively change the balance of legal power, and give environmental quality (and the human race) at least an even chance in the coming years.

Appendix C

Questions and Answers Document Distributed Prior to the Public Referendum on the Environmental Amendment

FRANKLIN L. KURY, MEMBER
142 MARKET SQUARE
SUNBURY, PENNSYLVANIA 17801

COMMITTEES
BUSINESS AND COMMERCE
CONSERVATION
LOCAL GOVERNMENT

HOUSE OF REPRESENTATIVES
COMMONWEALTH OF PENNSYLVANIA
HARRISBURG

JOINT RESOLUTION 3

SHALL ARTICLE 1 OF THE CONSTITUTION BE AMENDED BY ADDING A NEW SECTION GUARANTEEING THE PEOPLE'S RIGHT TO CLEAR AIR AND PURE WATER AND THE PRESERVATION AND CONSERVATION, BY THE COMMONWEALTH, OF THE STATE'S NATURAL RESOURCES FOR THE PEOPLE'S BENEFIT?

YES ? OR NO ?

Joint Resolution 3 is, I believe, an important piece of legislation for the benefit of Pennsylvanians. It should be passed at the May 18 Primary Election. However, voter apathy or confusion could easily defeat it, particularly since there are four other amendments to be voted on at the same time.

To promote full public understanding of Joint Resolution 3, I have prepared a Question and Answer sheet explaining it. Other background material is also enclosed. Please feel free to publish or reprint any of this material.

If you would like further information, please call or write me at 142 Market Street, Sunbury, Pennsylvania, 17801 (AC 717/286-5866) or Box 115, House of Representatives, Harrisburg, Pennsylvania, 17120 (AC 717/787-3528).

Your active support of Joint Resolution 3 can make a substantial contribution to its approval on May 18.

Sincerely,

Franklin L. Kury
Chief Legislative Sponsor

Joint Resolution 3:

Shall Article 1 of the Constitution be amended by adding a new section guaranteeing the people's right to clean air and pure water and the preservation and conservation, by the Commonwealth, of the State's natural resources for the people's benefit?

Yes? or No?

Joint Resolution 3 is, I believe, an important piece of legislation for the benefit of Pennsylvanians. It should be passed at the May 18 Primary Election. However, voter apathy or confusion could easily defeat it, particularly since there are four other amendments to be voted on at the same time.

To promote full public understanding of Joint Resolution 3, I have prepared a Question and Answer sheet explaining it. Other background material is also enclosed. Please feel free to publish or reprint any of this material.

If you would like further information, please call or write me at 142 Market Street, Sunbury, Pennsylvania, 17801 (AC 717/286-5866) or Box 115, House of Representatives, Harrisburg, Pennsylvania, 17120 (AC 717/787-3528).

Your active support of Joint Resolution 3 can make a substantial contribution to its approval on May 18.

Sincerely,
/s/ Franklin L. Kury
Franklin L. Kury
Chief legislative Sponsor

JOINT RESOLUTION 3: MAY 18 PRIMARY ELECTION

Q. What is Joint Resolution 3?
A. This is one of the five referendum questions which will appear on the ballot for voter approval or rejection at the May 18 primary election. It deals with conservation and it will read: "Shall Article I of the Constitution be amended by adding a new section guaranteeing the people's right to clean air and pure water and the preservation and conservation, by the Commonwealth, of the State's natural resources for the people's benefit?"

Q. If approved, what will this resolution or amendment do?
A. Joint Resolution 3, as a Constitutional Amendment, would add a new section to our State Constitution's Declaration of Rights. The basic provision of the amendment would give the people of Pennsylvania a fundamental *legal* right to a decent environment. The amendment also establishes that the public natural resources of the Commonwealth belong to all the people, including future generations, and that the Commonwealth is to serve as Trustee of our natural resources for future generations.

Q. Will the amendment make any real difference in the fight to save the environment?
A. Yes, once Joint Resolution 3 is passed and the citizens have a legal right to a decent environment under the State Constitution, every governmental agency or private entity, which by its actions may have an adverse effect on the environment, must consider the people's rights before it acts. If the public's rights are not considered, the public could seek protection of its legal rights in the environment by an appropriate law suit. The Resolution would benefit all of the people, and would go a long way toward tempering any individual, company, or governmental body which may have an adverse impact on our natural or historic assets.

In short, the amendment will incorporate three broad principles into our legal system:

1. The people have the right to a decent environment.
2. Our public natural resources belong to all the people, including future generations.
3. The State is the trustee of these natural resources for future generations.

Q. How do you read all of this into the short Resolution 3 stated on the ballot?
A. Because of space limitations on the ballot, the Secretary of State is required to condense the actual text into as brief a space as possible. The

complete text of the Resolution, which was passed twice, and unanimously, by both Houses of the State Legislature, reads in its entirety: "Section 27. Natural Resources and the Public Estate.— The people have a right to clean air, pure water, and to the preservation of the natural, scenic, historic and esthetic values of the environment. Pennsylvania's public natural resources are the common property of all the people, including generations yet to come. As trustee of these resources, the Commonwealth shall conserve and maintain them for the benefit of all the people."

Q. Will there be any "teeth" in the law, if passed?
A. It will be up to the courts to apply the three broad principles to legal cases. However, having this law passed will strengthen substantially the legal weapons available to protect our environment from further destruction. In the words of Robert Broughton, Associate Professor of Law at Duquesne University, the amendment "will, if passed, effectively change the balance of legal power and give environmental quality (and the human race) at least an even chance in the coming years."

Q. Is this bill supported by both Democrats and Republicans?
A. Yes, it has bi-partisan support. Joint Resolution 3 passed two successive sessions of the legislature with *unanimous* support by members of both parties. Both our Democratic and Republican legislators apparently feel that we need this bill to protect our environment against air, water and land pollution, and because it will expand the base for citizens' legal action.

Q. What organizations are supporting this amendment?
A. Leading organizations are quite interested in seeing that Joint Resolution 3 is passed. Among them are: The Pennsylvania Bar Association, The Pennsylvania Federation of Sportsmen's Clubs, the Pennsylvania Environmental Council, and the League of Women Voters of Pennsylvania—all known for their vigor in championing and protecting the rights of the individual. It should be noted that New York and Michigan have already enacted a similar amendment.

Q. Will Joint Resolution 3, if passed, benefit individual citizens personally?
A. Yes. At present individual citizens' legal rights in the environment are basically limited to protecting their property or person from actual or threatened damage. Joint Resolution 3 broadens these legal rights to include a legally protectable interest in the whole environment -- including the water we drink, the air we breathe, and the esthetics of the landscape.

Q. Will there be any cost involved?
A. No. Joint Resolution 3 will cost the taxpayer nothing. Resolution 3 will create no new state agency, bureau or commission. The amendment

strengthens peoples' rights; it does not expand the government. It is a rare form of legislation. It will give, you won't.

Q. If passed by the electorate, how long will it take to make Resolution 3 law?
A. Resolution 3 becomes part of our State Constitution immediately. It will be an amendment to Pennsylvania's Declaration of Rights which is the State's version of the Federal Bill of Rights.

Q. Won't the right of eminent domain still exist?
A. Yes, however, it will have to be exercised in conformity with this amendment. A highway department or utility company could not take land without fully considering the public's right to a decent environment. Joint Resolution 3 should force a much more judicious use of eminent domain.

Q. Do most Pennsylvanians know about this resolution?
A. Not enough! This is why it is so important to spread the word. It has been proved that when people see referendums on the ballot, if they do not understand the question as stated, they may automatically vote "no." In this instance a "no" vote would be a tragic mistake. This is why we are trying to make every Pennsylvanian aware that he is vitally needed at the May 18 Primary, and that he should vote "yes" on Joint Resolution 3 which deals with conservation of our state's natural resources.

Appendix D

A Report of the Special Senate Committee to Study Confirmation Procedure, November 1973

> It will readily be comprehended, that a man who had himself the sole disposition of offices, would be governed much more by his private inclinations and interests, than when he was bound to submit the propriety of his choice to the discussion and determination of a different and independent body, and that body an entire branch of the legislature.
>
> Alexander Hamilton, Essay Number 76, *The Federalist*

**SPECIAL SENATE COMMITTEE
TO STUDY CONFIRMATION PROCEDURE**

Appointed pursuant to 1973 Senate Resolution Serial No. 11, adopted February 6, 1973

Franklin L. Kury
Chairman

Joseph S. Ammerman
Majority Caucus Secretary

Richard C. Frame
Minority Leader

Henry C. Messinger
Majority Whip

Stanley G. Stroup
Minority Whip

Letter of Transmittal to the Members of the Senate

In Essay No. 51 of *The Federalist*, James Madison stated that "If angels were to govern men, neither external nor internal controls on government would be necessary. In forming a government which is to be administered by men over men, the great difficulty lies in this: you must first enable the government to control the governed; and in the next place oblige it to control itself."

The confirmation requirement was placed in the Constitution of Pennsylvania as such an obligation of the government to control itself. However, as is often the case in a government "administered by men over men," the most carefully devised provisions when carried out do not always effectively achieve the results intended.

Members of the Senate—aware of the inefficiencies and serious abuses that now undermine the confirmation process—by resolution established a special committee to conduct a study and suggest measures to improve the procedure. This report presents the committee's findings and its unanimous recommendations for procedural change. The appendix includes a comprehensive study by the staff of the Joint State Government Commission. Since no other document is now available which intensively explores this topic, this publication will serve scholars in Pennsylvania and elsewhere as a prime reference for future research on the confirmation process.

In undertaking this assignment, the members of the committee agreed wholeheartedly that reforming the Senate's confirmation procedure is not a matter to be handled on a partisan basis between two competing political parties. Rather, we agreed that this reform is an institutional problem for the Senate that bears equally on both parties and on every Senator. In short, we acted on the basis that reform of the confirmation procedure should be done with the idea of making the Senate a more effective and respected governmental body.

In that spirit the committee submits this report.

The committee expresses thanks to Peter M, Coleman, special assistant to the Senate Majority Leader; Thomas W. Corbett,* legal and research counsel to the Senate Minority Whip; Donald C. Steele, research director of the Joint State Government Commission, and the staff of the commission for their substantial assistance.

> Respectfully submitted,
> /s/ Franklin L. Kury
> Franklin L. Kury,
> Chairman Special Senate Committee to Study
> Confirmation Procedure
> November, 1973

---

*The father of the current (2010) attorney general, Thomas W. Corbett.

REPORT OF THE SPECIAL SENATE COMMITTEE TO STUDY CONFIRMATION PROCEDURE

At the Federal Constitutional Convention of 1787 in Philadelphia, our country's Founding Fathers drafted into the Constitution the requirement of Senate confirmation of executive appointments. They developed the concept as a check and balance of the President's appointive power, to insure nomination of qualified men to positions of governmental responsibility.

In 1838 a limited version of the federal requirement was written into the Pennsylvania Constitution. The state provision mandated Senate confirmation of gubernatorial appointments to judicial offices of courts of record and permitted the Governor to fill without senatorial consent vacancies happening during recess of the Senate.

Exactly 100 years ago, on November 3, 1873, delegates to the State Constitutional Convention in Harrisburg adopted a Constitution extending the Senate confirmation requirement and interim appointment privilege to include all offices for which the Constitution or statutes required appointment by the Governor. In addition, they inserted the provision requiring a two-thirds vote of members of the Senate for confirmation, apparently agreeing with the delegate from Lycoming County who argued that this requirement would lift the confirmation process further above the "influence of politicians" and guarantee that appointees were confirmed "upon their merit and not as a reward merely of political services."

As a result of the constitutional revisions made in 1967, Article IV, Section 8, of the Constitution now requires confirmation only for those appointed officers whose confirmation is specifically mandated by the Constitution or the statutes. Under this provision—which is substantially augmented by general provisions in Section 207 of the Administrative Code of 1929, as amended, and 32 separate statutes—approximately 2,000 appointments are now subject to Senate confirmation.[1]

Careful review of confirmations over the past decades reveals that actual practice has not always been in consistent compliance with the constitutional and statutory requirements governing confirmation of gubernatorial appointments. Confusion exists concerning which appointees require confirmation and why some positions require confirmation and others do not.

Furthermore, even the most casual observer of today's Pennsylvania government will sadly note that the confirmation process as it has evolved is not the effective check and balance originally envisioned. To the

---

1. A detailed review of the current constitutional and statutory provisions pertaining to gubernatorial appointment and senatorial confirmation requirements are found in the appendix, pp. 23 to 45. The constitutional provisions are presented in full on pp. 63 to 64. (NOTE: These page references refer to the original Report's appendices, which while not reprinted here can found in the full Report, available in the Senate Library.)

contrary, the process has become characterized by indefensible delay by the Senate, circumvention of the constitutional requirement by the Governor and excessive political maneuvering by the Senate and the Governor. It has opened both the executive and legislative branches of Pennsylvania government to deserved criticism.

Clearly, reform is needed. The Senate has recognized the need for change by creating the Special Senate Committee to Study Confirmation Procedure and directing it in particular to investigate "The entire Senate confirmation procedure that the Senate follows upon receipt of a nomination."[2]

Deliberations of the Committee

Following its appointment, the committee undertook a thorough study of the federal and state historical background of Senate confirmation of executive nominations and of current requirements and practices. Committee members also met to evaluate the confirmation history and the responsibility of each position required by the Constitution or by statute to be filled by gubernatorial appointment.

The research of the Joint State Government Commission which served as a basis for much of the committee's study is found in the appendix of this report.

On May 3, 1973 the committee held a public hearing in the Capitol at which the following individuals testified (in order of appearance):

Ralph D. Tive, Esquire
  The Governor's Special Assistant for Legislation
Honorable Ernest P. Kline
  Lieutenant Governor of Pennsylvania
Jack R. Weinrauch, Esquire
  Chief Counsel to the Senate Majority Leader
Mrs. Roberta Ehrenberg
  Chairman of the Legislative Study for the League of Women Voters of Pennsylvania
Dr. Daniel J. Elazar
  Professor of Political Science and Director of the Center for the Study of Federalism, Temple University
Honorable Helene Wohlgemuth
  Secretary of Public Welfare
Honorable John C. Pittenger
  Secretary of Education

---

2. Senate Resolution Serial No. 11, adopted February 6, 1973, is presented in full in the appendix, p. 66 of the Senate Report (not reprinted here).

Joseph E. Gallagher, Esquire
Chairman of the Pennsylvania Bar Association Judiciary Committee, who was assisted in responding to questions by
Frederick H. Bolton, Esquire
Secretary and Executive Director of the Pennsylvania Bar Association

While stressing the importance of Senate confirmation of the Governor's major appointments to Pennsylvania's system of checks and balances, all of the distinguished persons testifying suggested measures to improve the process. They generally called for a reduction in the number of appointments requiring confirmation to include only offices of cabinet status and those involving important policy-making and discretionary powers. Most expressed preference for a constitutional majority vote for confirmation, and several recommended time limitations for the submission and confirmation of nominations. Also recommended were open committee meetings (whenever appropriate) and public hearings on major nominations, thorough screening of important nominations by appropriate standing committees of the Senate and stringent limitations on and Senate review of interim appointments.

Problem Areas Delineated

As a result of the public hearing and the committee's detailed study, members have pinpointed a number of current requirements and practices which interact to impede the confirmation process in Pennsylvania.

First of all, the statutes in a haphazard fashion require Senate confirmation for an extremely large number of positions, many of which vary greatly in importance and degree of responsibility. Altogether the Senate must advise and consent to at least 1,910 appointments to 264 boards, commissions and other bodies. Adding to this burden is the constitutional requirement of a two-thirds majority vote for the confirmation of each appointment, a difficult assignment indeed considering the political composition of the Pennsylvania Senate as well as the number of confirmations required. Little wonder that "gubernatorial appointments gather dust waiting for confirmation that never comes" (as Mr. Tive stated in his testimony) and that governors—frustrated by the time lag and inaction in the Senate—traditionally have grossly misused the interim appointment privilege.

These practices are highlighted by a review of the Session of 1971, during which Governor Shapp submitted 54 nominations to the Senate for confirmation. The Senate held these from 1 to 247 calendar days and had not yet considered 16 when the General Assembly adjourned. Subsequently, in the period from December 29, 1971 to January 4, 1972, the Governor made

864 interim appointments, thus practically negating the senatorial role in the confirmation process.

The record for the 1972 Legislative Session is equally discouraging. During the 1972 Session, the Governor submitted 887 nominations and recalled 3. The Senate confirmed 41. However, these statistics must be considered in light of the fact that during the first 10 months of the session only 58 nominations were submitted (with one recall) and the Senate confirmed 36 of these. But in the last 18 hectic days of the session—between November 13 and 30—829 nominations were submitted by the Governor and 2 recalled. During this period, the Senate confirmed five. Following the adjournment of the 1972 Session sine die on November 30 as provided by the Constitution, the Governor made 1,047 interim appointments.

No limitations or prohibitions have prevented these undesirable practices of the Governor and Senate. The Senate has no limitation on the amount of time it may take to confirm or reject a nominee submitted by the Governor. Rather than defeat a nominee, the Senate is more apt to "hold" the nomination. The Governor often has made interim appointments to vacancies that actually existed for many months while the Senate was in session. Interim nominees assume office, receive compensation and are reappointed—again on an interim basis—without senatorial consent.

In addition, no provisions specifically prohibit nominees rejected by the Senate from serving in office. For example, one appointee to an independent board was rejected by the Senate in 1970 but served in office for several years because the Governor reappointed him twice on an interim basis. In the absence of clear legal prohibitions to unconfirmed appointees taking office, one might conclude that confirmation by the Senate is a meaningless and unnecessary exercise.

Several internal Senate rules and procedures do not encourage a thorough, open and expeditious review of nominations.[3] The present Senate rules provide that nominations are handled exclusively by the Committee on Rules and Executive Nominations. The standing Senate committees concerned with legislation administered by administrative departments or agencies have no opportunity to review nominations to these executive bodies.

Public hearings on nominations are almost never held, and little information is made available to the individual Senators, let alone the public, on the background and qualifications of any except the most important and controversial nominations. Often only the Senator in whose district a nominee resides knows of his qualifications—or lack of them.

The present Senate rule dealing with "Information concerning nominations" (Rule XXX, Sec. 2) is of questionable value and has been criticized

---

3. Rule XXX on executive nominations is presented in full in the appendix, p. 65, of the Senate Report (but not reprinted here).

on the grounds that it is unfair to nominees and the public-at-large. This rule requires that information concerning the character and qualifications of a nominee be kept secret, except that specific charges against him may be revealed to the nominee at the discretion of the Rules and Executive Nominations Committee.

Committee Recommendations

It is the intent of the special Senate committee to formulate changes that will infuse efficiency and meaning into the confirmation process, preclude abuse by either the legislative or executive branches and increase public confidence in the Senate's role as the confirming body on gubernatorial appointments. With these goals in mind the committee recommends that the Senate consider favorably measures which would:

1. Amend the statutes to remove at least 473 positions with primarily advisory responsibilities from the confirmation requirement (see pp. 17 to 19). This would reduce by approximately 25 percent the number of positions now subject to Senate confirmation but would not remove from the requirement positions with significant administrative or regulatory duties.

    One exception to the recommendation for a reduction in the number of appointments requiring Senate confirmation is that approximately 60 deputy secretaries in administrative departments—who are now appointed by department heads with the approval of the Governor—are added to the list of offices for which confirmation is proposed. The committee recommends that in the future deputy secretaries be appointed by the Governor with Senate confirmation, paralleling the federal practice in which the President appoints, subject to Senate confirmation, certain departmental undersecretaries and assistant secretaries. Members of the committee feel that there is now a regrettable lack of communication between the individuals holding the policy-making deputy-secretary positions and the standing committees concerned with the programs they administer. Senate review and confirmation could result in a meaningful interchange of views regarding problems and goals and a closer relationship between the legislative committees and their correlative executive departments.

2. Amend the Constitution to allow the designation by statute of certain positions as requiring a two-thirds confirmation vote and others as requiring a constitutional majority vote. It is recommended that, in contrast to the approximately 2,000 positions now subject to two-thirds confirmation, this requirement be confined to less than 200 positions. The confirmation process would be expedited and the

interests of the public and all of the members of the Senate adequately protected by limiting the two-thirds confirmation requirement to the most important nominations. Although the committee members are in unanimous agreement concerning the types of positions which should be subject to a two-thirds confirmation vote and a majority vote and which should be excluded from the confirmation process, no attempt was made to obtain unanimous agreement on the status of each and every position. The 192 recommended for the two-thirds requirement include the heads of departments, judicial vacancies, members of powerful independent administrative boards and commissions and members of departmental administrative bodies with extraordinary discretionary or regulatory powers. All of the remaining—approximately 1,312—are recommended for confirmation by majority vote only. The committee's suggestions are presented on pp. 13 to 16.

3. Amend the Constitution to remove provisions permitting interim appointments and to insert time limits of 90 calendar days within which the Governor must submit a nomination following a vacancy (and not thereafter) and 25 legislative days within which the Senate must act on a nomination submitted by the Governor. If the Senate fails to act within 25 legislative days, the appointee would take office as if confirmed.

4. Prohibit by statute an appointee from serving in office if his nomination has been rejected by the Senate.

5. Amend the Senate Rules to encourage an expeditious, thorough and public examination of the qualifications and character of nominees. This would be accomplished by:

   (a) Permitting the Rules and Executive Nominations Committee to refer nominations to appropriate standing committees of the Senate, which would hold public hearings when advisable, scrutinize the qualifications of nominees and report back their recommendations.

   (b) Requiring each nominee to set forth under oath on a questionnaire prepared by the committee his qualifications and such other information as may be determined by the committee, which questionnaire shall be available for the use of any Senator and for inspection by the public.

   (c) Requiring a confidential State Police report to be made on all nominees, which report shall be available for inspection by all Senators.

   (d) Providing that all information concerning a nominee (except the State Police Report) be available to the public unless the committee shall by majority vote determine that any information which is of an unsubstantiated but damaging nature shall be withheld.

   (e) Enabling any three members of the Rules and Executive Nominations Committee to demand in writing that the chairman of the committee call a meeting for the purpose of taking action on a nomination which has been before the committee more than 15 legislative days. The committee's recommendation concerning the acceptance or rejection of the nomination shall be reported to the Senate immediately thereafter.

The committee is preparing appropriate legislation and rule changes to implement these recommendations. The entire Senate confirmation procedure as it would result with the inclusion of the committee's recommendations is outlined on pp. 20 to 22 [in the original report but not reprinted here].

In conclusion, members of the Special Senate Committee to Study Confirmation Procedure wish to point out that their work has been directed solely toward making the Senate confirmation process a truly effective check and balance of the gubernatorial appointive power. Neither partisan considerations nor present officeholders were taken into account in the conduct of this study and in the formulation of recommendations. To maintain this objective, bipartisan approach, the effective date of legislation and rule changes introduced to reform the confirmation process will be set for January 1975, when the next gubernatorial term will start. The committee intends that proposed constitutional amendments be submitted to the electorate at the earliest possible date—May 1975.

Respectfully submitted,

SPECIAL SENATE COMMITTEE TO STUDY
CONFIRMATION PROCEDURE

Franklin L. Kury, Chairman

Joseph S. Ammerman

Richard C. Frame

Henry G. Messinger

Stanley G. Stroup

Appendix E

Article IV, Sec. 8 of the State Constitution as Revised to Implement the Committee Report

ARTICLE IV: THE EXECUTIVE

Appointing Power

Section 8. (a) The Governor shall appoint a Secretary of Education and such other officers as he shall be authorized by law to appoint. The appointment of the Secretary of Education and of such other officers as may be specified by law, shall be subject to the consent of two-thirds or a majority of the members elected to the Senate as is specified by law.

(b) The Governor shall fill vacancies in offices to which he appoints by nominating to the Senate a proper person to fill the vacancy within 90 days of the first day of the vacancy and not thereafter. The Senate shall act on each executive nomination within 25 legislative days of its submission. If the Senate has not voted upon a nomination within 15 legislative days following such submission, any five members of the Senate may, in writing, request the presiding officer of the Senate to place the nomination before the entire Senate body whereby the nomination must be voted upon prior to the expiration of five legislative days or 25 legislative days following submission by the Governor, whichever occurs first If the nomination is made during a recess or after adjournment sine die, the Senate shall act upon it within 25 legislative days after its return or reconvening. If the Senate for any reason fails to act upon a nomination submitted to it within the required 25 legislative days, the nominee shall take office as if the appointment had been consented to by the Senate. The Governor shall in a similar manner fill vacancies in the offices of Auditor General, State Treasurer, justice, judge, justice of the peace and in any other elective office he is authorized to fill. In the case of a vacancy in an elective office, a person shall be elected to the office on the next election day appropriate to the office unless the first day of the vacancy is within two calendar months immediately preceding the election day in which case the election shall be held on the second succeeding election day appropriate to the office.

(c) In acting on executive nominations, the Senate shall sit with open doors. The votes shall be taken by yeas and nays and shall be entered on the journal.

Appendix F

The Witnesses and Persons Consulted in the Investigation of the PUC

Public hearings were conducted by this Committee and testimony was heard on these dates from these witnesses:

April 24, 1974, Harrisburg, Pennsylvania

        Commissioner Louis J. Carter
        Commissioner James McGirr Kelly
        Commissioner Robert Bloom

May 1, 1975, Harrisburg, Pennsylvania

Peter Brown, counsel to the Public Utility Commission
Bernard T. Helhowski, director, Bureau of Rates and Research
Will Ketner, secretary
Jerry Rich, director, Bureau of Investigations Service and Enforcement
Merle A. Forst, director, Bureau of Transportation

May 13, 1975, Harrisburg, Pennsylvania

    George I. Bloom, former chairman, Public Utility Commission
    David Dunlap, Esq., Harrisburg
    Philip Kalodner, chairman-designate, Public Utility Commission

May 14, 1975, Harrisburg, Pennsylvania

> Frank Jones, Citizens Committee for Ethical Insurance
> Walter M. Creitz, President, Pennsylvania Electric Association
> President, Metropolitan Edison Electric Company

Note: Former PUC Commissioner Herbert Denenberg was invited by correspondence, April 16 and April 30, to testify before this Committee at its May 14, 1975 hearings. He declined. By subsequent correspondence, May 20, Mr. Denenberg was offered the opportunity to submit written testimony for the consideration of the Committee. He chose not to do so.

June 12, 1975, Harrisburg, Pennsylvania

> Stuart E. McMurray, President, People's Natural Gas Co.
>   member, Board of Directors, Pennsylvania Gas Association
> Joseph C. Zwerdling, Chief Administrative Law Judge, Federal Power Commission Washington, D.C.
> Albert Herbert, Executive Vice President Pennsylvania Independent Telephone Association
> Mary Ann Klein, SCCA consumer organization, York, Pennsylvania

June 19, 1975, Harrisburg, Pennsylvania

> Jack K. Busby, President, Pennsylvania Power and Light Company
> Jacob G. Kassab, Secretary of Transportation
> Jean Ann Fox, Director, Allegheny County Bureau of Consumer Affairs
> Paul Garver, People's Power Project, New American Movement, Pittsburgh
> William H. Wilcox, Secretary of Community Affairs
> Peter F. Pugliese, General Solicitor, Bell Telephone Company of Pennsylvania

July 10, 1975, Harrisburg, Pennsylvania

> John Childs, Vice President, Kidder, Peabody and Co. New York, New York
> Richard D. Cudahy, Chairman, Wisconsin Public Service Commission

In addition, inspection visits were conducted by members of this committee and committee staff to the headquarters of the Wisconsin Public Service Commission, Madison, Wisconsin, and the California Public Utilities Commission, San Francisco, California. Extensive interviews were conducted with:

Wisconsin:

    James Bailey, executive director, Public Service Commission
    Fred Huebner, director, Division of Finance and Accounts
    James Tanner, director, Division of Rates
    Robert Malko, economist

California:

Vernon Sturgeon, Commissioner
William Symons, Commissioner
Leonard Ross, Commissioner
William Johnson, executive secretary
William Foley, assistant general counsel
Kenji Tomita, director, Division of Finance and Accounts
Russell Leonard, rate of return specialist, Division of Finance and Accounts
Walter Cavagnaro, chief engineer, Division of Utilities
Donald Houck, assistant chief engineer, Division of Utilities

Appendix G

Senator Franklin L. Kury, "Rendezvous with Disaster," *Pennsylvania Township News* Magazine, May 1977

Pennsylvania has a rendezvous with disaster. It is only a matter of time until another major flood devastates Pennsylvania as Agnes and other great floods have devastated our state in the past. Floods are a permanent threat to Pennsylvania. Every year increased development reduces the ability of the land to absorb water and causes the runoff to increase flood potential.

All of the flood control measures that we have built to date may be inadequate to meet the next flood disaster. In Hurricane Agnes alone, the property damage far exceeded all of the money invested in flood control and protection to that time.

The hard fact is that there is no way to stop flooding. There is no way to eliminate completely the damage and grief which flooding brings. The only thing we can do is minimize the damage by taking appropriate action now.

What, then, can be done?

First, and by far the most important, we must recognize that we are dealing with irrevocable laws of nature. The laws of nature are permanent. They cannot be amended or repealed by any legislative body. We have two choices—we can work in harmony with the laws of nature or we can work in defiance of them. So far, we have chosen the latter course and we have paid the price for it.

There are three laws of nature to be considered in dealing with floods. The first law is that rivers will flood when an excess of water enters them and that this water will spread out and temporarily occupy the flood plains. *Building on a flood plain is therefore about as logical as building on a railroad track.* It is just a matter of time until there will be a violent collision.

The second law of nature is that rivers and streams, like the veins and arteries of the human body, must be treated as a whole system. To deal with streams on a community-by-community basis is like a surgeon operating on an arm as if it were not connected to the rest of the human body. If we are to deal effectively with flooding, we must, therefore, deal with the streams on a watershed basis.

The third rule of nature is that streams are constantly changing, flowing, filling, forming and reforming almost as if they were a living organism. Mark Twain's book, "Life on the Mississippi," vividly describes this phenomenon. Dredging, removing of islands' and similar suggestions often made are therefore in defiance of a law of nature. Such suggestions are at best short-term expedients which cannot permanently reduce flood damage.

Having recognized these fundamental laws of nature, it is obvious that we have for centuries lived and built in defiance of them. Virtually every major community in Pennsylvania is built right in the middle of the flood plain. It is estimated that 2,100 of Pennsylvania's 2,800 communities have been built in the 100-year flood zone. In contrast, the ancient Egyptians built their cities out of the Nile River's flood plain.

Having built in so many of our communities in defiance of a fundamental law of nature, we have then spent over a billion dollars in dams, dikes and other flood control projects to protect ourselves from the mistakes we made.

As the public becomes increasingly aware of the permanent danger of flooding, suggestions are made to increase our emphasis on flood control projects—more dams, dikes and walls.

As a means of protecting existing communities in the flood plain, these suggestions have merit. As a means of dealing permanently with the problem, they are inadequate.

There is no way to assure that additional flood control projects assure protection. The City of Sunbury, for example, has an eight-foot high flood wall built by the U. S. Army Corps of Engineers in 1946. Hurricane Agnes brought the Susquehanna to within two inches of "topping" that wall. Who knows how high the next Agnes will be? That is the point that is too often missed. Flood control projects, no matter how well thought out, are still fundamentally acting in defiance of the laws of nature. So long as we rely on them, we are at the mercy of the rivers and the waters' flow.

It has also been suggested that requiring every flood prone community to qualify for the federal government's flood insurance program is sufficient. This suggestion is also misleading.

The federal flood insurance program is a limited means of dealing with the flooding problem. Basically, federally endorsed flood insurance offers partial compensation for damage to property already in a flood zone. One of the unfortunate effects of flood insurance is that it may create the false impression that it is safe to build in the flood zone as long as flood insurance is purchased. Flood insurance should be looked on for exactly what it is—*partial* compensation for the property value protection of structures already built in the flood zone. It does nothing for mental anguish, grief, loss of life, resulting unemployment or community blight. It should not be a basis for expanding construction in flood zones.

It is true that the federal government requires communities to pass flood plain zoning ordinances to qualify for flood insurance. But this is no solution to the problem. The federal government's flood insurance program does not deal with the streams and rivers on a watershed-by-watershed basis. Rather, it deals with flood insurance on a community-to-community basis. In addition, the federal flood insurance program *does not* insure that communities in each watershed are complying with flood plain zoning ordinances or that there is any coordination between them. If there is no coordinated response throughout the watershed, all the good one community may do to protect itself may be washed away by the action or inaction of its upstream neighbors.

Finally, municipal flood plain zoning—the basis for flood insurance—cannot apply to utilities or state agencies. Yet utilities and state agencies build structures which significantly affect flooding.

The federal flood insurance program can be an effective basis for meeting Pennsylvania's flood problem only if there is a state law mandating uniformity of compliance and enforcement on a watershed-by-watershed basis.

Having recognized the permanent laws of nature, and the limitations of flood control and flood insurance programs, we can now act effectively. The first step is to make a bold decision—to regulate further construction in the flood plains. This decision must be made so that we do not compound the already difficult problem which we have created for ourselves. By concentrating new building out of flood zones, we, like the Egyptians, will not need dams or dikes for protection.

This can only be accomplished by an effective state flood plain management law which brings the law of Pennsylvania into harmony with the laws of nature. Such a law must deal with the flood plain on a watershed-by-watershed basis and require each community in each watershed to live up to uniform standards for development and regulation of the flood plain. This state law can use the federal flood insurance structure, provided the state insures uniformity of enforcement in each watershed. Having made the fundamental decision to check uncontrolled construction in the flood plains, we must also take appropriate action to protect the communities already in the flood plain. Additional flood control and protection measures can be planned on the basis of existing construction.

At the same time, we should pass a strong law requiring all developers of real estate to hold back water runoff from their developments at the peril of significant penalties. The law should require that water runoff after development be no greater than before development. Existing Pennsylvania law of runoff water is confusing and difficult to fathom. Developers out of the flood plain have little, if any, incentive to hold back increased runoff which results from their construction and improvements.

This three-point program—checking uncontrolled new construction in flood zones, protection of existing communities, and the control of water flow from new developments out of the flood plain—will do as much as we can hope to do to minimize future flood damages. Enacting this program will be difficult and expensive. Considering that Pennsylvania has incurred flooding damages averaging $100 million a year since 1936, the taxpayers of our state have a legitimate interest in seeking effective state action.

Great controversy and emotion envelops proposals for a comprehensive state flood plain management bill. But we cannot let the controversy deter firm action to regulate the flood plain and the storm waters that run off into it. Only by acting firmly now can we hope to cushion our rendezvous with flood disaster.

Sure it's in the flood plain, but you can't beat the view!

Appendix H

The Study of Historical "Flood Disaster Prevention in the Commonwealth of Pennsylvania," Prepared by Senator Kury and Inserted in the *Senate Legislative Journal*, 1974

FOREWORD

Few issues in the Commonwealth of Pennsylvania are as important and as pressing to its citizens as is the task of limiting future flooding disasters in our State. This can only be achieved through a comprehensive program including new legislation to implement flood plain land use regulation, a now missing aspect of Pennsylvania's flood management program.

For the past several months my office and I have been in the process of working with Secretary Goddard and the Department of Environmental Resources in drafting "The Pennsylvania Flood Disaster Prevention Act." This bill (Senate Bill 1122) was introduced September 17 in conjunction with this work, I have been gathering and analyzing the information contained in this report so as to better explain the bill and the urgent need for its enactment.

This report is a review of the total flood picture in Pennsylvania today, including flood history, water resources, flood controls, and ideas for flood management.

The purpose of this report is to bring together facts that show the total picture of flood disasters in the Commonwealth. These facts dramatically show why the enactment of a sound flood plain management law such as Senate Bill 1122 deserves the highest priority.

Senator Franklin L. Kury
State Capitol
Harrisburg, Pennsylvania
November 1973

TABLE OF CONTENTS

1. Introduction
2. The Water Resources of Pennsylvania
3. History of Flooding in Pennsylvania
   A. Flood History
   B. Early Flooding History, Including the Floods of March 1936
   C. Flooding Since 1936
4. Historic Flood Damage in Pennsylvania
5. Flood Control and Protection in Pennsylvania
   A. Current Pennsylvania Law with Regard to Flood Prevention
   B. Flood Control by the Commonwealth
   C. Water Resources Development in Pennsylvania by the U.S. Army Corps of Engineers
   D. Soil Conservation Service
6. Flood Plain Management
7. Flood Plain Zoning in Pennsylvania
   A. Flood Plain Zoning Law in Pennsylvania
   B. Present Flood Plain Zoning in Pennsylvania
   C. The Courts: The Present Status of Flood Plain Zoning in Pennsylvania
8. Questions and Answers Regarding Senate Bill 1122, The "Pennsylvania Flood Disaster Prevention Act"
9. Summary of Senate Bill 1122 Pennsylvania Flood Disaster Prevention
10. Sources of Information Used in Preparing This Report
11. Appendix, Example Flood Plain Zoning Ordinances

1. INTRODUCTION

As Senator from Pennsylvania's 27th Senatorial District, flood plain management is of special importance to me and my constituents, for it is in the heart of my district that the waters of West and North Branches of the Susquehanna River join. It is for this reason and for the recognition that steps must now be taken to limit the scope of future flooding disasters, that I have introduced in the Senate of Pennsylvania Senate Bill 1122, entitled "The Pennsylvania Flood Disaster Prevention Act."

It is said that "floods are acts of God, and flood damages are results of the acts of man." And how true this statement is, for as early as 1687 floods have been recorded on the Delaware River in "Historic Tales of Olden Times Concerning the Early Settlement and Progress of Philadelphia and Pennsylvania." Despite the early knowledge of floods, growth continued on the flood plains of the Susquehanna and other Pennsylvania rivers and streams in defiance of the laws of nature.

In spite of the early floods, the founding settlers of Penn's Woods chose to settle by streams and rivers, directly on the flood plains. This was done largely as a matter of convenience for reasons of transportation, communications, water supply and sewage disposal. This habit of settlement and development of flood plains has never been questioned or checked. As a result, there are 663 flood-prone communities in Pennsylvania today.

Despite Pennsylvania's extreme and record flooding history no government action came until sometime after what was for many years thought to be the record flood, set in March 1936. At most points on the Susquehanna River and its tributaries in 1936 two free-flowing high water records were set within one week. Damages from the floods of March 1936 amounted to $67 million just in the Susquehanna River Basin. Flood waters in Carbondale, Olyphant, Wilkes-Barre, Kingston, Plymouth, Williamsport, Lewistown, Sunbury, Harrisburg, and Steelton flooded as much as 70 percent of the area of these communities.

Government so often only responds after the crisis and it was not until after major flooding again in 1942 that any flood control measures were actually begun in Pennsylvania. Late in the 1940's we then saw the creation of the Division of Flood Control within the Department of Forest and Waters. A concentrated and coordinated effort to develop flood control and flood protection however did not come until after again another crisis, with severe flooding in Stroudsburg in 1955. Since then Pennsylvania has proceeded at an even pace developing an effective system of flood works and has become a leader among the states in flood control and flood protection measures.

Hurricane Agnes, however, inflicted $3 billion in property damages and clearly demonstrated that just being a leader is not enough. What is needed is a broader and more unified program for managing flood losses within the river basin and within the State.

Since the initiation of flood control measures in the State, the Commonwealth has spent more than $82 million on such projects. The U.S. Army Corps of Engineers has spent over $1 billion in Pennsylvania; and there have been numerous watershed and flood control projects constructed by the U.S. Soil Conservation Service, and other local government and private interests. Adding to the money spent on these flood works the $1.5 billion set aside by the Federal Government for Agnes flood relief, the $209 million set aside by the Commonwealth for recovery, and include all the funds spent on previous flood recovery; we come up with a grand total way over 2 billion of the taxpayers' dollars being spent in Pennsylvania. In effect, we have been subsidizing the residents of the flood plains, private citizens and businessmen alike.

The intent of Senate Bill 1122, "Pennsylvania Flood Disaster Prevention Act" is to limit the scope of future flooding disasters in the State by regulating the use and development of land on the flood plain. This bill would put an end to the current crazy cycle of "build, flood loss, and rebuild," and as a result save lives, property, and tax dollars.

We must remember that government policies in the past have encouraged development of the flood plain, and therefore we must recognize our responsibility and continue our support of the residents already located on the flood plain. Any further development should be controlled to minimize damages upstream and down, however, and the developers should assume full responsibility for their losses on the flood plain hereafter.

Flood plain management is only one aspect, but unfortunately it is the missing aspect, of a balanced flood control program. "Reduction of flood damages can he achieved through measures that are either structural or nonstructural or appropriate mixes of both."[1] This is the answer to the flooding problem in Pennsylvania. Flood losses can never be fully eliminated, but the extent of the flood disaster can be greatly reduced through "appropriate mixes of" more structural measures, additional upstream detention projects, flood plain land use regulations, and a reliable flood warning system.

These four measures can provide the balanced flood management program we need and can be achieved through continued flood control and protection projects, and the passage of Senate Bill 1122, "Pennsylvania Flood Disaster Prevention Act."

No matter how comprehensive the flood protection program is though, total protection and elimination of flood damages is probably impossible. It has been estimated that to protect the Susquehanna River Basin from a flood of Hurricane Agnes' dimension would require the construction of 522 new dams on 98,449 acres of land. (See Franklin S. Adams "Hurricane Agnes: Flooding vs. Dams in Pennsylvania." Bulletin of the Atomic Scientist, April 1973, p. 30 et seq.). Who can predict what storms and floods will come in the future? Who can say with certainty what effect is had on rainfall and run-off by our society's technological advances and continuing spread of asphalt and concrete? And remember that much of Pennsylvania's population—663 communities—resides in flood-prone areas. The forecast for future flood damages is indeed grim, unless effective action is taken now.

In short, Senate Bill 1122 asks us to break the historic habit that keeps our society building and developing in flood-prone areas. The bill says, in effect, that whatever we have built in the flood plain heretofore not with-

---

1. Susquehanna River Basin Commission, Proposed Comprehensive Plan for Management and Development of the Water Resources of the Susquehanna River Basin (Mechanicsburg, Pa. June 4, 1973), p. 13.

standing future development must be regulated in conformance with the logic of nature and not the dictates of man's convenience.

Finally, I want to acknowledge the excellent research assistance of John Showers, New Berlin, Pa., in preparing this report; he has my thanks for a job well done.

Franklin L. Kury
State Senator

2. THE WATER RESOURCES OF PENNSYLVANIA[2]

Pennsylvania is blessed with several great rivers. There are five major river basins or areas in. Pennsylvania. Of the Commonwealth's 46,044 square miles, 45,309 square miles are classified as the drainage system. The remaining 735 miles are contained in the Pennsylvania portion of Lake Erie, which also attributes to the State its few miles of shoreline. This shoreline presents Pennsylvania with its only shoreline flood control and beach erosion problems. The rest of Pennsylvania's waterways are inland and subject to different conditions.[3]

Pennsylvania receives high annual precipitation and is also affected by hurricanes. Its rivers and streams are winding, sometimes with rapid rates of fall, and often restricted by the rugged mountain ranges in which they flow. All these factors, coupled with the early development of towns, industries, roads and railroads on the valley floors have led to serious loss of lives and property damage from flooding.

Within these river basins the population is presently shifting to the suburban areas and is creating strong competition for land between the rural interests and the ever increasing population. This competition in many cases causes haphazard utilization of the land and further creates many and varied water resources and related land use problems.

Water availability is affected by the amount of water impounded by dams and reservoirs. The high flows of the Commonwealth are affected by the dams constructed to prevent flood damage by temporarily storing the water. The low flows are affected by the dams and reservoirs constructed to augment anticipated drought or low flows. In addition, other dams have been constructed for combination multiusage such as flood control, water supply and recreation. Others serve such single purpose functions as recreation, water supply, agriculture, electric power and other related uses.

---

2. The information in this section is largely from "Programs and Planning for the Management of the Water Resources of Pennsylvania," Pennsylvania Department of Environmental Resources. (Harrisburg, Pa., November 1971)

3. Ibid., p. 5.

Table FP.1. The Major River Basins and Areas of Pennsylvania

Major River Basins in Pennsylvania	Total Drainage Area in Penna. (square miles)	Percent of Pennsylvania
Susquehanna	21,038	46%
Ohio	15,614	35%
Delaware	6,465	14%
Potomac	1,584	4%
St. Lawrence	608	1%

Source: "Programs and Planning for the Management of the Water Resources of Pennsylvania," Pennsylvania Department of Environmental Resources (Harrisburg, Pa., November 1971), page 5.

Table FP.2. Current Major River Basin Population in Pennsylvania

Basin	Current Population (millions)	Percent of Total Population	Percent of the Total Land Area
Delaware	4,900	42%	14%
Ohio	3,700	31%	35%
Susquehanna	2,800	24%	46%
St. Lawrence	220	2%	4%
Potomac	180	1%	1%

Source: "Programs and Planning for the Management of the Water Resources of Pennsylvania," Pennsylvania Department of Environmental Resources (Harrisburg, Pa., November 1971), page 35.

Table FP.3 Existing Land Use in Pennsylvania (in square miles)

	Forests and Woodlands*	Cropland	Urban and Built-up Areas	Pasture	Water Areas**	Other Lands	Total
	17,100	6,185	2,375	1,772	900	1,068	29,400
Total percentages	58%	21%	8%	6%	3%	4%	100%

* Includes highways, lanes, mine spoil areas, strip mines, and farmsteads.

** Includes Lake Erie (470), rivers and streams (259), and dams, reservoirs, and natural lakes (171).

Source: "Programs and Planning for the Management of the Water Resources of Pennsylvania," Pennsylvania Department of Environmental Resources (Harrisburg, Pa., November 1971), page 41.

Table FP.4. Location and Storage of the Dams, Reservoirs, and Natural Lakes of Pennsylvania

	No.	Percent of Dams	Volume of Storage in Billion Gallons	Percent of Volume	Natural Lakes	Volume in Billions of Gallons
Ohio	461	20%	1,040	64%	6	9
Susquehanna	933	40%	332	20%	30	6
Delaware	879	38%	244	15%	39	11
Potomac	33	2%	9	1%	–	–
St. Lawrence	7	Less than 1%	Small	Less than 1%	–	–

Source: "Programs and Planning for the Management of the Water Resources of Pennsylvania," Pennsylvania Department of Environmental Resources (Harrisburg, Pa., November 1971), page 75.

At the present there are approximately 2,700 dams, reservoirs and natural lakes in Pennsylvania. Of this number several hundred dams have been filled by silt and/or other natural material. In addition, there are numerous natural lakes located primarily in Pike, Wayne and Monroe Counties that have a surface area of less than 20 acres in size. For the purpose of this report those lakes of less than 20 acres are not considered as being dams and/or reservoirs.[3]

The 2,318 dams and reservoirs impound approximately 1,625 billion gallons of water. In addition the 75 natural lakes contain 26 billion gallons of water. The reservoirs created by these dams and natural lakes represent approximately 171 thousand acres of 235 square miles of surface area, which is a small portion of the State's total area of 46,044 square miles.[4]

Private impoundments represent 93 percent of the total number of structures and contain 20 percent of the total water stored. Commonwealth structures represent 6 percent of the total number and impound 11 percent of the total storage. Federal structures represent 1 percent of the total number, but represent 60 percent of the total storage. In terms of storage, impoundments for multi-purpose usage contain 43 percent of the total, with flood control containing 21 percent and miscellaneous usage representing an additional 15 percent. The remaining 21 percent of storage is devoted to water supply and recreational purpose.[5]

In summary, the average precipitation rate of 40 inches per year produces approximately 33,000 billion gallons of water per year. Of this figure 14,200 billion gallons, or 42 percent, is received by the rivers and streams of the State. The Commonwealth can currently impound 1,625 billion gallons of water to satisfy its water oriented needs. Therefore, 12 percent of

3. Ibid, p. 5.
4. Ibid., p. 5.
5. Ibid., p. 41.

average surface run-off can be impounded for later usage with the remaining 83 percent or 12,575 billion gallons available for usage for water supply, agriculture, electric power generation and other water oriented needs.[6]

3. HISTORY OF FLOODING IN PENNSYLVANIA

A. Flood History.

All flood records in the Commonwealth of Pennsylvania are kept by the United States Geological Survey. Peak stages and discharges are recorded rather than specific statewide flood records. These records are recorded at individual gaging stations along Pennsylvania's streams maintained by the Geological Survey and the statistics are reported by major river basin, and broken down by tributary.

Floods and high water have been recorded officially in Pennsylvania since 1890 with the establishment of the oldest gaging station in the Commonwealth at Harrisburg. Systematic collection of streamflow records in Pennsylvania began at a few other mainstream locations during the period 1890–1900. However, it was not until about 1914 that a fairly representative network of gaging stations was operated throughout the State. Since 1914 the number of gaging stations has been increased gradually, a relatively large number being established during the decade 1930–1940. All unofficial records, before 1890, were obtained through other written accounts of that period.

The United States Geological Survey compiles an annual water year report. This water year runs from October 1 thru September 30. The Geological Survey also compiles information of record floods like Agnes. After floods like Agnes the Survey also sends engineers into the field to determine record water levels from high water marks in areas where there are no gaging stations.

B. Early Flooding History, Including the Floods of March 1936.[7]

Before the floods of March 1936 and earlier flooding, there was no effective coordinated system of flood control and flood protection works in the Commonwealth. After the 1936 crisis State and local governments began to install appropriate measures to control flood waters. Before the advent of the white man the Indians had gathered knowledge concerning the behavior of the streams upon which they lived and traveled, and there

---

6. Ibid., p. 75.
7. The source of the following information is "The Floods of March 1936 in Pennsylvania," Pennsylvania Department of Forests and Waters (Harrisburg, Pa., 1936), pp. 121–29.

was a tradition among them that "great floods" occurred on the Delaware and Susquehanna Rivers at regular intervals of 14 years. Early writings contain occasional references to the warning given by Indians to white settlers concerning the height of extreme floods, which were too often unheeded.

Delware River

The floods of 1687 and 1692 on the Delaware River are mentioned in a letter written by Phineas Pemberton on February 27, 1692 and is included in the "Historic Tales of Olden Times Concerning the Early Settlement and Progress of Philadelphia and Pennsylvania." The flood of 1692 he described as having risen 12 feet above the usual high-water mark at the Delaware Falls (Trenton, N.J.), the water reaching the upper stories of houses on the lowlands. A detailed account of this flood appears in "History of the City of Trenton," by John O. Raum, in 1871, which mentions the danger of inundations as foreseen by the Indians.

The early flood heights on the Delaware River were observed at various localities, but the records collected in the vicinity of Phillipsburg, N.J., cover the longest period prior to the establishment of the Weather Bureau gage in 1904, when systematic daily observations began. Although the early records at Phillipsburg were observed at gages set to different datums and at some distances apart, certain deductions and corrections have been made to be comparable with those observed in recent years. The greatest recorded flood as of 1936 on the Delaware River was that of October 10, 1903, which reached a stage of 35.9 feet referred to the present Phillipsburg gage. It was 4.8 feet above the high recorded state of December 1901, and exceeded the flood of March 1936 by 5.2 feet. Other great floods on the Delaware River were those of January 1841 and June 1862, which reached 28.5 feet, and that of March 1902, which reached 29.5 feet. Smaller floods that attained the height of 24.5 feet occurred in October 1869 and December 1878, and a stage of 25 feet was recorded in August 1933.

Lehigh River

Our knowledge of floods on the Lehigh River begins with a reference to one in 1739. The greatest recorded flood as of 1936 on this stream occurred on February 28, 1902, when a stage of 25.9 feet was reached at New Street Bridge in Bethlehem. Fifteen other floods were recorded for the Lehigh River between 1739 and 1902. At Bethlehem the flood of January 1841 and October 1869 reached 23 feet and in June 1862 a stage of 23.3 feet was observed. A stage of 18 feet was recorded in October 1786. In 1902 a gaging station was established at Bethlehem, and systematic observation of gage height began at that time. A stage of 20.8 feet was reached in August

1933, and 20.7 feet in July 1935. A near record flood during the term of the station record was that of March 1936, which was 19.0 feet.

Schuylkill River

The earliest recorded flood for the Schuylkill River was that of July 15, 1757. The highest stages in the upper reaches of this stream have not given the greatest flows near its mouth. One of the highest recorded stages at Reading was 23 feet in September 1850. A stage of 21.6 feet was recorded in October 1869. At Conshohocken there were floods in 1869, and in 1895. The flood of February 1902, which reached 21.5 feet at Reading, was one of the highest on the stream in both its upper and lower reaches. Other exceptional floods at Reading, not including those caused by ice jams, occurred in October 1786, July 1850, and August 1933, when stages at 17.3, 18.6, and 17.5 feet respectively were reached.

Susquehanna River

Our record of floods on the North Branch of the Susquehanna River begins with that of March 15, 1784, which was described in a letter by Rev. Jacob Johnson of Wilkes-Barre, mentioning twenty-one floods on the stream, with some information relating to 16 of them. Two great known floods on this stream were those of March 18, 1865, and March 20, 1936, when 33.1 feet was reached at Wilkes-Barre on both occasions. A stage of 28.8 feet was reached 7 days before the flood of March 20, 1936, and was the highest recorded in 34 years. Other great floods at Wilkes-Barre, not including those caused by ice jams, occurred in October 1786, April 1807, May 1933, March 1902, March 1913, and March 1914, when stages of 29, 30, 28, 31.4, 28.5, and 28.3 feet respectively were recorded.

Before March 1904, when the greatest of all known ice gorges on the North Branch of the Susquehanna River occurred, there is mention of 19 floods at Wilkes-Barre that were amplified by ice conditions. The flats opposite Wilkes-Barre were often flooded by these ice gorges and in March 1875 all bridges at Pittston were destroyed.

For the period 1692 to 1895, when regular gage-height observations began at Williamsport on the West Branch of the Susquehanna River, there are references to 32 floods, but little information is available concerning 20 of them. During the 48 years, 1846 to 1894, crests were recorded for nine floods that include eight of the greatest known on this stream in 244 years, not including those in March 1936. The 1936 flood crest on the West Branch of the Susquehanna River was reached on March 18, when a stage of 33.57 feet was reached at Williamsport. However, this stage was only 1.2 feet higher than June 1889. The outstanding feature in connection with the flood of March 18, 1936, was the fact that on March 12, 6 days previous to its occurrence, the stream reached 23.66 feet and was at its highest stage in 42 years. Other exceptional floods at Williamsport were those which reached a stage of 24 feet in March 1846 and September 1861; 26 feet in March 1865; and 30 feet in May 1894.

The first mention of floods on the main stem of the Susquehanna River was found in Hazard's Register, which states that at Harrisburg the flood in 1740 was higher than that of March 15, 1784. Systematic observations of river heights began at Harrisburg on January 1, 1874. There are references to 22 floods before that time with some information relating to the height of eight that were not caused by ice jams and reached stages ranging from 16 to 24.6 feet on the Harrisburg gage.

The highest known flood on the Susquehanna River between Sunbury and its mouth during the 196 years, 1740 to 1936, occurred on March 19, 1936, when 30.33 feet was reached at the Walnut Street gage in Harrisburg. This flood exceeded any previous known height at Harrisburg by 3.5 feet. Six days prior to this flood, however, a stage of 21.76 feet was reached, the highest water with free-flow conditions in 42 years. The three previous great floods at Harrisburg occurred in March 1865, June 1889, and May 1894, when stages of 24.6, 26.8, and 25.4 feet respectively were recorded. Other exceptional floods at Harrisburg, exclusive of those caused by ice jams, were those of October 1786 and March 1846 when 22 feet was reached on each occasion, and that of December 1901, for which 21.2 feet was recorded.

Juniata River

For the Juniata River there are references to 18 floods during the period 1802 to 1894, including the one of June 1889 which reached 35.9 feet at Newport, the highest known as of 1936. At Newport on March 19, 1936, 34.24 feet was reached, and it followed a gage height of 20.41 feet on the 12th, one week before, which was the highest stage, exclusive of those caused by ice jams in 28 years. Other floods of unusual magnitude on the Juniata River were those of November 1810, October 1847, and May 1894, when 28.0, 28.5, and 31.0 feet respectively were recorded at Newport.

Allegheny River

Historic writings first mention floods on the Allegheny River by referring to the one of April 10, 1806. Unfortunately there are no recent gage height records for localities where the early observations were made, as the most authentic flood heights of years ago were referred to gages that have been discontinued or that are not comparable under present conditions. The five outstanding floods on the Allegheny River that were not the results of backwater from ice gorges and have not been exceeded by quantity of flow, as of 1936, were those of April 1806, March 1865, February 1883, March 1905, and March 1913. The flood of 1865 gave the highest free-flow stage at Franklin, while that of 1913 broke all records at Kittanning. The flood of 1806 is said to have reached 30 feet at Kittanning; in 1913 a stage of 24.5 feet was reached at Franklin and 30.4 feet at Kittanning. Other exceptional floods on the Allegheny River were those of December 1873, June 1881, and February 1884, when 27.0 feet was reached at Kittanning on the first date and 28.0 feet on the others. Backwater from ice jams reached a stage of 26 feet at Franklin in February 1971 and 1926. There has not been a great flood with free-flow conditions above the lower reaches of the Allegheny River since that of March 1913, as of 1936.

Kiskiminetas River

The record of floods on the Kiskiminetas River begins in March 1824, but there is very little information for the period before 1884, when observations of river stages were started at Saltsburg by the U.S. Signal Service. The flood of March 18, 1936. which reached a stage of 47.2 feet at Avonmore, exceeded by 13.4 feet the highest previously known height of 33.8 feet which occurred in March 1907. This extreme difference between a maximum stage and a previous maximum is unprecedented in the records for any other stream in Pennsylvania. At the time of the first destructive flood at Johnstown, in June 1889, known as the "Johnstown Flood", the stage at Avonmore was only 29.8 feet. Other floods of unusual height at Avonmore were those of August 1888, February 1891, and March 1908, when .ages of 31.8, 30.4, and 30.8 feet were reached.

Youghiogheny River

Early floods on the Youghiogheny River that were caused by ice gorges are said to have destroyed the highway bridge at Connellsville on February 1816 and again in 1831. In May 1865 the dams of the Youghiogheny Slack Water Company failed. However, there is no detailed information relative to the heights which the river may have attained. The Youghiogheny River has a lower range between its high and low flows than any other major stream in Pennsylvania. During the 24 years prior to March 1912 when the river reached 17.3 feet at Connellsville, the crests were 17.8 feet in August 1888 and 18.4 feet in March 1907. The highest known stage for Connellsville was that of March 18, 1936, when 21.0 feet was recorded. In March 1924 a stage of 20.5 feet was reached, and in April 1860 and February 1897 there were floods that reached 16.5 and 16.7 feet respectively.

Monongahela River

The early mention of floods on the Monongahela River began with that of May 18, 1807, but there is little information concerning the ten known floods previous to May 4, 1873. There is no justification from all that is known to warrant a belief that any of them exceeded or even reached the 43.5 feet recorded on July 11, 1888, at Old Lock No. 4. The second highest known stage at Old Lock No. 4 was 42.5 feet on February 23, 1897, and the next in magnitude was that of March 18, 1936, when 40.1 feet was reached. Other great floods on the Monongahela River were those of January 1877, July 1896, March 1907, and January 1911, when 38.3, 39.5, 38.9, and 38.2 feet respectively were recorded. In January 1907, November 1913, and March 1924 a stage of 38.1 feet was reached.

Ohio River

For the Ohio River the history of floods begins with the occupancy of Fort Duquesne by the French in 1756. Frequent mention of trouble from floods appeared in letters that emanated from that fort and later from Fort Pitt. The flood record for the Ohio River at Pittsburgh covers a period of over 174 years. The highest recorded stage was 46.0 feet on March 18, 1936, which exceeded by 6.1 feet the second highest flood on record, which occurred in March 1763. Other great floods at Pittsburgh were those of January 1762, February 1832, and March 1907, when stages of 39.0, 38.0, and 38.5 feet respectively were recorded. The floods of April 1809, February 1816, and February 1884, reached 36.9, 36.0, and 36.3 feet respectively. Stages ranging from 34 to 35.4 feet have been observed on seven occasions during the long term of record.

C. Flooding Since 1936

There is a tendency to look upon a great flood, as the floods of March 1936, as unprecedented and not likely to occur again. As a matter of fact, great floods at long intervals of time are as much a part of the normal course of events as are smaller ones which occur at more frequent intervals. The floods of 1936 are now history and have been surpassed by the 1972 flood of Hurricane Agnes.

Since 1936 there have been numerous other floods. The storm of July 18, 1942, which unleashed over 30 inches of rainfall in less than 24 hours, caused record flooding on the Sinnemahoning Creek. There were also floods caused by the storm of November 25, 1950.

Other Hurricanes have also pounded at the Commonwealth and left a toll of damages. Hurricane "Hazel" in October 1954 caused record flooding on the Juniata River. The following year Hurricane "Connie" on August 12 and 13, and Hurricane "Diane" on August 17–19 flooded the Lackawanna River and other tributaries in the northeastern Susquehanna River Basin.

Record high flows were caused by the January 22, 1959 storm on some northern and western tributaries of the West Branch of the Susquehanna and the Cowanesque River. March 5 thru 10 also saw flooding in Pennsylvania in 1964. There have also been numerous other storms and ice gorges since 1936. And then there was Agnes in June 1972.

Even since Agnes the streams of the Commonwealth have again been flooded. Less than one year and one week after the wrath of Agnes, Bloomsburg as well as several other communities, was once again assaulted by flood waters and the community was declared a limited disaster area by Governor Shapp. Other Pennsylvania communities have also been ravaged by flood waters since Agnes.

There is, therefore, no historical pattern or cycle of flooding which can be safely relied on for protection from damages.

4. HISTORIC FLOOD DAMAGE IN PENNSYLVANIA

Pennsylvania has an historical record of extensive flood damage. And with population centers increasing and unwise use of the flood plain continuing damages are steadily on the rise, despite massive Federal and State efforts to protect the Commonwealth from the flooding waters of its many streams.

Over the years it has been recorded that approximately $5.3 billion of property damages have been caused by flooding in the Commonwealth. This total includes the $3 billion toll of Agnes.

The most widespread loss of life occurred in 1936. In the Ohio Basin over 100 lives were lost. In the Susquehanna River Basin 20 lives were lost. In 1955 in the Delaware River Basin two hurricanes hit the basin two days apart, and resulted in the loss of 100 lives and damages of over $140 million.

The most serious loss of life occurred in May of 1898 when a dam located above Johnstown failed, causing the loss of more than 2,220 lives and a missing list of over 1,000 residents of the area.

The total losses in 1936 were about $67,000,000 in the Susquehanna River Basin. Urban and industrial losses constituted about 72 per cent of the total losses, utility losses about 5 percent, rural losses about 4 percent, public losses about 16 percent, and railroad losses about 3 percent. Large portions of Carbondale, Olyphant, Wilkes Barre, Kingston, Plymouth, Williamsport, Lewistown, Sunbury, Harrisburg, Steelton, and many smaller communities were inundated. More than 70 per cent of some of the areas of these towns were flooded. In the principal damage centers the total number of buildings which incurred damages to structure and content exceeded

31,000 residential buildings, 4,000 commercial buildings and buildings of 400 manufactories. In addition, many public buildings, schools, churches, and other institutions were damaged. Anthracite mines in the vicinity of Wilkes-Barre and Scranton were flooded, and unwatering required several weeks. Electric, gas, telephone, telegraph, and water systems at many communities were put out of commission by the flood and their services were curtailed during the rehabilitation period. Transportation routes and bridges were seriously crippled by inundation and wash-outs, and some communities were complete[ly] isolated.

Estimates for the June 1972 Agnes Disaster range anywhere from $2.5 to 6 billion, with the average figure of $3 billion plus most often used. In the Commonwealth, 49 persons lost their lives, and this total is low due to the outstanding rescue efforts by citizens and the National Guard.

Agnes forced 100,000 persons in 50 towns to flee their homes in the wake of rising waters. 23,305 went into temporary HUD housing, and today 6,000–7,000 still remain in HUD trailers in the Wyoming Valley alone with the possibility that these might be in use for several more years. 30,000 homes were destroyed or suffered some form of water damage. 3,500 commercial buildings were devastated, and 44 public schools, 12 libraries, 2 hospitals. 50 churches and synagogues, 3 colleges, 10 bridges, hundreds of miles of roads, and thousands of miles of telephone and electric cable were damaged.

In the Wyoming Valley, which took the brunt of the Agnes waters, 150 factories were inundated resulting in the temporary loss of employment for 11,335 workers. In Kingston only 28 of the seven thousand homes and buildings did not sustain any water damage.

The Federal Government has appropriated $1.5 billion for flood recovery efforts. One third of this amount is in the form of Small Business Association Loans (SBA) and will be repayed back to the government with interest. The Commonwealth of Pennsylvania has appropriated $290 million for flood relief. This is the largest amount of money ever made available by any state for relief after a natural disaster.

5. FLOOD CONTROL AND PROTECTION IN PENNSYLVANIA

Responsibility for flood control and protection measures in Pennsylvania is in the hands of a number of local, State, and Federal agencies.

State responsibility for flood works lies with the Department of Environmental Resources.

The United States Army Corps of Engineers is responsible for the most extensive flood control work in the Commonwealth.

Table FP-5. Historic Flood Damage in Pennsylvania

	Past Structures Damaged by Flooding											
Basin	Residential Dwelling (in 1,000)	Percent by Basin	Commercial (in 1,000)	Percent by Basin	Industrial (in 1,000)	Percent in Basin	Totals	Total Percent by Basin	Number of Communities Effected	Percent by River Basin	Past Flood Damage (in Millions of dollars)	Percent of Damage by Basin
Ohio	73	72%	17	81%	.6	46%	90.6	73%	290	44%	1,132	50%
Susquehanna	22	22%	3	14%	.4	31%	25.4	20%	200	30%	890	40%
Delaware	7	6%	1	.5%	.3	23%	8.3	7%	170	26%	231	10%
St. Lawrence	Small	—	Small	—	Small	—	—	—	2	Less than 1 %	2	Less than 1%
Potomac	Small	—	Small	—	Small	—	—	—	1	Less than 1%	Small	Small
Totals	102	100%	21	100%	1.3	100%	124.3	100%	663	100%	2,255	100%

Source: Department of Environmental Resources

The Soil Conservation Service, under the United States Department of Agriculture, is also concerned with the problems of flooding in Pennsylvania. The Soil Conservation Service takes over where the U.S. Army Corps of Engineers leaves off and aids in the protection of the local watershed with flood control and land conservation practices. The Soil Conservation Service projects are not as extensive or costly as those carried out by the Army Corps.

Bridging the gap between State and Federal agencies are the three River Basin Commissions located in Pennsylvania. These commissions are made up of the different signatory state members of the river basins, plus Federal representatives. The commissions serving Pennsylvania are the Susquehanna River Basin Commission, the Delaware River Basin Commission, and the Ohio River Basin Commission. These Commissions are concerned with the total picture of water resource management in the basin.

Serving all State and Federal agencies is the United States Geological Survey which makes historic and hydrological information available for flood plain delineation studies. The Geological Survey is currently doing a number of flood plain studies of Pennsylvania communities.

A. Current Pennsylvania Law with Regard to Flood Prevention

There are over 200 statutes on the record in Pennsylvania with sections pertaining to flood prevention, control, and management which give the State governmental agencies, and local communities many flood management powers. Government is clearly given the power of eminent domain in the placement of flood control measures and is given the power to finance these projects. Legislation gives specific powers and duties to the Department of Environmental Resources, its subdivisions, and other agencies. Legislation also creates multistate river basin commissions to effectively develop the potential of the river basins.

B. Flood Control by the Commonwealth

Flood control was not initiated in the State until after the flooding in 1942. It was after these floods that the first control projects and channel improvements were started. The Water and Power Resources Board of the Department of Forest and Waters first constructed these flood control measures. Late in the 1940's as demand for flood control works increased, the Division of Flood Control was created to meet the demand for these projects. After another disastrous flood at Stroudsburg in 1955 the State became a prime mover in flood control and protection, and since that time Pennsylvania has been a leader among the states in developing a comprehensive network of flood control and protection measures.

Today the Department's flood control work is under the Office of Resources Management. Most of its work entails stream clearance and channel improvements. Emergency work and alleviation of temporary or new problems is also done. On a larger scale the Office is usually involved in 4–6 major engineering projects a year. These projects include flood control work, flood protection, upstream measures, and detention projects. The 1973–1974 fiscal year budget calls for the expenditure of $2,300,000. The budget varies from year to year with anywhere from $2-5 million being spent annually.

The Department's awareness of a flood situation generally manifests itself in one of two ways: (1) by request from local government officials or citizen groups, and (2) by first hand observation by Department personnel during major floods.

Flood problems generally fall into two categories: (1) those which require extensive protective works and permanent structures, and (2) those where relief can be extended by removal of channel blockages through their stream improvement program. Such work is performed with rented equipment and local hired labor.

The second program is the Comprehensive Local Flood Protection Program. If extensive protection works are required to provide flood protection, a comprehensive engineering study is recommended. This study includes damage studies, hydrologic characteristics and flood history, topographic mapping, preliminary project design, economic justification, environmental impact, and planning report. To be economically justified a project must prevent more damages than the project costs.

After the planning report is submitted to the local government, engineers from the Department meet with local officials to explain the proposed project in detail, and to discuss the items of local participation and responsibility. It is the community's responsibility to choose from several alternatives proposed by the Department and pass a resolution of sponsorship. In choosing the best suited flood protection solution, financing and local citizen desires are taken into account.

The Department has the authority to finance up to 50 per cent of land acquisition and certain other costs which are usually the responsibility of the local government. In addition, the State assists local governments in costs associated with Public Law 566 Flood Control Program of the U.S. Soil Conservation Service.

Approximately 75 major projects, consisting of local protection facilities and/or dams, have been constructed by the Commonwealth of Pennsylvania, at a total cost of over $48 million.

C. Water Resources Development in Pennsylvania by the U.S. Army Corps of Engineers

The United States Army Corps of Engineers has done quite extensive water resources development in the Commonwealth of Pennsylvania.

Table FP.6. Flood Control Expenditures By The Commonwealth of Pennsylvania (1959–1968)

1959	$ 834,658.34
1960	7,418,278.72
1961	8,147,564.51
1962	7,807,090.67
1963	10,817,060.67
1964	12,826,117.08
1965	7,173,544.40
1966	9,243,659.04
1967	8,750,130.36
1968	7,848,717.31
TOTAL	$ 80,866,821.10*

*Total expenditures for flood control by the Commonwealth 1959–1968. These expenditures were incurred when there was a Flood Control Division within the Department of Forest and Waters. This Division was eliminated in 1968.

Through their three Divisional Offices in Philadelphia, Baltimore, and Pittsburgh that are responsible for the water resource development in the Delaware, Susquehanna, and Ohio River Basins respectively, the Army Corps has spent over one billion dollars in Pennsylvania.

The Army Corps comes to the assistance of local governments in aiding them in flood protection and control works. Local sponsorship is required and initial and/or matching funds are necessary in some cases, although many of the projects are totally Federal funded.

Army Corps work ranges from navigation projects to flood control, snagging, and clearing projects. Many projects are multi-purpose and include recreation features.

Table FP.7. Expenditures for Flood Control Projects By The Commonwealth of Pennsylvania (1969–1972)

1969	$ 364,691.21
1970	467,568.33
1971	354,163.28
1972	841,033.90
TOTAL	$ 2,027,456.72*
TOTAL 1959–1972	80,866,821.10
	$ 82,894,277.82

*Total expenditures representing only project costs within the Department of Environmental Resources for flood control, not representing administrative costs.

D. Soil Conservation Service

Multiple-purpose watershed projects, under Public Law 566, are administered by the Soil Conservation Service of the U.S. Department of Agriculture. Experience in hundreds of localities demonstrates that these multiple-purpose projects are an effective means for rural and urban communities to deal with land use and water problems.

Since 1954, when the Watershed Protection and Flood Prevention Act (Public Law 566) was enacted, many communities have shown that they can halt unchecked erosion and excessive water runoff, stop destructive floods, improve drainage conditions on land in agricultural production, provide for more effective irrigation, supply water for municipal needs, enhance fish and wildlife resources, and provide developments for recreation.

Small watershed projects protect, manage, improve and develop water and related land resources in watersheds up to 250,000 acres in size through a project-type undertaking.

A project is planned and carried out jointly by local, State, and Federal agencies with the full understanding and support of a large majority of the landowners and citizens of the community. Projects are based on: (1) local initiative and responsibility, (2) Federal technical, cost-sharing, and credit assistance, and (3) State review and approval of local proposals and opportunity for State review and approval of local proposals and opportunity for State financial and other assistance.

Multiple-purpose watershed projects include land treatment and structural measures such as dams, levees, and channels.

Multiple-purpose watershed projects bridge the resource-development gap between the soil and water conservation work of individual landowners and large federal and State projects for water resources development in the major river basins.

6. FLOOD PLAIN MANAGEMENT[8]

A large percentage of the Commonwealth's population and tangible property is concentrated in flood-prone areas. Public policy should seek to foster efficient use of the bottom lands for the common good but it will fail in this so long as it is out of harmony with certain principles. These principles relate to the unalterable characteristics of geographical location and hydrologic events, conditions of economic efficiency, and the recognition of individual, as well as social, responsibility in managing flood plains.

---

8. The source of much of the material in this section is taken from "A Unified National Program For Managing, Flood Losses," the Task Force on Federal Flood Control Policy, 89th Congress, 2nd Session, House Document No. 465. (U.S. Government Printing Office, Washington, D.C., 1966).

A stream-bed and the flood plain lands immediately adjacent to it are integral parts of every natural watercourse. Overbank flows are not abnormal. The flood plain acts as a natural reservoir and temporary channel for the excess water. In the economy of nature, the channel efficiently conveys the day-to-day flow and calls upon its flood plain when needed. Typically, a river uses some portion of its flood plain about once in 2 to 3 years. At average intervals of, say, 25, 50, or 100 years, the river may inundate its entire flood plain to a considerable depth. Although records of floods permit estimation of frequency of flooding, it is not possible to forecast the year a flood will occur on any given watercourse. Flood records suggest that the frequency of natural overbank flows in the United States has not changed significantly in the years since flood losses became so large as to justify a Federal effort to control them.

Man-made development may so encroach upon a natural watercourse as to retard its capacity to pass flood flows. Silt deposits in the stream channel may have a similar effect. Flood heights are raised, velocities are increased, and additional areas are subject to damage. Unless encroachment lines are enforced by public agencies or such encroachments are made clearly uneconomical to the individual developer, these constrictions will continue.

The configuration of a flood plain has a bearing on the economic and engineering feasibility of flood protection works. The layout of many areas render it impossible to provide adequate flood protection through physical works such as dams, levees, channel improvements, and upstream land-treatment measures.

Even a perfectly designed engineering project on stream-bank or shore line may be subject to damage from a flood exceeding the expected maximum.

For these reasons, so long as flood plains are occupied, the Commonwealth will be faced with the problems of flood damages.

Use of flood plains involving periodic damage from floods is not, in itself, a sign of unwarranted or inefficient development. It may well be that the advantages of flood plain location outweigh the intermittent cost of damage from floods. Further, there are some kinds of activity which can only be continued near a watercourse.

Principles of national economic efficiency require, however, that the benefit of flood plain occupants exceed all associated costs, not merely those borne by the individual or enterprise which so locates. Total associated, or full social costs include: (1) immediate expenses of development, (2) damages to be endured by the occupant or the expense of protective measures undertaken to reduce the frequency and extent of flood damage, and (3) damages. forced on others as a result of encroachment, and public costs involved in disaster relief and rehabilitation.

Flood plain occupation in which benefits do not exceed the estimated total costs, or which yields lower returns than other uses such as recreation and wildlife conservation, is undesirable, because it causes an eventual net loss to society. Any public policy which encourages submarginal development adds to those losses.

Flood damages are a direct consequence of flood plain investment actions, both private and public. Floods are an act of God; flood damages result from the acts of man. Those who occupy the flood plain should be responsible for the results of their actions.

To the degree that State and local governments sanction unfettered flood plain development, including new construction of public facilities, they share responsibility for excessive flood damages. In this regard, State activity unintentionally nurtures apathy with respect to the most economic solutions for avoiding or abating flood damages. It can not be overemphasized that the mere supply of information as to where the water has reached and when, does not necessarily lead decision makers to avoid the flood threat. In the absence of clear and present danger, the typical citizen is not easily persuaded to protect himself from the flood hazard.

In its concern for the general welfare, the Commonwealth has a proper interest in measures to hold damages to an economic minimum. It has a responsibility to discourage flood plain development which would impose a later burden on the Pennsylvania taxpayer, which would benefit some only at the expense of others, and which would victimize unsuspecting citizens. It does not follow, however, that the state government should be held solely responsible for success of a program to make wise use of flood plains.

Attempts to resolve the problem of rising flood losses within the framework of the state's traditional value system should focus on promotions, sound investment decisions by individuals, local governments, and the State. They should concentrate on bringing the moral, legal, and fiscal responsibilities of all parties involved into effective alignment.

To coordinate the use and development of the flood plain while furthering meaningful flood damage prevention requires effective participation of the Federal, State, and local governments in programs directed to these concerns. Each level of government must see its respective responsibilities as part of a total effort. Continuing community planning now is recognized as an imperative for rational land use and development. Flood plain planning and appropriate consideration of water resources should be regarded as an integral part of that process and reflected in the resulting community action.

Policies now governing the Commonwealth flood control program fail to achieve the necessary integration and equitable apportionment of responsibilities. Principal shortcomings are: (1) there is inadequate recognition of the nature of the flood threat and the limitations of engineering works; (2) a river control approach is championed to the virtual exclusion of other applicable means such as flood proofing and land regulation; and (3) individual beneficiaries from engineering protection works do not, in many instances, bear an adequate share of the costs.

This latter factor, combined with the bias in favor of river control alternatives, has relieved many individual flood plain occupants of responsibility, in a fiscal sense, for the consequences of their actions. Under existing policies flood plain property owners in unprotected areas may bear only a portion of the cost, their price being exacted when damage occurs. Some shoulder the full losses; others rely on public relief and assistance in rehabilitation. No matter how serious their encroachment on the watercourse, the occupants bear few of the costs resulting from encroachment. They bear a minor fraction, through payment of general taxes, of the public cost of relief and rehabilitation. The general public, by bearing all or a major part of the cost of flood protection works and lessening the individuals' damage costs, further subsidizes their use of the flood plain. Principles of economic efficiency and social equity thereby are violated.

7. FLOOD PLAIN ZONING IN PENNSYLVANIA

A. Flood Plain Zoning Law in Pennsylvania

Presently, Pennsylvania counties, cities, boroughs, townships, and towns are authorized, but not required, to do flood plain zoning. See the Pennsylvania Municipalities Planning Code, Section 603-605, 53 P. S., Sec. 10000 et seq.

Pennsylvania Municipalities Planning Code
Act 247 As Amended By Act 93/1972
(53 P. S. Sec. 10000 et seq.)

ARTICLE VI
Zoning

Section 601. General Powers.—The governing body of each municipality, in accordance with the conditions and procedures set forth in this act, may enact, amend and repeal zoning ordinances to implement comprehensive plans and to accomplish any of the purposes of this act.

Section 602. County Powers.—The powers of the governing bodies of counties to enact, amend and repeal zoning ordinances shall be limited to land in those cities, boroughs, incorporated towns. and townships, wholly or partly within the county, which have no zoning ordinance in effect at the time a zoning ordinance is introduced before the governing body of the county and until the city, borough, incorporated town or township zoning ordinance is in effect. The enactment of a zoning ordinance by any municipality, other than the county, whose land is subject to county zoning shall act as a repeal protanto of the county zoning ordinance within the municipality adopting such ordinance.

Section 603. Ordinance Provisions.—Zoning ordinances may permit, prohibit, regulate. restrict and determine:

1. Uses of land, watercourses and other bodies of water;
2. Size, height, bulk, location, erection, construction, repair, maintenance, alteration, razing, removal and use of structures;
3. Areas and dimensions of land and bodies of water to be occupied by uses and structures, as well as areas, courts, yards, and other open spaces and distances to be left unoccupied by uses and structures;
4. Density of population and intensity of use.

In addition, zoning ordinances may contain:

1. Provisions for special exceptions and variances administered by the zoning hearing board, which provisions shall be in accordance with this act;
2. Provisions for conditional uses to be allowed or denied by the governing body after recommendations by the planning agency, pursuant to express standards and criteria set forth in the ordinances;
3. Provisions for the administration and enforcement of such ordinances; and
4. Such other provisions as may be necessary to implement the purposes of this act.

Section 604. Zoning Purposes.—The provisions of zoning ordinances shall be designed:

1. To promote, protect and facilitate one or more of the following: the public health, safety, morals, general welfare, coordinated and practical community development, proper density of population, civil defense, disaster evacuation, airports, and national defense facilities, the provisions of adequate light and air, police protection, vehicle parking and loading space, transportation, water, sewerage, schools, public grounds and other public requirements, as well as
2. To prevent one or more of the following: overcrowding of land, blight, danger and congestion in travel and transportation, loss of health, life or property from fire, flood, panic or other dangers. Zoning ordinances shall be made in accordance with an overall program, and with consideration for the character of the municipality, its various parts and the suitability of the various parts for particular uses and structures.

There are also other statutes that regulate, or mention the regulation of the flood plain such as the River Basin Compacts, and several different statutes which provide for the preservation of Pennsylvania's forests, waters and State parks. One additional Pennsylvania statute that regulates the development and construction in the area of the flood plain, or watercourse is known as the "Pennsylvania Channel Encroachment Law" and deals mainly with obstructions in the waterway.

B. Present Flood Plain Zoning in Pennsylvania

Early efforts in the Commonwealth to encourage local communities to adopt flood plain zoning ordinances came from the U.S. Soil Conservation Service. The Soil Conservation Service activity in this area though lacked guidance and the proper technology and as a result produced some haphazard flood plain zoning ordinances on the local government level. Montgomery County and Berks County in particular have numerous flood plain zoning ordinances on the books from this period. There are also several other counties in the State that have adopted ordinances. These early ordinances have resulted in three court tests in Pennsylvania of the government's ability to regulate land use on the flood plain.

Since the early efforts of the U.S. Soil Conservation Service, there was no state-wide campaign to encourage the adoption of flood plain land use regulations until 1970 when National Flood Insurance became available to all citizens of the Commonwealth who live in communities which have acceptable flood plain zoning ordinances in use. Since then the Division of Community Planning, of the Pennsylvania Department of Community Affairs, has been responsible in assisting and encouraging local governments in the adoption of flood plain zoning ordinances in compliance with guidelines of the National Flood Insurance Act of 1968.

The National Flood Insurance Act of 1968 states in section 1315 that, "no new flood insurance coverage shall be provided under this title in any area (or subdivision thereof) unless an appropriate public body shall have adapted adequate land use and control measures (with effective enforcement provisions) which the Secretary of (HUD) finds are consistent with the comprehensive criteria for land management and use under Section 1316." Section 1316 states that "No new flood insurance coverage shall be provided under this title for any property which the Secretary finds has been declared by a duly constituted state or local zoning authority, or other authorized public body, to be in violation of state or local laws, regulations, or ordinances which are intended to discourage or otherwise restrict land development or occupancy in flood-prone areas." The U.S. Department of Housing and Urban Development is responsible for the administration of this program and has granted several grace periods to local communities in meeting compliance with land use regulations. Currently communities are deemed eligible if they adopt two resolutions, one expressing a desire for flood insurance coverage, and a second expressing an intent to adopt land use regulations on the flood plain. Flood insurance policies are then made available and thousands have already been sold to citizens living in eligible Commonwealth communities. It is after a community has been deemed eligible that Community Affairs assumes its role as consultant to the local government and aids them in developing the required land use regulations.

The Division of Community Planning began in 1970 to assist local governments in their efforts to comply with the National Flood Insurance Act of 1968. The efforts of Community Planning have been financed mainly with Federal 701 funds, which are granted for local community development. Using these funds and several staff members of Community Planning a "shoestring" operation was begun to get the 663 Pennsylvania flood-prone communities on the eligibility roles for flood insurance and to see these communities adopt flood plain zoning. Although a "shoestring" operation it was and is quite an effective and efficient operation with 420 communities meeting the eligibility requirements as of July 1973. Several communities to date have completed the process and have fully enacted flood plain zoning ordinances. In November of 1972, Milton, Pennsylvania, which suffered severe losses in 1972 when Hurricane Agnes struck the Susquehanna Valley, was the first local government to fully comply with the enactment of its ordinances.

The first step in drawing up flood plain zoning ordinances requires the delineation of the flood plain. Flood plain studies are quite expensive and present a financial burden to the local communities. Mapping costs run about $2,500 to $3,000 a linear mile. These studies are done by private or Federal engineers and are the basis of all future land use regulations. No State agency does mapping. The U.S. Army Corps of Engineers and the U.S. Geological Survey do some flood plain delineation studies. On June 21, 1973 the U.S. Department of Housing and Urban Development announced the spending of $933,272 for mapping the communities along the Susquehanna River. The project, financed by HUD's Federal Insurance Administration, is being carried out by the Susquehanna River Basin Commission. This project affects some 90 communities and will take about 18 months to complete.

After the study is complete Community Planning assists the local community in drawing up their ordinances. Community Planning has four model ordinances for the local government leaders to use as a guide in drawing up their own flood plain zoning regulations.

The process of adoption requires that all ordinances be submitted to public inspection and approval, and also meet the standards set by Community Planning as required by the National Flood Insurance Act.

The efforts by Community Planning have come as a result of the National Flood Insurance, which serves as a greatly needed inducement to encourage the regulation of land use in flood-prone areas. But something more than just an inducement is needed if the damages of future floods are to be brought within tolerable bounds. Under the present State zoning law the Commonwealth lacks the power, the responsibility, and the enforcement capability to insure the wise development of Pennsylvania's flood-prone areas in accordance with the laws of nature.

The Courts: The Present Status of Flood Plain Zoning in Pennsylvania. Flood plain zoning ordinances and flood plain legislation are new statutes on the record in most states. Accordingly, the number of court decisions on the legality of flood plain zoning are few. In Pennsylvania there have been three court decisions regarding the regulation of flood plain land use.

Essentially, flood plain regulation is based on the state's police powers and the state's responsibility to promote the "General Welfare."

The separation of incompatible land uses and the orderly development of the community are the usual purposes of zoning, and flood plain zoning is no exception. The primary objective of flood plain zoning is to separate land uses from land that is incompatible with those particular uses. This in itself, however, is probably not enough to withstand constitutional attack, since the scope of the police power does not include the prevention of unwise decisions by individuals. However, the disallocations and disruptions that the community suffers as a result of this basic incompatibility of the land and the use to which it is put does provide justification for application of the police power.[9]

Invocation of flood plain zoning is warranted to prevent or reduce the following social problems: (1) excessive governmental expenditures on flood control projects and relief; (2) victimization of persons who do not have adequate knowledge of the flood plain; (3) damage to land not on the flood plain caused by use of the flood plain; (4) crippling disruptions of the local economy; (5) the onset of urban blight; and (6) health problems and loss of life."[10]

The use of the police powers to regulate the development and use of the flood plain generally invokes several constitutional questions. The constitutional problems involved are: (a) substantive due process; (b) equal protection of the law; (c) conflict between the state and Federal laws under the supremacy clause of the United States Constitution; and (d) taking without compensation.

Pennsylvania's three decisions come from the flood plain zoning ordinances adopted by municipalities some years back under the guidance of the U.S. Soil Conservation Service.

---

9. Clifford L. Bertholf, "Ecological and Legal Aspects of Flood Plain Zoning," *Kansas Law Review*, Volume 20 (1972), pp. 268–82.
10. Ibid, 268–82.

The first two decisions deal with the zoning ordinances of Whitemarsh Township in Montgomery County, Pennsylvania.

The first decision, *Hofkin et. al. v. Whitemarsh Twp.*, 88 Montg. Co. L.R. 63, (1967) went against the township supervisors attempts at flood plain regulation. The court declared the ordinance invalid as a confiscatory taking without compensation.

In this case the plaintiff was prevented from building three six-story apartment houses on 17.8 acres of land zoned as part of the flood plain. The court found that there was no threat to life or property which could not be eliminated by piping the small stream in question to a culvert. In the court's view, the statute was so broad as to prevent any use of the land without providing significant protection to the public health, safety and welfare.

In *Solomen et. ux. v. Whitemarsh Twp.*, 92 Montg. Co. L.R. 69, (1969), the plaintiff had purchased some land in a flood plain zoned area adjacent an industrial park. The plaintiff wanted to change the course of the stream, drain a marsh, and rezone the flood plain to industrial use. The plaintiff was denied a change in zoning because it would constitute an exception to the law. Also it was not proven that the changes to the stream bed would reduce the flooding dangers, and in fact the flood dangers would probably be increased.

Plaintiffs, as in Hofkin, contended the ordinance served to take their property without just compensation by restricting the dispositions of its use.

This time the court upheld the validity of the ordinances, and in doing so, drew four differences from the Hofkin case: (1) In Solomon, the court noted the ordinance invalidiated in Hofkin had been amended so as to provide an avenue of appeal to the zoning board from a decision of the zoning officer; (2) plaintiffs in Solomon had acquired the land after the enactment of the ordinance and hence knew of the hardship they were acquiring; (3) unlike Hofkin, no man-made factor is singularly responsible for the flood danger, and (4) the uses of the land available to the plaintiffs, unlike Hofkin, were not "utterly impractical and completely profitless."

The third Pennsylvania case, *Gaebel v. Thornbury Twp.*, Delaware Co. 8, Pa. Commonwealth 379, was decided on April 6, 1973. The ruling came as an appeal by landowners from an order of the Common Pleas Court, which sustained preliminary objections filed by the township to a petition for appointment of viewers and an order appointing a board of viewers to ascertain and award just compensation under the Eminent Domain Law. The land in question was governed by a flood plain zoning ordinance which plaintiffs believed to be confiscatory and a "taking." The court held that after owners' land, which had been zoned commercial, was rezoned as flood plain (which limited the use of land to such activities as cultivating and harvesting crops, and grazing animals) owners' exclusive recourse was to challenge the constitutionality of the zoning ordinance under provisions of review established by the Municipalities Planning Code, and they could not avail themselves of compensation under provisions of Eminent Domain Code. The appeal was affirmed.[11]

8. QUESTIONS AND ANSWERS REGARDING SENATE BILL 1122, THE "PENNSYLVANIA FLOOD DISASTER PREVENTION ACT"

1. What is the purpose and policy of the "Pennsylvania Flood Prevention Act"?

Recurrent flooding causes great economic losses and human suffering, which vast public expenditures for flood control and relief have failed to control adequately. (In the past 15 years the federal and state governments spent $1.08 billion for flood control in Pennsylvania. Yet Hurricane Agnes caused $3 billion in property damage alone.) Unregulated development in the flood-prone areas reduces and interferes with the carrying capacity of a stream thereby causing more flood damages.

The purpose of this act is to regulate development in flood-prone areas by limiting new construction to structures which are flood proof and which will not contribute to more damage in the next flood. To accomplish this, the act establishes management by local governmental bodies under standards established by the state.

2. What is the State's role in the administration of this act? What is the local community's role?

The Pennsylvania Environmental Quality Board shall set the standards and regulations for the State's flood plain management program. The Department of Environmental Resources shall enforce these regulations, coordinating and supervising statewide efforts to regulate the development of the land in the flood plain. The major responsibility lies, however, with the local municipalities which will be responsible for drafting their own flood plain zoning ordinances and laws. The responsibility for drafting, adopting and enforcing the flood plain zoning ordinances rests with the municipalities subject to compliance with state standards.

3. Will the act regulate existing housing of the flood plain?

Existing housing will not be regulated by the act as long as there is no extensive modification that would impair the stream's flood carrying capacity,

---

11. *Gaebel v. Thornbury Township*, Delaware County, Pa., Pa. Commonwealth, 303 A. 2d. 57.

or as long as the building is not removed. The main thrust of the act is to regulate future development so that it is flood proof and will not contribute to future flood damage. This will be done under a system of permits. To build in a flood plain will require a permit.

4. Will the act regulate farm ponds?

No, farm ponds and other privately owned bodies of water of five acres or less are specifically excluded from the Act. (Sec. 104(2) (d)).

5. Will local communities be assisted financially in the administration of this act?

No, but the Act does authorize state assistance in providing information and technical help to municipalities.

6. What powers of enforcement are included in this act?

If a municipality fails to adopt an adequate flood plain zoning ordinance, the county will be authorized to act for the municipality. As a last resort, the Department of Environmental Resources can adopt a plan. See Sec. 202 (C).

Individuals violating the approved flood plain zoning ordinance or the act are subject to criminal (Sec. 406) and civil penalties (Sec. 404).

7. Does the Commonwealth have the right of eminent domain ender this act?

No. The Commonwealth can only purchase land from funds specifically appropriated by the legislature for that purpose.

8. What about the bill's provisions for inspection warrants?

The bill allows employees of the Department or the municipalities to inspect land (not buildings) in flood areas to make surveys and to locate possible obstructions in the watercourse on flood-prone area. The only entry authorized for buildings is for those buildings under construction and then the entry can only be to determine compliance with flood proofing requirements. (Sec. 303).

9. Will the act bring coordination to the Commonwealth's flood management program?

Yes. The act calls for local government to adopt flood plain zoning ordinances and calls for the Department to insure uniformity among the different communities. It also gives the Department the authority to coordinate all flood management programs with the federal government, interstate agencies, and to accept federal monies and spend them appropriately.

10. Will the "Pennsylvania Flood Disaster Prevention Act" reduce the limit and scope of future flooding disasters in the Commonwealth?

Yes. By insuring that only those structures which are flood proof and which will not obstruct the free "run off" of flood water are built on flood plains, the act will reduce future flood damage to property and lives.

9. SUMMARY OF SENATE BILL 1122: PENNSYLVANIA FLOOD DISASTER PREVENTION ACT

Senate Bill 1122, the "Pennsylvania Flood Disaster Prevention Act" was introduced in the hope that government does not need one more crisis to act, and in the recognition that steps must now be taken to limit the scope of future flooding disasters.

The following is a summary of the "Pennsylvania Flood Disaster Prevention Act" as introduced in the Senate of Pennsylvania.

Article I. The General Assembly finds that recurrent flooding causes economic losses and human suffering, and vast public expenditures for flood control and relief measures are costly and that these flood control measures have failed to adequately reduce public and private losses.

The General Assembly finds that development in the floodway reduces and interferes with the carrying capacity of a stream, causing more damages upstream and down. The General Assembly also finds that a comprehensive program of flood and area management, including the reasonable regulation and prohibition of new construction, is fundamental to the public health, safety, and welfare and the protection of the people of the Commonwealth, their resources and the environment.

In accordance with these findings, the purpose of this act is to encourage planning and development in flood-prone areas which is consistent with sound water and land use practices. It is further the policy and purpose of this act to authorize a comprehensive program of flood area management, encouraging local administration and management of flood areas consistent with state supervision.

Article II. The Environmental Quality Board shall have the power and its duty shall be to adopt regulations to insure comprehensive flood area management in the Commonwealth and to establish minimum standard for delineation and management of flood-prone areas.

The power to coordinate and supervise the management of flood-prone areas shall be vested in the Department of Environmental Resources.

The major responsibility shall lie, however, with the local municipality, whose responsibility it shall be to administer flood area management in conformity with the regulations of the Environmental Quality Board and the provisions of this act and subject to the approval of the Department of Environmental Resources.

Each municipality shall submit to the Department an official plan for the flood area management within the territorial jurisdiction of the municipality. This plan shall include the results of engineering studies, historic data, proposed implementation plans, and procedures for revision and updating. After the plan is officially approved each municipality shall administer the management of their flood areas.

If a municipality fails to administer the provisions of this act or of an official plan the Department may require the county in which such municipality is located to act as an agent of the municipality, or as a last resort, the Department can assume administration of the flood area management program.

On or after July 1, 1974 no person shall construct, modify, remove, abandon or destroy an obstruction in a flood area unless such person has first applied for and obtained a permit from the Department or municipality which has an approved flood area plan.

No person shall construct, maintain, or operate an obstruction authorized pursuant to a flood area permit except in accordance with the term and conditions applicable hereto.

The Department shall temporarily or permanently issue flood area permits.

Each flood area permit application shall be published, at the applicants' expense, in such periodicals and manner as the Board shall determine.

Permits shall be filed in the Office of the Recorder of Deeds for the county in which the subject property or obstruction is located.

A municipality or the Department may modify, suspend or revoke a permit, or refuse to renew or may withhold the issuance of a permit where the permittee or applicant is engaging or has engaged in any unlawful conduct as defined in this act.

The Board may, by rule or regulation, designate certain classes or categories of obstructions for which flood area permits requirements may be waived; provided that such waiver shall in no way affect the rights of the Commonwealth.

The Department shall acquire in the name of the Commonwealth, by purchase, gift, or lease, such lands or other property as are determined by the Environmental Quality Board to be necessary to and consistent with implementation of the purposes of this act.

The Board may, by regulation, require the posting of a sufficient performance bond or other security as a condition upon the issuance of any category or categories of flood area permits issued by a municipality or the Department.

Article III. In addition to the powers and duties established in other sections, the Department and every municipality shall have the power and duty to investigate complaints, institute and conduct survey programs to identify and define flood areas, conduct and supervise educational programs with respect to flood hazards, and institute legal proceedings under this act.

An agent or employee of the Department or a municipality shall have the power and duty to enter any land or building in flood areas for the purpose of surveying land, noting obstructions in the waterway or floodway, and to ascertain the compliance or noncompliance with the flood proofing regulations adopted by the Board. If entry is denied, they have the power and the duty to apply for an inspection warrant from the appropriate Commonwealth official.

The Department shall cooperate with appropriate agencies of the United States or of other states or any interstate agencies with respect to flood management. The Department shall receive Federal monies and be responsible for the expenditure of them. The Department shall also provide advisory consultation services to the county and municipal agencies.

All civil penalties collected under this act shall be paid into the Treasury of the Commonwealth in a special fund known as the "Flood Area Disaster and Relief Fund." Such monies collected shall be expended to aid the Department in achieving the purposes of this act.

Article IV. It is the duty of the Department and the municipalities to restrain or prevent any activity or condition declared by this act or official plan as unlawful conduct, and shall issue such orders as necessary for the enforcement of this act.

Civil penalties of an amount not less than $100 nor greater than $10,000 per violation plus $500 for each continuing day of violation shall be assessed any person who fails to respond to an order of the proper hearing board. Any respondent who fails to pay the above fine shall have a lien entered by the prothonotary on said property.

Anyone aggrieved by such decision shall have the right to a hearing before the proper municipality hearing board within 30 days. An appeal before the Environmental Hearing Board must be taken within 30 days after the final decision of the municipality.

Any person engaging in unlawful conduct as defined in this act is guilty of a summary offense and shall be subject to a fine of not less than $100 and not more than $1,000 for each offense, and in default of payment of such fine, such person shall be imprisoned in the county jail for a period of not more than sixty days.

Any person found guilty of a second summary proceeding within two years for unlawful conduct as defined in this act shall be subject to a fine of not less than $500 and not have more than $5,000 for each offense or imprisonment in the county jail for a period of not more than one year.

Article V. One million dollars is hereby appropriated to carry out the purposes of this act.

This act shall take effect immediately.

10. SOURCES OF INFORMATION USED IN PREPARING THIS REPORT

1. Bibliography

Adams, Franklin S. "Hurricane Agnes: Flooding vs. Dams in Penna." Bulletin of the Atomic Scientists, April 1973, p. 30 et seq.

Dunham, Allison, "Flood Control Via the Police Power," University of Pennsylvania Law Review, (vol. 107, 1959), p. 1098-32.

Hess, Clarke F., "The Present Status, of Flood Plain Zoning in Pennsylvania," Pennsylvania Bar Association Quarterly, (vol. SL, No. 4, June 1969), p. 578-83.

Kansas Law Review, "Ecological and Legal Aspects of Flood Plain Zoning," (vol. 20, 1973), p. 268-82.

Minnesota Law Review, "Minnesota's Flood Plain Management Act, State Guidance of Land Use Controls," (vol. 55, No. 4), March 1971, p. 1163-200.

Pennsylvania Department of Environmental Resources, Flood Control Manual, October 1971.

Pennsylvania Department of Environmental Resources, Programs and Planning For The Management of the Water Resources of Pennsylvania, November 1971.

Pennsylvania Department of Forest and Waters, The Floods of March 1936 In Pennsylvania, 1936, p. 113-29.

Susquehanna River Basin Commission, "Proposed Comprehensive Plan For Management and Development of the Water Resources of the Susquehanna River Basin, Mechanicsburg, Pennsylvania," June 5, 1973.

The Task Force on Federal Flood Control Policy, "A Unified National Program for Managing Flood Losses," 89th Congress, House Document No. 465, U.S. Government Printing Office, 1966.

U.S. Army Corps of Engineers, The Susquehanna River Basin, Baltimore.

U.S. Army Corps of Engineers, Water Resources Development in Pennsylvania, January 1971.

U.S. Department of Agriculture Soil Conservation Service, Watershed Progress Report in Pennsylvania, September 1972.

University of Wyoming College of Law, "County and Municipal Flood Zoning Under Existing Wyoming Legislation," Land and Water Law Review, (vol. VII, No. 1, 1972), p. 103-14.

2. Legal Cases

Gaebel v. Thornbury Township, Delaware County 8 Pa. Commonwealth 379.
Hofkin et al. v. Whitemarsh Township, 88 Montg. L. R. 63, (1967).
Solomon et ux. v. Whitemarsh Township, 92 Montg. L.R., p. 114-118, (1969).

3. Personal Interviews

Mr. Dallas A. Dollase
  Director, Community Planning, Department of Community Affairs
Mr. Vernon M. Beard
  Director of Engineering, Department of Environmental Resources
Mr. Robert Adams
  Bureau of Engineering, Department of Environmental Resources
Mr. Bruno J. Chiesa
  Comptroller, Department of Environmental Resources
Mr. Frank Ullyon
  Special Accounts, Comptroller's Office, Department of Environmental Resources
Mr. David Brown
  Community Planning Bureau, Department of Environmental Resources

11. APPENDIX EXAMPLE FLOOD PLAIN ZONING ORDINANCES

Enacted by the Borough of Milton, Northumberland County, the first municipality in Pennsylvania to comply fully with the flood plain zoning requirements of the National Flood Insurance Act.

Ordinance No. 640

An Ordinance Amending Ordinance No. 536, The Building Code Of The Borough of Milton. To include Flood Damage Controls For Construction Within The Borough's Flood Plain Conservation District(s).

BE IT ENACTED AND ORDAINED by the Council of the Borough of Milton, Northumberland County, Pennsylvania, and it is hereby enacted and ordained by the authority of the same:

Section 1—In order to prevent excessive damage to buildings and structures due to conditions of flooding, the following restrictions shall apply to all construction occurring within the Borough's designated flood plain district(s) :

A. No first floor of any building or structure, including basement, shall be constructed at an elevation of less than one (1) foot above the elevation of the one hundred (100) year flood.

    1. Where fill is permitted, it shall consist of soil and rock materials only.

    2. In addition, fill shall be permitted only when the applicant has demonstrated that his proposal, when combined with all other existing and anticipated uses, will not increase the water surface elevation of the one hundred (100) year flood more than one (1) foot at any point.

B. All buildings and structures shall be firmly anchored to prevent flotation, thus reducing the threat to life and property and decreasing the possibility of the blockage of bridge openings and other restricted sections of the watercourse.

C. All buildings and structures shall be constructed and placed on the lot so as to offer the least reasonable obstruction to the flow of water and shall be designed to have a minimal effect upon the flow and height of flood water.

D. Special precautions shall be taken so that no buoyant, flammable or explosive materials are stored in a manner that would be injurious to human, animal or plant life. Such precautions shall include firm anchoring of these materials to prevent flotation and/or storing these materials at an elevation one (1) foot above the elevation of the one hundred (100) year flood.

E. Utilize water supply systems and sanitary sewage systems designed to preclude infiltration of flood waters into the systems and discharges from the system into flood waters.

F. Adhesives shall have a bonding strength that is resistant to inundation.

G. Doors and all wood trim shall be sealed with a water resistant paint or similar product.

H. Basements shall be permitted in non-residential buildings only if they are designed to preclude inundation by the one hundred (100) year flood.

I. In new construction or substantial improvements, water heaters, furnaces, electrical-distribution panels, and other critical mechanical or electrical installations shall be prohibited in basements.

J. Plywood used at or below the first floor level shall be of an "exterior" or "marine" grade and of a water resistant or water proof variety.

K. Wood flooring used at or below the first floor level shall be installed to accommodate a lateral expansion of the flooring, perpendicular to the flooring grain, without incurring structural damage to the building.

Section 2—To insure that the aforementioned flood damage controls are being employed in all construction within the Flood Plain Conservation District(s), the Borough Building official shall require the following specific information to be included as part of an application for a building permit.
  A. A plan which accurately locates the construction proposal with respect to the district limits, stream channel, and existing flood plain developments.
  B. Such plan shall also include contours and elevation of the ground, size of the structure, location and elevations of streets, soil types and flood proofing measures.
  C. A document certified by a registered professional engineer or architect that adequate precautions against flood damage have been taken with respect to the design of any building or structure, and that the plans for the development of the site adhere to the restrictions cited in Section 1 of this Ordinance.

Section 3—A copy of all plans for development of the Flood Plain Conservation District(s), to be considered for approval shall be submitted by the building official to the Northumberland County Soil and Water Conservation District for review and comment prior to the issuance of a permit. The recommendations of the Soil and Water Conservation District should be incorporated into the plan to provide for protection against one hundred (100) year flood hazard.

Special Note to Section 1. A-2.
  To assist in determining the effects of fill on the water surface elevation of the one hundred (100) year flood, the applicant can utilize the information provided in the Type 15 Flood Insurance Study issued in March, 1972, as prepared by the United States Department of Interior, Geologic Survey for the Borough of Milton.

Section 4.—All Ordinances inconsistent herewith are hereby repealed.
  ENACTED AND ORDAINED into an Ordinance this 14th day of November, A.D., 1972.

Ordinance No. 641

An Ordinance Amending Ordinance No. 625, The Milton Borough Zoning Ordinance, To Modify The existing Flood Plain District Regulations,

Establish an Additional Flood Plain District In the Borough, Regulate The Use Of Land in the Flood Plain Districts, Provide For The Modification Of The Flood Plain Boundaries By Agents and Employees from Liability For Permits Issued In Any Flood Plain District.

BE IT ENACTED AND ORDAINED by the Council of the Borough of Milton, Northumberland County, Pennsylvania, and it is hereby enacted and ordained by the authority of the same.

Section 1—Article 3—Schedule IV of Ordinance No. 625, the Milton Borough Zoning Ordinance is hereby modified to read as follows:
 3,500—Schedule IV
  This Schedule governs development and the use of land in all areas which are subject to flooding.
 3,510—Introduction
 3,511—Declaration of Legislative Intent
  In conjunction with the overall objectives as stated in Article I of this Ordinance, the specific intent of this section is to:
   A. Reduce financial burdens imposed on the community, its governmental units and its individuals by preventing excessive development in areas subject to periodic flooding.
   B. Minimize danger to public health by protecting water supply and natural drainage;
   C. And promote responsible flood proofing measures within the Flood Plain Districts.
 3,512—Abrogation and Greater Restrictions
  This section supersedes any zoning provisions currently in effect in flood-prone areas. However, any underlying zoning shall remain in full force and effect to the extent that those provisions are more restrictive.
 3,520—Establishment of the Flood Plain Districts
 3,521—Description of Districts
  The districts are as follows:
  District FP-1 (Special Flood Plain Conservation District)
  This district shall include all those areas zoned as flood plain on the official Zoning Map located in the Milton Borough Office.
   A. District FP-2 (General Flood Plain Conservation District)
    1. This district shall include all areas subject to inundation by flood waters of the one hundred (100) year frequency. This shall be deemed an overlay on any district now or hereafter applicable to any lot.
    2. The source of this delineation shall be the Type 15 Flood Insurance Study, issued in March of 1972, as prepared by United States

Department of the Interior, Geologic Survey for the Borough of Milton, Northumberland County, Pennsylvania.

3,522—Change in Flood Plain Districts

The delineation of any Flood Plain District boundaries may be revised and modified by the Borough Council where there are changes, through natural or other causes, in either district or where changes can be validated by further detailed engineering studies employing on-site survey techniques as approved or recommended by the U.S. Army Corps of Engineers, Baltimore District, or the Northumberland County Soil and Water Conservation District.

3,530—Permitted Uses in District FP-1 (Special Flood Plain Conservation District)

The following uses and no other shall be permitted in District FP-1:

A. Agricultural uses (excluding structures) such as: general farming, outdoor plant nurseries, horticulture, truck farming, sod farming, forestry, lumbering (excluding storage and mill structures), and wild crop harvesting.

B. Public and private recreational uses not requiring "permanent or temporary structures" designed for human habitation such as: beaches and swimming areas, parks, day camps, picnic groves, golf courses, circuses, carnivals and fairs of a temporary nature, fishing preserves, boating clubs, game farms, fish hatcheries, wildlife and nature preserves, hiking areas and arboreta.

C. Parking lots where required by this Ordinance.

D. Water related uses such as: docks, piers, bridges and river crossings of transmission lines.

E. Front, side and/or rear yards and uses customarily incidental thereto, except that no structures shall be permitted. Inclusion of flood plain lands within residential lots in order to meet minimum lot area or yard requirements is contingent upon complying with the objectives and standards set forth in Section 3,511 of this Ordinance.

F. Utility facilities such as: power plants, flowage areas, transmission lines, pipe lines, water monitoring devices, outlet installations for sewage treatment plants, sealed public and private water supply wells, and accessory uses customarily incidental to any of the foregoing permitted uses.

3,540—Uses by Special Exception in District FP-1 (Special Flood Plain Conservation District)

The following uses may be permitted in District FP-1 as a special exception when authorized by the Zoning Hearing Board (subject to Articles 5 and 8 of this Ordinance) and after review by the Planning Commission:

A. Sewage treatment plants and sewage pumping stations provided they are protected from flooding by dikes or other equally effective means.

B. Dams, culverts, and bridges approved by the Pennsylvania Department of Environmental Resources.
C. Paved roads and driveways.
D. Impoundment basins.
E. Storm sewers.
F. Other uses similar to the above, provided the effect is not to alter substantially the cross-sectional profile of the flood plain at the point of the proposed construction or use.

3,550—Permitted Uses in District FP-2 (General Flood Plain Conservation District)

In District FP-2, the development and/or use of any land will be permitted provided that the development or use adheres to all the requirements of the underlying district. In addition, all structural development in this district shall adhere to the floodproofing provisions stipulated in the "Building Code of the Borough of Milton."

3,560—Uses by Special Exception in District FP-2 (General Flood Plain Conservation District)

In District FP-2, all provisions for special exceptions in District FP-1, (Section 3,540) shall apply; except those restrictions pertaining to paved roads and driveways. These uses shall be permitted in District FP-2 because of their importance as an accessory use to structural development.

3,570—Special Regulations

3,571—Boundary Disputes

A. In the case of any dispute concerning the boundaries of a Flood Plain Conservation District, an initial determination shall be made by the Zoning Officer.

B. Any party aggrieved by a decision of the Zoning Officer as to the boundaries of a Flood Plain Conservation District, as defined in Section 3,520, which may include the grounds that the said data referred to therein is or has become incorrect because of changes due to natural or other causes, may appeal to the Zoning Hearing Board as provided in Section 5,810. The burden of proof in such an appeal shall be on the appellant.

3,572—Severability

Should District FP-2 (General Flood Plain Conservation District) be declared inapplicable to any tract by reason of the action of any court of competent jurisdiction in determining the legal effect of the same, the zoning applicable to such lot shall be deemed to be the District to which it is located without consideration of this Section.

3,580—Municipal Liability

The grant of a zoning permit or approval of a subdivision plan in the Flood Plain Conservation District shall not constitute a representation, guarantee, or warranty of any kind by the Borough or by any official or employee thereof of the practicability or safety of the proposed use, and shall create no liability upon the Borough, its officials or employees.

Section 2—Article II is hereby amended to include the following definition:

Flood Plain

The relatively flat or low land area adjoining a river, stream, or water course which is subject to partial or complete inundation by flood waters of the one hundred (100) year frequency.

Section 3—All Ordinances inconsistent herewith are hereby repealed.

ENACTED AND ORDAINED into an Ordinance this 14th day of November A.D., 1972. Approved the 30th day of November, A.D., 1972.

Ordinance No. 642

An Ordinance Amending Ordinance No. 497, The Milton Subdivision Ordinance, To Include Regulations For The Subdivision Of Land In A Designated Flood Plain Conservation District, And To Provide For The Administration Of Such Regulations.

BE IT ENACTED AND ORDAINED by the Council of the Borough of Milton, Northumberland County, Pennsylvania, and it is hereby enacted and ordained by the authority of the same that Ordinance No. 497, The Milton Subdivision Ordinance is amended as follows:

Section 1

Section 4. Definitions

Is hereby amended to include the following definitions:

Flood Plain

A relatively flat or low land area adjoining a river, stream, or watercourse, which is subject to partial or complete inundation by flood waters of the one hundred (100) year frequency as shown on the official Milton Borough Zoning Map.

Section 2

Section 12. Pre-Application Plans and Data: Procedure is hereby amended to read as follows:

1. These shall include any features of the .... , but not limited to .. . . drainage reservations, "flood plain areas", shopping centers, and school sites.

Section 3
   Section 13. Pre-Application Plans and Data: Specifications
      Is hereby amended to read as follows:
         1. General information describing or outlining existing covenants, land characteristics including flood plain area, community facilities and utilities, and street improvements.
Section 4
   Section 14. Preliminary Plats: Procedures
      Is hereby amended to read as follows:
         2. The Commission may submit copies of the preliminary plat to the Engineer, "the Northumberland County Soil and Water Conservation District", public utilities, . . . for approval.
         4. Before taking final action on any submitted plat the Commission shall submit copies of the preliminary plat and accompanying data to the Engineer who shall advise the Commission as to the suitability of all engineering details and specifications "including those for any flood plain areas", . . . of the utility easements.
         In addition, a copy of the preliminary plat plan and accompanying data shall be submitted to the Northumberland County Soil and Water Conservation District for review and comment on any measures needed to control erosion and sedimentation. In the event the proposed subdivision is in a flood plain area, the district recommendations should be incorporated into the plan to provide protection against inundation by flood waters of the one hundred (100) year frequency.
Section 5
   Section 15. Preliminary Plats: Specifications
      Is hereby amended to add the following:
         2. d.
         A plan which accurately locates the subdivision proposal with respect to flood plain limits, stream channel and existing flood plain developments, shall also include elevations, soil types and floodproofing measures needed.
Section 6
   Section 17. Final Plat: Specifications
      Is hereby amended by adding the following:
         16. Other data: "g"—Plans which accurately locate the subdivision proposal with respect to flood plain limits, stream channel and existing flood plain developments. It shall also include elevations, soil types and any floodproofing measures required.
Section 7
   Section 39. Erosion and Sediment Control
      Is hereby amended by adding the following:

In the event that any developer shall intend to make changes in the contour of any land proposed to be subdivided, developed or changed in use by grading, excavating or the removal or destruction of the natural topsoil, trees or other vegetation covering thereon, the developer shall submit to the Commission for approval, a plan for erosion and sedimentation controls, unless there has been a determination by the Commission that such plans are not necessary.

Erosion and sedimentation control measures used to control erosion and reduce sedimentation shall as a minimum meet the standards and specifications adopted for use by the Northumberland County Soil and Water Conservation District.

Section 8

All Ordinances inconsistent herewith are hereby repealed.

ENACTED AND ORDAINED into an Ordinance this 14th day of November, 1972.

Ordinance No. 647

An Ordinance Amending Ordinance No. 640, Which Amended Ordinance No. 536, the Building Code of the Borough of Milton, to Provide for a Flood Plain at an Elevation of the One Hundred (100) Year Flood.

BE IT ENACTED AND ORDAINED by the Council of the Borough of Milton, Northumberland County, Pennsylvania, and it is hereby enacted and ordained by the authority of the same that:

Section 1 of Ordinance No. 640, adopted November 14, 1972, shall be amended to read as follows:

Section 1—In order to prevent excessive damage to buildings and structures due to conditions of flooding, the following restrictions shall apply to all construction occurring within the Borough's designated flood plain district (s):

A. No first floor of any building or structure, including basement, shall be constructed at an elevation of less than the elevation of the one hundred (100) year flood.

1. Where fill is permitted, it shall consist of soil and rock materials only.

2. In addition, fill shall be permitted only when the applicant has demonstrated that his proposal, when combined with all other

existing and anticipated uses, will not increase the water surface elevation of the one hundred (100) year flood.

B. All buildings and structures shall be firmly anchored to prevent flotation, thus reducing the threat to life and property and decreasing the possibility of the blockage of bridge openings and other restricted sections of the watercourse.

C. All buildings and structures shall be constructed and placed on the lot so as to offer the least reasonable obstruction to the flow of water and shall be designed to have a minimal effect upon the flow and height of flood water.

D. Special precautions shall be taken so that no buoyant, flammable or explosive materials are stored in a manner that would be injurious to human, animal or plant life. Such precautions shall include firm anchoring of these materials to prevent flotation and/or storing these materials at an elevation above the elevation of the one hundred (100) year flood.

E. Utilize water supply systems and sanitary sewage systems designed to preclude infiltration of flood waters into the systems and discharges from the system into flood waters.

F. Adhesives shall have a bonding strength that is resistant to inundation.

G. Doors and all wood trim shall be sealed with a water resistant paint or similar product.

H. Basements shall be permitted in non-residential buildings only if they are designed to preclude inundation by the one hundred (100) year flood.

I. In new construction or substantial improvements, water heaters, furnaces, electrical distribution panels, and other critical mechanical or electrical installations shall be prohibited in basements.

J. Plywood used at or below the first floor level shall be of an "exterior" or "marine" grade and of a water resistant or waterproof variety.

K. Wood flooring used at or below the first floor level shall be installed to accommodate a lateral expansion of the flooring, perpendicular to the flooring grain, without incurring structural damage to the building.

Section 2—All Ordinances or portions thereof inconsistent herewith are hereby repealed.

ENACTED AND ORDAINED into an Ordinance this 13th day of March, A.D., 1973.

Acknowledgments

John Pittenger several years ago urged me to write my legislative story. I had been thinking about it for a year or so, but "Pitt," as his friends knew him, prompted me to move on the project. Although he died in December 2009, I am pleased that he read and critiqued the first draft a year before then. As the text shows, I have the highest regard for him and salute his memory.

In writing the book I have received considerable assistance from a number of friends. Vincent Carocci was particularly helpful in suggesting the organizational framework and in editing the initial draft. Former Representatives Robert Wise and David Steil gave me helpful information from their experiences. Former Governor George Leader gave me the benefit of his experience as a senator from 1951–1955.

I also received substantial aid in fact-checking and suggestions from Michael Aumiller, John Showers, Neil McAuliffe, James Cawley, Stephen MacNett, William McLaughlin, Irwin "Sonny" Popowsky, and Al Santor, Northumberland County Elections Clerk in 1970 and later a commissioner of Coal Township; former Northumberland County Commissioner William Rumberger; former Shamokin *News Item* reporter Harry Dietz; Kenneth C. Larson, former chief engineer for Penn DOT District 3; F. B. Paulsen, former owner of the Paulsen Wire Rope Corporation; Dan Fitzpatrick, flood plain management law administrator for the Department of Community and Economic Development; and Barry Newman, storm water management law administrator for the Department of Environmental Protection. My late brother, Dr. Wendell Kury, gave me the benefit of his recollection of family matters.

Betsy Lark and Tony May gave me their insights into Northumberland County politics of the Lark era, as did Representative Merle Phillips.

I appreciate the time and attention each of them gave to this project.

A special note of thanks goes to Heidi Mays and her capable staff at the Pennsylvania House of Representatives Archives and Records Center. They were most helpful over a period of several months in locating and making available the *House* and *Senate Journals* for the debate excerpts used. I recommend Ms. Mays and her office to anyone researching the Pennsylvania General Assembly.

Special thanks also go to Micheline Leininger and Lisa Dishong of the Malady and Wooten state government affairs office (where I work), who were very helpful in preparing the photographs.

I am grateful to Susquehanna University Press. Rachana Sachdev and Sarah Bailey, the editors at Susquehanna, provided great encouragement and cooperation in moving the manuscript through the publishing process. Donald Housley, the university's historian, gave extensive editorial comments that prompted me to rethink and improve the manuscript.

I also want to thank Scott Paul Gordon and Monica Najar of the Lehigh University Press for enthusiastically moving forward with the manuscript when Susquehanna University closed it press.

A special note of appreciation goes to my wife, Beth, who enthusiastically and effectively took part in all of my campaigns and also gave her professional skill in reviewing the manuscripts.

Much of the story is drawn from my memory and files. Whatever mistakes are found are mine, and I take the responsibility for them.

Notes

PROLOGUE

1. The Coal and Iron Police were terminated by a progressive Republican governor, Gifford Pinchot, in 1928.
2. Reed M. Smith, *State Government in Transition: Reforms of the Leader Administration, 1955–1959*, University of Pennsylvania Press, 1961, at page 13.
3. As governor, Leader led a wide-ranging reform of state government that began the dismantling of the patronage system and brought state government into the twentieth century. For example, he quickly brought 12,000 state positions out of the patronage system by an executive board order. He directed that state automobile insurance be purchased on a "fleet" basis, rather than individual cars, and reduced the commissions. The county highways sheds, however, were left in patronage as a concession to the Democratic county chairmen. The highway sheds continued in the patronage system in the governorships of Lawrence, Scranton, Shafer and Shapp. Governor Thornburgh in 1979 finally removed them from patronage, as is described in chapter 16.

CHAPTER ONE: GETTING READY

1. Although it would not grant excused absences to see President Truman, four months later the Sunbury School District sent the High School Marching Band to Washington to march in the Inaugural Parade for President Eisenhower.
2. Shroyer, along with Dr. George Deitrick Sr., began an insurrection against the Lark organization (which dominated county politics) that briefly took control of the County Commissioners' office away from Lark. Shroyer's son, Lawton, became the minority county commissioner in the late 1960s. Deitrick's son, George Deitrick Jr., became my Republican opponent for the Senate seat in 1972.

3. Ulrich was the son of Dr. Henry Ulrich, the Northumberland County Coroner, elected on the Lark organization ticket.

4. Jack N.X. Oanh, a Vietnamese and assistant professor of economics, was one of the faculty who served as a judge during our practice sessions. Fourteen years later Oanh served in the Vietnamese government as acting prime minister for several days in the turmoil before U.S. forces withdrew. In describing Oanh's brief term as prime minister, the author Stanley Karnow reported:

> Only after two days did paratroopers, their bayonets fixed, restore order. Meanwhile, Khanh had appointed an amiable Harvard-educated economist, Nguyen Xuan Oanh, to act as prime minister in his absence. Oanh's prospects were dim from the start. For one thing, he spoke fluent English, which tainted his nationalist pretensions. And American officials in Saigon did not help by nicknaming him "Jack Owen."
>
> [Oanh's tenure lasted five days but on January 27—days later—he was reappointed and served until being replaced on February 16.]

See *Vietnam: A History*, by Stanley Karnow, at pages 396 and 400.

When my wife and I visited Saigon in 2004 we hoped to call on Professor Oanh, but he died a month before we arrived. We did, however, visit with his widow at their home and paid homage to him at a Buddhist mourning shrine she maintained.

5. Norcross later ran unsuccessfully for a U.S. Senate seat from New Jersey.

6. *Commonwealth v. Schuck*, 401 Pa. 222 (1960). In Pennsylvania the State Supreme Court automatically reviews every death penalty sentence. This was Schuck's Supreme Court review, and it unanimously affirmed the trial court's sentence.

7. *Abington School District v. Schempp*, 374 U.S. 203 (1963).

8. The value of the wall was demonstrated in June 1972 when the rising waters from Hurricane Agnes rose to within two inches of topping the walls and flooding Sunbury. The Sunbury *Daily Item* published a photograph showing the river within two inches of going over the wall. During the debate of my flood plain and storm water bill in the State Senate in 1977, I placed an enlarged copy of the photo on a tripod on the Senate floor and used it to bolster my arguments in favor of the bills.

9. Senators then had twenty scholarships to be awarded at their discretion to four state-related universities: Pennsylvania, Pittsburgh, Temple, and Penn State. See my discussion in chapter 11 of the scholarships and how I awarded them.

10. The manner in which Lark obtained the nomination for Davis rankled some Republican leaders from outside of Northumberland County. When I ran for the Senate nine years later, one of them, Harvey Murray Sr., a Snyder County party stalwart, quietly supported me to get back at Lark.

11. I believe Beth was one of the first women to serve as a city solicitor in Pennsylvania.

12. When Governor Scranton signed the bill, the amendment became part of the law. See 35 P.S. Section 691.4.

13. *Legislative Journal*—House, Volume 1, at page 670. Every other House member from the 27th Senate District voted for the bill—Murray, Purnell, Shelhamer, Kessler, and Ruane. Kessler, from Montour County, made a short speech in favor the bill.

CHAPTER TWO:
CRACKING GIBRALTAR, THE LARK "MACHINE"

1. Since 1954 five other lieutenant governors tried unsuccessfully to succeed their Governor: Lloyd Wood(1954), Raymond Broderick(1970), Ernest Kline (1978), William Scranton II, (1986) and Mark Singel (1994).

2. For a detailed chronicle of the Lark family since its arrival in Pennsylvania from Switzerland, see "Genealogical and Biographical Annals of Northumberland County, Pennsylvania," J. L. Floyd, Chicago, 1911, at pages 573-74 and 633-34.

3. As a college student I was assigned by my political science professor to write a paper on a public issue and have it critiqued by a public official. I took my paper to then Judge Troutman, who graciously reviewed it with me. A few years later Judge Troutman and Judge Fortney administered the oath to me when I was sworn in to practice law.

4. WISL is the acronym for Lark's wife, Isabelle S. Lark.

5. In 1954 Lark and Sunbury Wire Corporation filed a lawsuit in federal court seeking $7,775,000 in damages against U.S. Steel and eight other large steel manufacturers on the grounds that the defendants, in violation of federal antitrust law, conspired to drive the company out of business. (See *Wall Street Journal*, June 1, 1954.) According to the *Journal*, Lark claimed that the business was worth $2,100,000 prior to the alleged conspiracy and was worthless when the complaint was filed. Lark's claimed total net sales of $2,600,000 in the fiscal year ending January 1952 and net profits of $233,000. Lark reportedly settled the claim for $1 million. Later he sold the assets of the defunct company to Paulsen-Webber Cordage of Brooklyn, which became Paulsen Wire Rope Corporation.

6. Since the Civil War Northumberland County, like Snyder and Union Counties, had been a reliable Republican county in voter registration and voting. It is no coincidence that Cameron Park in Sunbury, next to the courthouse, is named for a Union Army general whose statue is there. The three counties were agricultural, mercantile, and overwhelmingly Protestant. Unlike Snyder and Union Counties, however, the cultural makeup of Northumberland began changing toward the end of the nineteenth century as Catholic immigrants from Ireland, Poland, Italy, and other eastern European counties came to the coal regions to work in the mines. At first the new arrivals tended to support the status quo, such as by becoming Republican, the dominant party. As the twentieth century moved on and the immigrant families became more secure and their children better educated they became open to the Democratic Party. The elections of John Stank to the House from the coal region district of Northumberland County illustrated this. But the balance of voting registration in the county as a whole continued to be Republican. Prior to Dr. Rumberger's election from Sunbury as county commissioner in 1967, the only Democrats elected to county office were from east of Trevorton and Shamokin, the coal region; for example, George Perles from Mt. Carmel as county commissioner, Larry Snyder from Coal Township as prothonotary, and James F. Kelley Sr. (father of the Commissioner James Kelley who worked with me) as commissioner before Perles.

CHAPTER THREE: RUNNING FOR THE HOUSE

1. After I was elected to the Senate, Governor Shapp nominated Raup for a Lycoming County judgeship. I was especially pleased to vote for him. Raup was elected and reelected as judge.
2. As pointed out earlier, Bower cast one of the six votes against H.B. 585 when it was before the House on final passage before going to the Senate. The Senate amended the bill and sent it back to concur in its amendments. Bower voted to concur.
3. I don't recall the source of the Nixon quote, but it was not fabricated. Nixon often made the same point in this campaign against Kennedy in 1960. See Nixon's response to a question by Harold L. Levy in the debate with Kennedy on October 7, 1960. Another example is Nixon's speech in West Memphis, Arkansas, on September 27, 1960.

CHAPTER FOUR: THE EDUCATION OF A FRESHMAN

1. Today the salary is $76,163 plus a per diem expense allowance based on a federal scale or actual expenses incurred.
2. Representative Jimmy Musto of Luzerne County found another way to respond to constituents. One morning I walked through the empty hall of the House. Seated at the clerk's desk, Musto was making phone calls on a phone that allowed long distance calls. He explained, "I call personally everyone who writes to me. It saves a lot of time."
3. I had been introduced to the legislative process when I participated in the Connecticut Intercollegiate Student Legislature, but the student legislature had no party caucuses. I came to Harrisburg ignorant of the importance of party caucuses.
4. In one early caucus Fineman was going through the bills on the calendar and asked if anyone had amendments to a particular bill. One member replied that he did. "What does it do?" Fineman asked. "Nothing. It's just a change of language," the legislator replied with a straight face as the caucus erupted in laughter.
5. Former Representative Robert Wise recalled for me that in his first session in the House, 1964–1966, the Democratic floor leader, Joshua Eilberg of Philadelphia, often called from the House floor to Philadelphia City Committee for guidance on how to vote. The Democratic Chairman of Philadelphia, Frank Smith, came to a House Democratic caucus and said he would be expecting the entire caucus to vote with Philadelphia. This message was not well taken by Wise and other upstate Democrats like Kent Shelhamer. They declared their independence through numerous votes and floor statements.
6. Bragdon, Henry W. and Pittenger, John C. *The Pursuit of Justice: An Introduction to Constitutional Rights.* Toronto, Macmillan Company, 1969

CHAPTER FIVE: ABSENTEE BALLOT REFORM

1. See the 1968 *House of Representatives Journal*, pages 866–87 and 906–12.
2. Ibid., page 872.

3. Act of Dec. 11, 1968, Act No. 375.
4. See 25 P.S. Sec. 3146.2 et seq.

CHAPTER SIX: BALLOT BOX REFORM IN NORTHUMBERLAND COUNTY

1. One of the meetings was held on January 20, 1970, a date I cannot forget. Shortly after 10 p.m., as the meeting was nearing its close, I received a telephone call from Beth, then nine months pregnant, telling me she was ready to deliver. I went home directly and took her to the Geisinger Medical Center. Within a few hours she delivered our first son, Steven.
2. Help America Vote Act, Public law 107–252.

CHAPTER SEVEN: CLEAN STREAMS AND THE ENVIRONMENTAL REVOLUTION

1. The deed can be found in *Northumberland County Deed Book* 138 at page 397, where it was recorded on January 26, 1905.
2. The Act of April 22, 1905, P. L. 260, No. 182.
3. Section 4 provided that "this act shall not apply to waters pumped or flowing from coal mines . . ."
4. The Act of June 14, 1923, P. L. 793, No. 311; the Act of June 22, 1937, P. L. 1987, No. 394; and the Act of May 8, 1945, P. L. 435, No. 177.
5. The 1923 law specifically exempted pollution from coal mines. Section 310 of the 1937 law exempted acid mine drainage until the Sanitary Water Board finds it practical to remove such pollution. Sections 6 and 7 of the Act of May 8, 1945, P. L. 435, No. 177, authorized pollution discharges to already polluted streams and taxpayers to provide conduits to coal companies to carry pollution away from clean streams to the already polluted ones!
6. This was H.B. 585, discussed above at pages 21–22. It became the Act of August 23, 1965, P. L. 372, No. 194.
7. H.B. 2652, which became the Act of June 12, 1958, Act. No. 92.
8. H.B.1416, which became the Act of June 19, 1968, Act. No. 446.
9. H.B. 2062, which became the Act of June 19, 1968, Act. No. 447.
10. S.B. 479, which became the Act of July 17, 1968, Act No. 181. The chief sponsors of the bill were Senators Z. H. Confair of Williamsport, Preston B.Davis of Milton, and Martin L. Murray of Wilkes-Barre.
11. *House Legislative Journal* for 1968 at page 1455.
12. Ibid.
13. Representative John Murtha of Johnstown was also a prime sponsor. He later became the senior member of the U.S. House of Representatives from Pennsylvania. He died in 2010.
14. Our decision not to make the speeches, but to insert them into the record, was in deference to the legislative axiom that, if you have the votes, you don't need a speech. We had the votes. No one voted no.

15. Senator McGregor's district included Wilkinsburg, Allegheny County, my wife's hometown. Beth's mother, Elizabeth Heazlett, held a coffee klatch for McGregor in his campaign for the Senate.

16. See 35 Pa. Cons. Stat. Ann. Sec. 691.1 et seq.

17. See Clean Water Act, as amended, 33 U.S. C. Sec. 1251 et seq., Public Law 92-500, October 18, 1972.

18. See 52 PA. Cons. Stat. Ann. Sec. 1396.1 et seq. (Purdon 1985 Supp.)

19. See 52 Pa. Cons. Stat Sec. 30.53 (Purdon 1985 Supp.) This was H.B. 2652 of the 1967-1968 session.

20. See 35 Pa. Cons. Stat. Ann Section 4001 et seq. (Purdon 1985 Supp.) This was H.B. 926 of the 1967-1968 session.

21. See 35 Pa. Cons. Stat. Ann. Sec. 6001.1 et seq. (Purdon 1985 Supp.). This was S.B. 514 of the 1967-1968 session.

22. 32 Pa. Cons. Stat. Ann. Sec. 820.21 et seq. (Purdon 1985 Supp.) This was H.B. 963 of the 1971-1972 session and I was its originator and chief sponsor.

23. See 71 Pa. Cons. Stat. Ann. Sec.510-1 et seq. (Purdon 1986 Supp.) This was H.B. 2213 of the 1969-1970 session and I was a prime sponsor.

24. See 32 Pa. Cons. Stat. Ann. Sec. 5101 et seq. (Purdon 1985 Supp.)This was S.B. 509 of the 1967-1968 session.

25. See 71 Pa. Cons. Stat. Ann. Sec. 512 (Purdon Supp. 1975-1976). This was S.B. 408 of the 1969-1970 session. The environmental assessment required by this law became the basis for the *Payne v. Kassab* test for implementation of Article I, Section 27, the Environmental Amendment to the Constitution.

26. Discussed in detail in chapter 8.

27. H.B. 385 (P.N. 2885), the Act of December 15, 1969, (P.L. 1779), Act 109.

28. For more information on the restoration of migratory shad to the Susquehanna, see the website of the Pennsylvania Fish Commission, www.fish.state.pa.us/shad.htm and the Chesapeake Bay Program website at www.chesapeakerbay.net

CHAPTER EIGHT: THE ENVIRONMENTAL AMENDMENT TO THE STATE CONSTITUTION

1. See Article 14, Sec. 3 of the New York Constitution, adopted November 4, 1969, eff. Jan. 1, 1970.

2. *Legislative Journal*—House, April 14, 1970, beginning at page 2,269.

3. See the *House Journal*, above, at page 2,272. The article was also published in the Pennsylvania *Bar Association Quarterly*, 421-38 (June, 1970). Sadly, Broughton died in a mountain climbing accident in the Himalayas in 1975.

4. The other proposed constitutional amendments on the ballot were (1) Res. 1, to permit civil jury verdicts of 5/6, rather than unanimous votes. The voters approved it 833,283 to 423,006, a two to one margin. (2) Res. 2, to prohibit discrimination based on sex, which received approval by 783,331 to 464,882. (3) Res. 4, to permit elected officials to raise their salaries during their term, was defeated. (4) Res. 5, to permit legislators to be appointed to executive positions during their elected terms, was also defeated.

5. For law review articles and legal publications analyzing how Article I, Section 27 has been interpreted by the courts and administrative agencies see, for examples: Gormly et al., *The Pa. Constitution: A Treatise on Rights and Liberties*, George T. Bisel Co., Inc., Philadelphia, 2006, chapter 29, beginning on page 683. Also, Dernbach, John C. "Taking the Pennsylvania Seriously When It Protects the Environment. Part I—An Interpretative Framework for Article I, Section 27." 103 *Dickinson Law Review*, Summer 1999, Number 4; and Part II—Environmental Rights and the Public Trust." 104 *Dickinson Law Review*, Fall 1999, Number 1. Also, Woodside, Robert E. "Pennsylvania Constitutional Law," Murrelle Printing Company, Inc, Sayre, Pa., 1985. My own analysis is in the Pennsylvania Bar Institute's "Pennsylvania Environmental Law and Practice," 4th ed., Harrisburg, 2006.

CHAPTER NINE: THE BRIDGE AT SUNBURY

1. S.B. 331 (P.N. 1464).
2. "The SPEAKER recognizes the minority leader, Mr. LEE:

Mr. Speaker, would the Chair inform us how long you are going to hold the switch open? We understand that at least half of the courthouse in Philadelphia has already fallen down.
 The SPEAKER. The Chair will hold the voting open for a reasonable length of time.
 Mr. LEE: . . . would a reasonable length of time be another three minutes? Everyone is in his seat. Everyone has voted.
 The SPEAKER. Reasonable has a wide range. It could be as brief as five minutes or it could be as long as fifty-five minutes. We are trying to expedite the business at hand, Mr. Lee."
Legislative Journal–House, December 28, 1971 at page 1,987–88.

3. Sunbury *Daily Item* of Wednesday, December 29, 1971.
4. *The New York Times* of February 14, 2009, at page A10 carried a headline "Specter, a Fulcrum of the Stimulus Bill, Pulls Off a Coup for Health Money." The story reported that Senator Arlen Specter, a Republican, leveraged his vote in favor of the Obama economic stimulus bill for a 34 percent increase in the funding for the National Institute of Health. Specter's action resonated completely with me.
5. The Act of December 8, 1982. This was S.B. 457(PN 2242). Section 3, the axle tax, provided for a $36 per axle tax on all trucks over 26,000 pounds. The proceeds were directed to paying the $9 billion bond obligations and building bridges.
6. While the bypass bridge was under design the department made plans to replace the white bridge (also known as the Charles Steele Bridge in honor of a previous state senator) between Northumberland and Snyder County over the west branch of the Susquehanna. To do this the existing bridge had to be demolished, which would result in that bridge's normal traffic being detoured down Front Street in Sunbury and across the old toll bridge. This would add significantly more traffic to the old bridge and create more traffic jams. The department announced that the

white bridge would be demolished in the week before the November 1976 election, when I was seeking a second term in the Senate. When I read the announcement I exploded with anger. I could visualize the Republicans running radio and newspaper ads blaming the traffic jam on Front Street on my inability to deliver the new bypass bridge. I placed a call to the governor's office and told him directly that the demolition had to be postponed until after election day. The administration agreed to my request. Several days after the election I had the pleasure of watching the white bridge demolished by expertly detonated explosives. When the new bridge was completed in 1978 I drove the first automobile across, carrying as my passengers Donald Morgan, the mayor of Sunbury, and Mrs. Charles Lewis, wife of the mayor of Northumberland.

CHAPTER TEN: DEFYING GRAVITY

1. Karl Purnell, a Republican Representative from Union County, did make a spirited but unsuccessful challenge to Davis in the primary election.

2. Abrams was constitutionally prohibited from running for senator from the 27th Senate District in 1972. Article II, Section 5, provides that senators must be "inhabitants of their respective districts one year next before their election." At the time he made his announcement to be a candidate (December 1971), Abrams was living in Camp Hill, Cumberland County, and his children were attending school there. If he had moved to the 27th Senate District that day he would still be a month short of one year before the 1972 election. He could not have survived a legal challenge to his nomination petitions if he had filed them.

3. The 27th Senate District stretched from Berwick on the east to Laurelton on the west, a distance of sixty-five miles; and from Allenwood on the north to just north of Liverpool, a span of forty-five miles. It consisted of all of Columbia, Montour, Northumberland, Snyder, and Union Counties, as well as four townships in Juniata County.

4. Candidates providing alcoholic beverages for the voters has been done since prior to the American Revolution. In George Washington's campaign for the Virginia House of Burgesses in 1758 it was estimated that, through his agent, he supplied 28 gallons of rum, 50 gallons of rum punch, 34 gallons of wine, 46 gallons of beer, and 2 gallons of cider royal. When John Marshall and John Clopton opposed each other for a seat in Congress in 1799 a barrel of whiskey with the head knocked in was on the courthouse green. See Charles S. Sydnor's *American Revolutionaries in the Making: Political Practices in Washington's Virginia*. New York, N.Y. Collier Books, 1952, at page 55.

CHAPTER ELEVEN: THE SENATE IS NOT THE HOUSE

1. Davis and Reiter were known as the 51st and 52nd senators.

2. When Senator Murray ordered all lobbyists off of the Senate floor, Mike Johnson, the AFL-CIO lobbyist, reportedly accosted him, declaring that labor had waited thirty years for a Democratic majority in the Senate and this was no way to reward them. When cooled, Johnson appreciated Murray's action.

Notes

3. John Scotzin, veteran legislative correspondent for the Harrisburg *Evening News*, was incensed by the move. "I want to be up front so I can see the whites of their eyes when they vote!" Robert Lauf, editor of the Sunbury *Daily Item*, called me to express his concerns. I invited him to visit the Senate and observe a Senate session from the new press seats in the rear. Lauf did, and when he left he told me he was quite satisfied. The press had no grounds to complain. Reporters still had the best seats in the chamber except for the senators and staff.

CHAPTER TWELVE: SENATE CONFIRMATION OF THE GOVERNOR'S APPOINTMENTS

1. See Vincent Carocci's *A Capitol Journey* at page 50 for another description of how the confirmation study committee came about. Pennsylvania State University Press, University Park, 2005.
2. Staff Report of the Joint State Government Commission, 1973, at page 52 of the Committee's Report.
3. Report of the Special Senate Committee to Study Confirmation Procedure, Session of 1973. Filed November 1973. A copy is in the Senate Library.
4. See the *Legislative Journal— Senate*, for March 8, 1976, pages 1317–25.
5. See the *Legislative Journal—Senate* for September 27, 1976, at pages 1962 and 1967–70.
6. Ibid., pages 1969–70.

CHAPTER THIRTEEN: THE "BLOODLESS COUP" BILL AND THE GOVERNOR'S DISABILITY

1. For a detailed discussion of the events leading to Casey's invoking the disability statute, see Carocci's *Capitol Journey*, chapters 22 and 23.
2. Feerick has written two books that provide a complete study of presidential disability and vice presidential succession. See *The Twenty-fifth Amendment: Its Complete History and Earliest Applications*. New York, Fordham University Press, 1976, and *From Failing Hands: The Story of Presidential Succession*, New York, Fordham University Press, 1965.
3. *Pennsylvania Bar Quarterly*, Vol. XXXVI, March 1965, No. 3.
4. *Legislative Journal—Senate*, June 26, 1974, at page 2067.
5. 71 P.S. Sec. 784.1 et seq.
6. For the dramatic circumstances faced by Governor Casey and his family, as well as the courage with which he did it, see Casey's autobiography, *Fighting for Life*, Dallas, Word Publishers, 1994.

CHAPTER FOURTEEN: RIGHTING A LISTING SHIP BY REWRITING THE UTILITY LAW

1. One of my best grades in law school was in Professor Louis Schwartz's course on monopolies and antitrust law, for which I wrote a paper on natural gas prices in the Permian Basin in Texas.

2. George Bloom did testify and provided us with the benefit of his insight and perspective. Denenberg, however, declined to appear before our committee, although we invited him twice.

3. Report and Recommendations of the Senate Consumer Affairs Committee to Reform the Pennsylvania Public Utility Commission, September 1975, filed in the Senate Library.

4. *Philadelphia Inquirer*, March 1, 1976, at page 11-A.

5. *Senate Consumer Affairs Report*, at page 29.

6. Final Report of Counsel to the Senate Consumer Affairs Committee's Investigation of the Pennsylvania Public Utility Commission, signed by James H. Cawley, Majority Counsel and Frederick R. Taylor and Susan M. Shanaman, Minority Counsel, filed in the Senate Library.

7. *Legislative Journal—Senate*, May 18, 1976, at page 1550.

8. *Legislative Journal—Senate*, June 22, 1976, at page 1767.

9. Shane represented Indiana County and was a law school classmate. He later served two terms as a PUC commissioner.

10. *Senate Consumer Affairs Report*, at pages 89–90.

11. Before becoming the first consumer advocate, Widoff had served as deputy attorney general for education and executive assistant to Education Secretary John Pittenger. Widoff served three years. His major challenge was to organize the office so it could take on utility "heavyweights" like Philadelphia Electric and Bell Telephone. He takes pride in the staff of attorneys he assembled, that included Richard Spiegelman (now counsel to Senator Robert Casey), William Lloyd (later a state representative and now small business advocate) and David Barasch (see note 13, below).

12. 488 U.S. 299 (1989).

13. Barasch later became a special assistant to Governor Robert Casey, the U.S. attorney for the Middle District of Pennsylvania, and an unsuccessful candidate for state attorney general.

14. Popowsky became the consumer advocate in 1990 and has held the position since then.

15. See Title 66, Pa. C. S. A., Public Utilities.

16. The Electricity Generation customer choice and Competition Act, Section 4 of H.B. 1509, signed into law December 3, 1996, as Act 128. 66 P.S. Sec.2801 et seq. I have always been skeptical of electric generation deregulation. My skepticism stems in part from the fact that this law is the fruit of a poisoned tree. Electric generation deregulation was conceived by Ken Lay and his associates at the infamous Enron Corporation in Texas. Enron employed platoons of lawyers and lobbyists to sell the scheme to legislatures throughout the country, including Pennsylvania. See David Cay Johnston's *Free Lunch*, chapters 17–19. Penguin Books, London, 2007. Johnston is a Pulitzer Prize-winning reporter for the *New York Times*. This law should not be judged by its title.

17. H.B. 2200, signed into law October 15, 2008, Act 129 of the 2008 session.

CHAPTER FIFTEEN:
OUR RENDEZVOUS WITH FLOOD DISASTERS

1. Consult the Missouri Flood of 1993 on Google or other Internet search programs.
2. *The Legislative Journal—Senate,* for June 11, 1974, at page 1,979. The research report was placed in the appendix to the *Senate Journal* and is also found in appendix H to this book.
3. See the *Legislative Journal—Senate,* for June 3, 1994, at pages 1,904 through 1,911 and June 11, 1974, at pages 1,979 through 1,985 for the debate on S.B. 1122, excerpts of which are used here.
4. Murphy later became a U.S. Congressman from southwestern Pennsylvania.
5. For the Senate debate and text of the amendments on S.B. 1, see the *Legislative Journal—Senate,* for June 9, 1975, at pages 384–97.
6. For the House debate, see the *Legislative Journal—House,* for October 1, 1975, at pages 2,847–80, from which excerpts used here are taken.
7. Wagner's widowed mother, Cleo Wagner, held a coffee klatch for me in one of my House campaigns. She later married Z. H. Confair, the former senator from Lycoming County.
8. *Legislative Journal—House* for October 1. 1975, at page 2,871.
9. *Legislative Journal—Senate* for November 25, 1975, at page 991.
10. The *Pennsylvania Township News* of May 1977, at page 13.
11. Weston later went into private law practice and developed a distinguished career as a water law attorney.
12. *Legislative Journal—Senate* for February 28, 1978, at page 3,203.
13. *Legislative Journal—Senate,* for March 7, 1978, at page 200 for S.B. 743 and April 4, 1978, at page 300 for S.B. 744.
14. For the House debate, see *Legislative Journal—House* for September 25, 1978, at pages 3,198 through 3,244, from which the excerpts used here are extracted.
15. The information on the current status of the flood plain and storm water management laws was provided by Dan Fitzpatrick of the Department of Community and Economic Development and Barry Newman of the Department of Environmental Protection. Fitzpatrick and Newman are responsible for administering the laws for their departments.
16. Former Representative David Steil, a Republican from Bucks County, tried persistently for five legislative consecutive legislative sessions to improve storm water management by strengthening the Act of 1978. His last proposal, H.B. 2266 of the 2008 session, would have made several major changes:
- storm water planning would become more comprehensive, bringing in other water uses so that the planning is coherent;
- municipalities could create storm water authorities to fund and manage implementation;
- give any citizen of Pennsylvania the standing to seek a mandamus order from a court against any municipality that fails to implement the law after funding is available.

Unfortunately, the 2008 session expired before H.B. 2266 could be considered by the Senate, and was therefore not passed by the House in the waning week of the session. Even more unfortunate, Rep. Steil voluntarily retired from the House after the 2007-2008 session.

Steil's storm water bills passed the House in two sessions and would likely have passed in the 2007-2008 session had it been voted. When I asked Steil why the Senate failed to act on his bills, he shrugged. "No one in the Senate sees storm water and flooding as a significant problem. I had no champion in the Senate." Steil added that local government was not the problem. "Local government is okay with my bill," Steil added.

As Steil spoke, I thought how his experience compared to mine a third of a century earlier. Unlike in his situation, local governments were the major critics of my legislation. Like Steil, there was no "champion" for flood plain and storm water management legislation in the other legislative body until the third Johnstown flood. Then three rose to the occasion: Majority Leader Manderino, Conservation Committee Chairman Fee, and, importantly, Adam Bittinger of Johnstown.

Pennsylvania has had numerous serious floods since 1978, but none of them has galvanized legislative attention as did the third Johnstown flood. Luck can be important in passing legislation, as the passage of my bills in 1978 demonstrated. Unfortunately, Steil was not so lucky.

CHAPTER SIXTEEN: THE THORNBURGH ADMINISTRATION AND FAREWELL

1. Thornburgh, Dick. *Where the Evidence Leads: An Autobiography*. Pittsburg: University of Pittsburgh Press, 2003, at page 140.
2. *Legislative Journal—Senate*, November 18, 1980, at page 2,230.

CHAPTER SEVENTEEN: POLITICAL LIFE AFTER THE LEGISLATURE

1. *The Insider*, Neri's political newsletter, October 14, 2005.
2. At that time the limit on personal contributions to federal candidates was $1,000.

CHAPTER EIGHTEEN: REFLECTIONS

1. Sunbury *Daily Item*, October 21, 2008.
2. Sunbury *Daily Item*, October 23, 2008.
3. To see partisan politics at its best, watch "The Prime Minister's Question Period," from the British House of Commons, shown Sunday evenings on the
CSPAN television channel. Every week Parliament is in session the prime minister stands for questions from any member of the House. The questions from the op-

position party leaders, who are seated directly across the aisle are particularly hard hitting, but always done in a manner consistent with the British code of civility. The responses from the prime minister are equally forceful. A neutral, but assertive, Speaker of the House serves as referee to keep the proceedings within the bounds of civility.

Bibliography

Beers, Paul B. *Pennsylvania Politics: Today and Yesterday*. University Park: Pennsylvania State University Press, 1980.
Carocci, Vincent. *A Capitol Journey*. University Park: Pennsylvania State University Press, 2005.
Casey, Robert P. *Fighting for Life*. Dallas: Word Publishers, 1994.
Commager, Henry Steele. *Documents of American History*. New York: Columbia University Press, 1949.
Genealogical and Biographical Annals of Northumberland County, Pennsylvania. Chicago: J. L. Floyd, 1911.
Johnston, David Cay. *Free Lunch*. London: Penguin Books, 2007.
Karnow, Stanley. *Vietnam: A History*. New York: Penguin Books, 1984.
Legislative Journals of the House and Senate of Pennsylvania. Harrisburg, Pennsylvania, from 1966–1980.
McGeary, Nelson M. *Pennsylvania Government in Action: Governor Leader's Administration*. State College, Pa.: Penn Valley Publishers, 1972.
Smith, Reed M. *State Government in Transition: Reforms of the Leader Administration, 1955–1959*. Philadelphia: University of Pennsylvania Press, 1961.
Stevens, Sylvester K. *Pennsylvania: Birthplace of a Nation*. New York: Random House, 1964.
Sydnor, Charles S. *American Revolutionaries in the Making: Political Practices in Washington's Virginia*. New York: Collier Books, 1952.
The Pennsylvania Manual, Harrisburg, Pennsylvania, Volumes 99 (1968–1969) and subsequent volumes.
Thornburgh, Dick. *Where the Evidence Leads: An Autobiography*. Pittsburgh: University of Pittsburgh Press, 2003.
Wildes, Harry Emerson. *William Penn: A Biography*. New York: Macmillan Publishing Company, Inc., 1974.
Woodside, Robert E. *Pennsylvania Constitutional Law*. Sayre, Pa.: Murrelle Printing Company, 1985.

Index

Abele, Ralph W., 65
Abrams, Terry T., 80
absentee ballot reform, 49–51
Agnes, tropical storm, 121–122, 127, 134
Ammerman, Joseph, 96, 100–101
Archimedes: levers and leverage, vi, ix, 49, 75, 163; water displacement, 124
Attorney General's office, Pennsylvania: Bible reading in public schools, defending, 15–16; death penalty, carrying out, 15; meeting Elizabeth Heazlett, 16–17
Aumiller, Michael L., 80, 159

Baran, Walter, 144, 159
Barasch, David, 118
Barney's Shoe Service: political incubator, 4–6
Beck, Basse A.: anger over Bower vote, 22; chair of Kury campaign, 28, 36; death of, 38; radio ad on Bower vote, 32; restoring shad to Susquehanna, 64–67; stroke and incapacity, 83; "Up and Down the River" columns, 20, 32, 65, 167–174

Becker, Paul, 28
Bell, Clarence, 110, 114
Berson, Norman, 100
Bible reading in public schools. *See* Attorney General's office, Pennsylvania
Bittinger, Adam, 126, 136–138
Blatt, Genevieve, 34
"bloodless coup" bill, 105
Bloom, George I., 108
Bodine, James, 144
Bower, Adam T.: campaign tactics, 35–36; election to House, 25, 27; help to author, 45, 47; vote on H.B. 585, 22
Brannon, Jean, 160
bridge at Sunbury, 73–76
Brittain, Richard C., 34
Broughton, Professor Robert, 70, 158; analysis of the environmental amendment, 175–179
Buchkowskie, Joseph, 55, 83
Buscemi, Peter, 118
Butera, Robert, 159

Carocci, Vincent P., 80, 92, 110, 159
Casey, Robert P. Jr., 155
Casey, Robert, 103, 106

Cawley, James H., 108, 112, 119–120, 160
Chamberlain, Peggy, 160
Charter of Privileges, xiii, 163
"checks and balances," Constitutional, 92, 95, 101, 161, 162
"Clean Streams" legislation in Pennsylvania: historical evolution, xv, 59–61; 1967–1968 Session, H.B. 2808, 61–62; 1969–1970 Session, H.B. 1353, 62–63
Columbia County, PA., conservative Democratic, 81
Community Affairs, Department of (DCA) (currently Department of Community and Economic Development), 127, 131, 133, 140–141
Confair, Z.H., 175
confirmation of Governor's nominees, Senate: Article I, Section 28, State Constitution, 95, 98–99; interim appointments, 96; other states and Texas, 97; Rule XXX, Senate, 96–98; special Senate Committee, 96–99; Two-Thirds Rule, 96–97, 100–101
confirmation procedure, special Senate committee to study, 96–99; committee report, 187–195
Connecticut Intercollegiate Student Legislature, 10–11
Conservation Committee, House, 62, 76
Constitution of Pennsylvania: Article IV, Section 8, Senate Confirmation of Governor's Appointments, 95–96, 98–102, 197–198; Article IV, Section 13, (Gubernatorial Disability), 104–105. See also environmental amendment (Article I, Section 27)
Consumer Advocate, Office of, 113–115, 118–119
Consumer Affairs Committee, Senate: admonitions of PUC, the public and industry, 117–118; Consumer Advocate and creation of, 113–115; investigation of PUC, 109–110,
199–201; legislation proposed, 111–113; PUC structure, reform of 115–117; report of investigation, 110, 158; staffing, 108
Cotner, Esther, 28, 83, 158
Cowell, Ronald, 136

Daily Item, Sunbury, 14, 19, 26, 31, 32
Davis, Preston B, 25, 79, 80
death penalty. *See* Attorney General's office, Pennsylvania
Deeter, William T., 28, 83
Deitrick, Dr. George Jr., 80–82, 86
Deitrick, Dr. George Sr., 81
Delaware River Basin Compact Commission, 141
Denenberg, Herbert, 108
Dildine, James T., 83
Dreibelbis, Galen, 130
Duffield, William, 127–128, 132, 134
Dunkin, Thomas, 86
Dunlap, David, 108–109

Ecenbarger, William, 110
Eisenhower, Dwight D., 21
environmental amendment (Art. 1, Section 27), Pennsylvania Constitution: amendments to, 70; analysis of, 175–179; impact of, 72; origination, 69; public referendum results, 71; questions and answers regarding, 181–185
Environmental Resources, Department of (DER), 125, 127; animosity toward, 126–128, 132, 134
environmental revolution in Pennsylvania: causes of, 59–60; legislation enacted, 63–64
Ertel, Allen E., 151–152
Ewing, Wayne, 108, 112, 114–115
ex parte communications, PUC, 111, 116–117
Eyster, Mollie Lou, 85, 158

fabridam, 35
Fairchild, Russell, 45

Federal Emergency Management Agency (FEMA), 140–141
Fee, Thomas, 136–138
Feerick, John D., 104
Fineman, Herbert: bridge at Sunbury, 74; environmental amendment, change to, 70; House minority leader, 41–42; Mazur and Pittenger appointments, 45–47; modernization of the legislature, 161; Speaker of the House, 62, 158–159
Fisher, Dean, 34
Fisher, Michael, 138
fish kills, Susquehanna River, 31–32
flood plan management law, 125–141
floods and flood disasters: central Pennsylvania from Agnes, 121–122; historical study of, 123–125; legislation to reduce its impact, 125–141; "Rendezvous with Disaster" article, 203–206; report on the prevention of, in Pennsylvania, 207–250
Foerster, Tom, 21
Frame, Richard, 96–97, 102, 158

Gekas, George, 134
General Assembly of Pennsylvania: beginnings, xiii–xiv; caucus system, 42–43; changes since 1980, 160–161; control of by coal, rail and steel industries, xv; future of, 161–163; under three constitutions, xiv; working conditions in 1967, 41
Gleason, Pat, 130–131
Goddard, Maurice K.: change to environmental amendment, 70; dedication of Island Park marina, 121; outstanding qualities, 159: secretary of Department of Environmental Resources (DER) and flood plain bills, 126, 134, 138
Goodman, James, 159

Haddon, Harry H., 14
Hager, Henry G, 100–101, 114, 126, 134

Haupt, Samuel W., 19
Help America Vote Act ("HAVA"), 57
Holl, Edwin, 132
House Bill 585 (1965–1966 Session), 20–22, 27, 36, 60, 61, 62
Howard, Edward, 134
Hunt, Margot, 132, 138
Hutchinson, William, 159

International Ladies Garment Workers Union (the ILGWU), 83–84
Irvis, K. Leroy: environmental amendment, support of, 70; House minority whip, 42; House majority leader, 158–159; invites author to dinner, 31; speaking ability, 90

Johnstown flood, the third, 132–133, 135–137
Jones, Clifford L., 45–47, 144, 159
Jubelirer, Robert, 115

Kalodner, Phillip, 113–114
Kassab, Jacob, 74
Kehler, Oscar, 25–26, 51, 55
Kelley, James P. (Northumberland County), 83–84, 159
Kelley, James (Westmorland County), 99, 114
Kennedy, John F., xi, 157
Kistler, Guy, 49–50
Klingman, Harriet, 29, 31, 33, 37, 158
Kury, Barney: death of, 11–12; education of children, 8; family background, 6–7; influence on author, 38; political involvement, 3, 9, 81. *See also* Barney's Shoe Service
Kury, Elizabeth ("Beth"): campaign planning, 29; "Choice is Yours" campaign photo, 32; meets author and marriage, 16–17; meets Henry Lark, 19–20; Mondale, Walter F., dinner with, 152; Obama, campaign, 155
Kury, Helen C., 6–9
Kury, Steven, 144

Lamb, Thomas, 89, 96, 158–159
Lark, Henry W.: campaign tactics and strategy, 24; family and businesses, 23–24; letter to voters, 35; meeting with author, 19–20; organization, "the Machine," 24–26, 144, 146; party "boss," xvii, 146
Larson, Thomas, 144–146
Laudadio, John, 21, 61, 136
Law School, University of Pennsylvania, 12–13
Leader, George M.: state senator, xvi–xvii; as governor, xvii, 11–12, 91
Lee, Kenneth B., 74
Leib, Richard C., 80
Lentz, William, 91
Linnet (Kondpka), Dr. John, 80–81
luck, role in success, x, 92, 146, 158

McAuliffe, Cornelius (Neil), 82–84, 86, 159
McClatchy, Richard, 130
McGovern, George, 83–87
McGregor, Jack, 62, 70
McLaughlin, William J., 55
Magna Carta, 148, 162
Manderino, James: conference committee on Senate confirmations, 100; flood plain and storm water management legislation, leadership in House passage, 125, 128–131, 137–138, 159
Mazur, John, 45, 90
Mellow, Robert, 135
Mertz, Neil, 86
Messinger, Henry, 100
migratory fish, restoring to Susquehanna, 64–67
Mondale, Walter F., 152–155
Montour County, PA, 27
Moore, William, 135
Murphy, Austin, 128
Murray, Martin L.: compared with Harvey Taylor, 91; confirmation reform, leadership in, 96; consumer advocate, Senate approval, 114; flood plain legislation, 125, 128, 132, 138; leadership qualities, 158–159; obtaining favorable votes, 135; policy towards senators, 91–92; rapport with new senators, 89

Neri, Al, 151
Nixon, Richard M., 37, 81, 87
Nolan, Thomas, 100, 108, 110
Northumberland County, PA: absentee ballot controversies, 49–50; ballot box controversies, 25–26, 53–57; citizens committee to reform paper ballot, 54–56
Noye, Fred, 136, 138

Obama, Barack, 155
O'Connell, Frank, 135–138

paper ballots, Northumberland County, 26, 53–55
patronage politics: "Boss" control, xvi–xvii; governors and, xvi; Northumberland County, 24; Thornburgh ends PENNDOT (Pennsylvania Department of Transportation) patronage, 144–146, 157
Penn, William: Charter of Privileges, xii, 163; beginning of elected legislature, xiii–xiv; environment of Penn's woods, 59
Pennsylvania Bar Association (PBA), 97, 104
Perles, George F., 25
Phillips, Merle, 45, 65
Pittenger, John, 29, 97, 159; public opinion questionnaire, 30; House Democratic Policy Director, 46
"police power," state government, 126
pollution, Susquehanna River. *See* "Clean Streams" legislation in Pennsylvania; fish kills Susquehanna River
Popowsky, Irwin ("Sonny"), 118
Powers, Joseph R., 160
Public Utility Commission, Pennsylvania (PUC): changes

subsequent, 119–120; investigation of, 109–113; legislation to reform, 111–113; structure, reform of, 115–117
PUC. *See* Public Utility Commission, Pennsylvania

Raup, Thomas C., 34
Reibman, Jeannette, 101
Rendell, Edward G., 102
Renwick, William, 65
Republican Party of Pennsylvania: "Bosses," xvi–xvii
Rhodes, George M., 17–18
Rhoads, C. Brewster, 104
Ruane, Paul G., 25, 55
Rule XXX, Pennsylvania Senate, 96, 98
Rumberger, Dr. William: challenges Lark machine, 25–26; citizens committee to reform the paper ballot, 55–56; experience with close elections, 37; relationship with author, 51
Ryan, Matthew, 100

Schaefer, Michael, 134
Scheiner, James, 144, 159
scholarships, State Senate, 90–91
Schmitt, C.L. ("Mr. Consumer"), 107, 113–114, 119
Scranton, William W., 35–36
Seaman, Thomas, 160
shad and other migratory fish, 64–67
Shafer, Raymond P., 23, 35, 50
Shanaman, Susan, 108, 112
Shane, William R., 116
Shapp, Milton: "bloodless coup" bill, 105–106; consumer protection, advocacy of, 107; consumer advocate bill, signing, 115; flood plain and storm water management bills, signing, 138; flooding from Agnes, response to, 122; interim appointments, 96; luck, part of Author's, 147; Philadelphia judges and bridge to Sunbury, 73–75; Republican distrust of, 100; Thornburgh's view of, 143–144
Shelhamer, Kent, 44, 86, 130–131
Showers, John R., 86, 123, 159
Singel, Mark, 103
Smith, Jackie, 158
Snyder, Richard, 105, 147
Sportsmen's Clubs, Pennsylvania Federation of, 36
Stank, John F., 25
Stauffer, John, 126, 135, 158, 159, 161
storm water management law, 121, 133, 137–141
Stroup, Stanley: alleged commitment with author, 101; co-sponsorship of gubernatorial disability bill, 105; open to compromise, 158–159; opposition to flood plain bills, 126–127
Susquehanna River: fabridam, 35; fishkills and pollution, 31–32; flooding, 121–122, 207–250; shad and other migratory fish, 64–67; writings about, 167–174
Sweeney, John, 107

Taylor, Frederick, 108, 112
Taylor, M. Harvey: defeat by William Lentz, 91; party "Boss," xvii, 146; president of State Senate, xvi–xvii
Thornburgh, Dick: ending highway shed patronage, 144–145, 157; inauguration and new style of government, 143–146; 1982 campaign and Ertel, 151; loses to Wofford for U.S. Senate, 155
Tilghman, Richard, 134
Tive, Ralph D., 96–97
Township Supervisors, the Pennsylvania State Association of (PSATS), 133
Trinity College, 10–12
Truman, Harry S., 3–4

United Steelworkers of America, 84
U.S. Army Corps of Engineers, 135

Van Kirk, Clara, 28

Wagner, George O., 129, 137–138
Wagner, Jack, 155
Weston, Timothy, 134
Whitney, Paul and Nancy, 34
Widoff, Mark, 118

Wilcox, William, 138
Winsor, Curtin, 138
Wilt, William, 62
Winters, David, 146
Wofford, Harris, 155
Wolfe, Samuel B., 19

www.ingramcontent.com/pod-product-compliance
Lightning Source LLC
Chambersburg PA
CBHW072127290426
44111CB00012B/1804